Mozambique: The Revolution Under Fire

Joseph Hanlon

Mozambique: The Revolution Under Fire

Joseph Hanlon

Zed Books Ltd., 57 Caledonian Road, London N1 9BU.

Mozambique: The Revolution Under Fire was first published by
Zed Books Ltd., 57 Caledonian Road, London N1 9BU in
1984.

Copyright © Joseph Hanlon, 1984

Typeset by Wayside Graphics
Proofread by A.M. Berrett
Cover designed by Lee Robinson
Maps by Lesley Gibbs
Photos by Kok Nam, Anders Nilsson and Joseph Hanlon
Printed by The Pitman Press, Bath
Permission was kindly given by Wheatsheaf for the quotation
    in Appendix 2 taken from *Revolutionary Socialist
    Development in the Third World.*

British Library Cataloguing in Publication Data

Hanlon, Joseph
    Mozambique: the revolution under fire.
    1. Mozambique – Politics and government
    — 1975 –
    I. Title
    967'.905   DT463.5

    ISBN 0-86232-244-8
    ISBN 0-86232-245-6 Pbk

US Distributor
Biblio Distribution Center, 81 Adams Drive, Totowa,
New Jersey 07512.

Contents

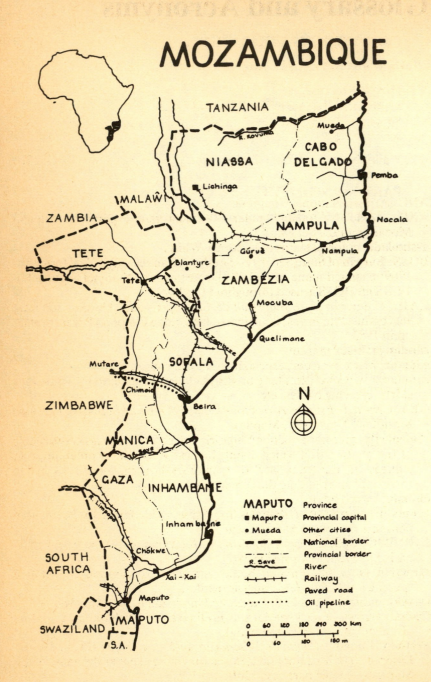

MOZAMBIQUE

TANZANIA

Mueda

R. Rovuma

CABO DELGADO

NIASSA

Lichinga

Pemba

ZAMBIA

MALAŴI

Nacala

NAMPULA

TETE

Blantyre

Gúruè

Nampula

Tete

ZAMBÉZIA

Mocuba

R. Zambeze

Quelimane

Mutare

SOFALA

ZIMBABWE

Chimoio

Beira

MANICA

R. Save

GAZA

INHAMBANE

R. Limpopo

Inhambane

MAPUTO   Province
■ Maputo   Provincial capital
● Mueda   Other cities
– – – –   National border
–·–·–·   Provincial border
R. Save   River
++++++   Railway
———   Paved road
········· Oil pipeline

SOUTH AFRICA

Chókwè

Xai-Xai

Maputo

SWAZILAND

MAPUTO

S.A.

0   60 120 180 240 300 km

0   60   120   180 m

N

Glossary and Acronyms

ANC: African National Congress.

ANP: *Acção* Nacional Popular – official fascist party in colonial Mozambique.

assimilado: colonial status of honorary White.

BOSS: Bureau of State Security – South African security police formed in 1969; changed name to DONS (Department of National Security) in 1978, but BOSS is used throughout this book.

CAIL: *Complexo Agro-industrial do Limpopo* – one of largest and least successful state farms, on irrigated land along Limpopo River; broken up in 1983.

candonga: black market.

capataz: black overseer, especially of forced cotton.

capulana: two yard (2m) long brightly coloured cloth used by women for skirts, carrying babies, etc.

CEA: *Centro de Estudos Africanos* – Centre of African Studies of Eduardo Mondlane University, Maputo.

cement city: area of permanent, high-rise, concrete buildings at the centre of the major cities, which mainly housed Whites in colonial times; in contrast to the 'cane city' of temporary housing for Blacks in the townships surrounding the cement city.

chibalo: forced labour.

colonato: resettlement schemes providing small farms to Portuguese peasants moving to Mozambique.

COREMO: *Comite Revolucionário de Moçambique* – unsuccessful alternative to Frelimo formed in 1965.

direction units: government bodies intended to plan and co-ordinate specific industrial areas, such as textiles.

escudo: monetary unit in Portugal, and in Mozambique until 1980.

flechas: arrows – Pide's special anti-Frelimo army which was independent of the normal military command.

Frelimo: initially, *Frente de Libertação de Moçambique* (Front for the Liberation of Mozambique), this acronym was kept as the name of the Marxist-Leninist party established in 1977.

Front Line States: Angola, Botswana, Mozambique, Tanzania, and Zambia; joined by Zimbabwe when it became independent in 1980.

GEP: *Grupo Especial das Páraquedistas* – special paratroops, an anti-Frelimo force.

GD: *Grupo dinamizador* – political action groups established by Frelimo during the 1974–75 Transitional Government in neighbourhoods and workplaces; largely replaced by other groups in 1978, they continue in cities as neighbourhood councils.

Gungunhana: last and most important feudal ruler in south of Mozambique, defeated by Portuguese in 1895.

intervene: a procedure similar to bankruptcy, in which the state appoints an administrator to run an abandoned or sabotaged private company; if the original owners do not reclaim the firm, it can be sold or converted into a state company.

Lourenço Marques: colonial name for the capital, now Maputo.

metical (pl. **meticais**): Mozambican currency introduced in 1980, in direct exchange for colonial escudo notes then still in use; colonial escudo coins continue in circulation along with new metical coins.

MFA: *Movimento das Forças Armadas* – Armed Forces Movement which carried out the 25 April 1974 coup in Portugal.

MNR: initially *Movimento Nacional de Resistência de Moçambique*, later *Resistência Nacional Moçambicana* (RNM or Renamo) – Mozambique National Resistance, an anti-Frelimo force created by Rhodesian security services and later backed by South Africa (see Chapter 21).

OMM: *Organisação da Mulher Moçambicana* – Mozambican Woman's Organization.

OPV: colonial Voluntary Police Organization, an anti-Frelimo militia.

palmatória: a wooden paddle with holes in it designed to raise weals when a person is hit with it.

People's Assemblies: parliament (*Assembleia Popular*) and provincial and local councils (*Assembleias do Provo*).

Pide: *Polícia Internacional e de Defesa do Estado* – Portuguese secret police; renamed DGS (*Direção de Segurança* in 1969, but Pide is used throughout this book.

régulo: traditional or Portuguese-appointed chief.

SADCC: Southern African Development Coordination Conference – founded 1980 to reduce dependence on South Africa; members: Angola, Botswana, Lesotho, Malawi, Mozambique, Swaziland, Tanzania, Zambia, and Zimbabwe.

Serli: *Secretário de Estado para o Desenvolvimento Acelerado para a Região do Limpopo e Incomati* – Secretariat of State for the Accelerated Development of the Limpopo and Incomati Regions, abolished 1983.

sipiao: 'native' policeman.

Frelimo Chronology

25 June 1962	Frelimo founded in Dar es Salaam
23–28 September 1962	First Congress, Dar es Salaam
25 September 1964	Armed struggle begins
20–25 July 1968	Second Congress, Machedje
3 February 1969	Assassination of Eduardo Mondlane
9–14 May 1970	4th Session of Central Committee elects Samora Machel as new President
4 March 1973	OMM First Conference
24 April 1974	Coup in Portugal
7 September 1974	Lusaka agreement between Portugal and Frelimo; settlers take over radio in Maputo
25 September 1974	Frelimo dominated Transitional Government
25 June 1975	Independence
24 July 1975	Nationalizations of health, education, law, funerals
3 February 1976	Nationalization of rented property; capital renamed Maputo
11–27 February 1976	8th session of Central Committee sets policy for transition to socialism
3 March 1976	Sanctions against Rhodesia imposed
3–12 October 1976	Co-operatives seminar
10–17 November 1976	OMM Second Conference
3–7 February 1977	Third Congress
October, November 1977	Elections for People's Assemblies
February–November 1978	Frelimo Party membership drive
August 1978	Joaquim de Carvalho dismissed as Agriculture Minister
1–4 August 1979	Council of Ministers declares 1980–90 the 'decade of victory over underdevelopment'
4 December 1979	President Machel's health speech
17 December 1979	Lancaster House Agreement ends Zimbabwe liberation war

20 March, 3 April 1980	Government reshuffle: two Party secretaries to work full time on Party, new Health Minister
26–31 March 1980	OMM Third Conference
April, May 1980	Elections
16 June 1980	Metical introduced as new currency
August 1980	First post-independence census
27–28 November 1980	First SADCC conference, Maputo
30 January 1981	South African commandoes raid the Maputo suburb of Matola
4 march 1981	CIA agents expelled
6–9 October 1981	People's Assembly approves ten year plan
14 October 1981	White man later identified as South African soldier killed trying to mine railway
29 October 1981	Bridges carrying road, railway, and oil pipeline from Beira to Zimbabwe sabotaged
4 March 1982	President Machel appoints provincial military commanders to strengthen fight against MNR
10–11 May, 3–7 June 1982	Meetings with 'the compromised' (collaborators)
17 August 1982	Ruth First assassinated
11 January 1983	First summary public executions of captured MNR men
10 April 1983	First public floggings
26–30 April 1983	Fourth Congress
21, 28 May 1983	Government reshuffle, including new agriculture minister and abolition of Serli, two Politburo members given additional tasks, other changes in security and economic ministries
23 May 1983	South African planes bomb the Maputo suburbs
July–September 1983	'Operation Production' expels unemployed from cities

Part I
Rebuilding under Fire

1. 'We Have Built Something'

'I joined Frelimo when I was only 13 years old. I have been a militant now for 19 years, and took part in the armed struggle and all of the changes in Frelimo,' explained José N'Chumali. Frelimo's leaders blame many of Mozambique's troubles on its 'enemies', ranging from South Africa to black marketeers. N'Chumali agreed, but he then turned to President Samora Machel and declared: 'I want to say that some enemies are also inside the Central Committee and inside the Council of Ministers, and if we don't unmask them, our revolution is headed for trouble.'

The President's mouth dropped open; even he was surprised by the harshness of this criticism. In many other countries, N'Chumali would have been locked up and never heard from again. Instead, he was elected to the Frelimo Central Committee.

This was at the Frelimo Fourth Party Congress in April 1983. Also elected to the Central Committee then was Aurélio Manhiça, who told the President that there was no point in imposing the new tougher laws he was advocating because they would simply 'join the other laws that are never applied, that remain only on paper'. Elected, too, was railway worker Benjamin Máquina, who asked the Congress how he could keep the trains running without tools and spare parts.

After four years in Mozambique, I am still impressed by the readiness to admit mistakes and change policies accordingly. Perhaps the best capsule summary of the Mozambican revolution comes from Information Minister José Cabaço: 'The number of errors we have made is enormous. But our success is that, despite the errors, we have built something.'

What they are trying to build is a developed, non-racial, socialist state – goals which, taken together, make Mozambique different from most of the African countries which have come to independence in the past three decades. But this makes it a direct threat to neighbouring white minority regimes; first Rhodesia and now South Africa have kept Mozambique under constant attack. This only adds to Frelimo's problems. After defeating the Portuguese in a ten-year guerrilla war, the Front for the Liberation of Mozambique inherited one of the most underdeveloped, backward and brutalized countries in Africa. It is hardly surprising that Frelimo has faced innumerable problems and made a host of mistakes.

The results can be seen in empty shops, long queues, failed cooperatives and the anger at the Fourth Congress.

Nevertheless, eight years after independence, Frelimo remains a vital and coherent force. It has not been rent by power struggles nor has it become a closed clique; the Fourth Congress showed it as open to criticism and willing to change. This, too, makes Mozambique unusual; it is not surprising that N'Chumali and the mass of the people still have faith in Frelimo.

Thus Mozambique is of special interest both because of its own history, and because of its position on the front line against South Africa. This book looks at the struggle to transform Mozambique, at how and why key choices have been made, and at people building new lives for themselves.

'We didn't want to be exploited any more. We saw this farm produce a lot in the time of Pinto. So we stopped producing cotton on our family plots and reopened Pinto's farm. But now the profits would be for us. And we would have a shop, like Pinto's, but it would be a consumer cooperative, and these profits would be ours, too.' A group of peasants in Assuate in Nampula Province were explaining how they decided to form their co-operative farm. They were talking to a team from the Centre of African Studies (CEA) of Mozambique's Eduardo Mondlane University.

Forced cotton growing had started in 1953. 'We received orders to leave our land and villages and open land for cotton along new roads. Each family had to cut the trees and clear the bush by hand. Those who refused were sent to the sisal plantations, or disappeared to São Tomé. Many hung themselves, preferring death to suffering along that road. The only ones left out were old men, widows, and the ill. When a man died or became too old to work, a son or nephew had to take his place.

'We were all forced to grow cotton and live along the roads. Each family had to produce two acres of cotton, two acres of sorghum, and two of cassava. We had to work from five in the morning till five at night, under constant supervision of the *capatazes* and *sipaios* (overseers and 'native' police). They never let us rest. When we couldn't endure the work any longer, we were denounced to the *régulo* (chief), arrested, bound, and taken by the sipaios to the administrator, who beat us with the *palmatória* (a paddle with holes in it designed to raise weals). We only escaped these punishments if we made "friends" with the sipaios by giving them chickens, money, and other things.

'In 1972 Pinto arrived here and appropriated the land and expelled us. He already had a shop. First he arranged workers to clean the land, which was easy because we had already done it. All he did was chop down our mango and cashew trees. He destroyed a lot, but what could we do?' For the next three years he grew cotton on a large area, with tractors and hired workers. But 'Pinto packed his bags in 1975, right after independence', abandoning his new farm.

Independence meant the end of forced cotton. 'No one was afraid of the palmatória any more. The régulos, capatazes, and sipaios couldn't order anyone. We grew cotton where we wanted, or stopped growing it. We had to rest a bit. In the first years after the arrival of Frelimo, cotton production dropped a lot. We went around with torn clothes, with no money. Exploitation had ended, but we suffered all the same. So we formed a group and called a meeting to try to figure out what to do to improve our life. The teacher António told us about collective production, and the idea came up to take over Pinto's old farm. At that first meeting we had to pick officials, and we decided on the people who were most determined and who spoke best in favour of collective production. Everyone agreed on Janta as head, and André was named bookkeeper because he was the only one of us who could read and write.'

They were dependent on help from the new locality administrator, because they had no experience. But the first season was a success. 'When the profits finally arrived, the administrator had to divide them, because there was so much money that even André couldn't figure it out.'

In the years that followed, this co-op and others faced many difficulties; most members dropped out, but the rest struggled on, constantly dogged by their own lack of knowledge and experience.

Sometimes it seems that everyone in Mozambique is in over their heads, like the barely literate 'bookkeeper' André, who was pushed into the job because no one else could write at all. Inevitably, education has become a national mania. School rolls are two-and-a-half times what they were before independence, and many schools run three shifts, with ordinary pupils during the morning and afternoon, and adults at night. There is a third rush hour at 10.30 pm with people going home from night school.

Angelo was a full-time student at the Industrial Institute in Maputo, sent back to school by the railways. He was 43 years old, and he and several of his nine children could be found round the dining table at night studying. The kids teased father about his low marks as he struggled to pass mathematics. When he went back to school in 1980, he hadn't studied for 20 years.

Angelo only had six years of primary school when he started to work for the railways in 1960, but he slowly worked his way up. The Portuguese had a complex system of job classification, and Angelo finally became a grade 2 technician, about as high as a black man could rise. Indeed, when he was sent to Quelimane to replace a white grade 2 technician, the railways refused to give him the house and salary to which his job entitled him, because he was black.

Eventually he returned to Lourenço Marques (now Maputo) and at independence joined the local Frelimo-organized action group, known as a Dynamizing Group (GD), and eventually joined the Party. Meanwhile, down at the railway, the thousands of white Portuguese who had held the skilled jobs left. The railways pushed people like Angelo into higher and higher jobs for which they were not trained, and they kept the ports and railways running. Many, like Angelo, were eventually sent back to school.

But no one does just one job. Angelo remained in the Dynamizing Group and active in the Party, which meant meetings every night. After the first South African raid, he had to do paramilitary training as well – from 3 am to 7 am every day before he went to school, for more than two months.

Not many 40-year-olds have Angelo's stamina. Revolutions are made by the young, and one of the most striking things about Mozambique is how many high officials and directors are in their late twenties or early thirties. Rogério was only 15 and living in the Maputo suburb of Matola when the rioting broke out in September 1974. The Portuguese Government had finally signed a peace treaty with Frelimo, but Portuguese settlers had taken over the radio station and were broadcasting virulent anti-Frelimo propaganda. Whites were driving around the suburbs shooting randomly into Blacks' houses; one of those severely injured was Rogério's brother. Black youth, including Rogério, set up roadblocks. There was no political line, just anger. He admits 'it was turning into a race war'. Then Frelimo representatives arrived to calm the backlash and preach non-racialism. Rigid Portuguese censorship meant Rogério himself knew little of Frelimo or politics, although he knew his father had listened to 'Voice of Frelimo' on the radio under the bedclothes at night.

A youth movement grew out of the kids on the barricades. First it was sustained purely by enthusiasm for independence, but later Frelimo became more involved and Rogério and his friends began to understand what Frelimo stood for. Later Rogério became a member of his neighbourhood GD. With independence, he went to the fifth and sixth years of primary school, and was increasingly active with the GD and youth group, gaining political knowledge and experience.

In 1977 he started seventh class at Francisco Manyanga secondary school in Maputo. 'We had very good students' and teachers' organizations. There was a lot of energy and enthusiasm. We started our own garden, designed a school emblem, etc.,' Rogério said. Most secondary teachers and administrators had been Portuguese and left Mozambique, yet school rolls were exploding. Rogério became secretary of the school GD and in 1979, at the age of 18, he became one of the three-person school directorate, running one of the largest schools in the country. And, with the shortage of teachers, he began to teach too – all while trying to study.

At the end of 1979 he finished secondary school and stayed on at Francisco Manyanga as a teacher. But he resigned from the directorate. 'I needed time to grow up,' he told me. What he really needed was time to be a teenager. For five years he had been an organizer, teacher, and director – doing work people twice his age would not normally do (especially while studying). Now he wanted time off to play football.

The break only lasted a few months. Rogério became a journalist and at the age of 23 became the bureau chief in Beira, the country's second largest city, of Mozambique's main daily newspaper, *Noticias*.

Everywhere you go in Mozambique, you find committed, enthusiastic people like Rogério and Angelo, who have risen to the demands of the jobs. But many have not, and bureaucracy has proved a refuge for the incompetent. The Portuguese left behind a complex system requiring formal petitions, tax stamps and rubber-stamped signatures. Frelimo never dismantled this system, and for anything difficult or unusual, the answer is often that the petition is not right, another signature is needed, or someone else is responsible.

Gardener Ricardo Sango never did penetrate the bureaucracy. He was quickly hired by Maputo's Commercial School after President Samora Machel in 1981 complained that this school was being allowed to deteriorate. But no one could figure out how to get Sango on the payroll. The school director met three times with the Maputo city director of education, then five times asked for an audience with the mayor, unsuccessfully. Finally, after 20 months on the job, Sango wrote to *Noticias* saying he had never been paid. The school director still could not get him on the payroll, but, prodded by the newspaper, it was decided to lend Sango money from the school social fund while the matter was being dealt with.

As they say in Mozambique, The Struggle Continues.

2. Bombs and Onions

The onions in Maputo come from South Africa. So does the electricity. And the planes that bombed Maputo on 23 May 1983 came from South Africa too.

South Africa has launched an undeclared war on Mozambique, yet it remains an important trading partner. This curious relationship is the result of history and geography, which have turned South Africa into the dominant military and economic power in the region.

In the colonial era, South Africa was made the region's economic heart. Mozambique was as closely linked to Johannesburg as to Lisbon. The port of Lourenço Marques was developed to serve South Africa, which also became one of the largest employers of cheap Mozambican labour. Portuguese settlers became dependent on South Africa even for basic foodstuffs. Lourenço Marques drew its electricity from the South African grid. Industry in Mozambique grew up dependent on South Africa for parts, raw materials and service. The Lourenço Marques oil refinery was designed to produce heavy fuel oil, not needed in Mozambique, to be sold to South Africa.

Eight years after independence, Lourenço Marques had been renamed Maputo, but the economic situation remains similar. South African cargo still passes through the port. Mozambique still imports spare parts, onions and a host of other items from its more developed neighbour. Part of Maputo's electricity still comes from South Africa.

The inevitable question is why does Mozambique deal with the enemy? Why not just close the border?

This would be an expensive and empty gesture which would only hurt Mozambique. Its trade with South Africa is tiny compared to that of the United States, Britain, Japan and West Germany; they must lead any imposition of sanctions.

Many items are cheaper and quicker to obtain from South Africa. Manufacturing costs there are higher than in Europe, but for bulky items shipping costs are much less. For some things, there is little choice: when a dredge sank in Maputo harbour, blocking the coal terminal, the only recovery equipment in the region was in South Africa. It would be possible to shop elsewhere, but it seems foolish for impoverished Mozambique to bear the brunt when richer countries continue to trade with South Africa.

South Africa remains a vital source of foreign exchange for Mozambique. In addition to the port traffic, there are Mozambicans working on South African farms, and more than 40,000 Mozambicans in South African mines. The miners send back £30 million ($50 million) per year, as important a source of foreign exchange as the biggest export, cashew nuts. However, Mozambique is different from South Africa's other neighbours in that there is a reciprocal dependence. Maputo is the closest port to the Transvaal and is cheaper for bulk exports like coal than South African ports, so considerable South African cargo still passes through Maputo. South Africa also treats Maputo as an 'internal port' – coal from the eastern Transvaal is railed to Maputo and transferred to coastal ships to be sent south to power stations along the South African coast, while oil products are sent from Durban and Capetown up the coast and transferred to rail tankers in Maputo to supply the eastern Transvaal. (The map on page 14 shows why this is done.) In 1979, the general manager of South African Railways, Jacobus Loubser, declared: 'It is an economic necessity that the railway line to, and harbour of, Maputo should remain accessible to South Africa.'

This must provide some protection to Mozambique. South Africa is unlikely to cut off the electricity if that disrupts the port handling its coal, or close the border and block its own exports.

In fact, both sides have been delinking, although in the case of Mozambique, breaking these ties requires restructuring the economy, a long and expensive task that is only possible as part of a general development programme.

Mozambique now imports maize, coal, seed potatoes and other items from Zimbabwe that it used to buy from South Africa. Sabotage has prodded it to find other sources for some strategic items. For example, deliveries of chlorine from South Africa for the Maputo water supply suddenly stopped just as a cholera outbreak was reported. Now Mozambique buys its chlorine from a safer supplier in Brazil.

For at least five years after independence, Mozambique continued to sell heavy fuel oil to South Africa, despite the oil embargo. There seemed a tacit acceptance by the oil suppliers, particularly Iraq, that this had to continue because the refinery was designed to produce this heavy oil for South Africa, that it was a low value product that had no other market, and that no one was prepared to give Mozambique millions of pounds to rebuild the machinery so it did not produce so much heavy oil. Recently, however, even this stopped; the heavy oil is now exported to Brazil –

9

inevitably for less money than South Africa would pay, due to the high transport costs.

South Africa, too, has cut back. Both the number of miners and the traffic through Maputo port are half what they were before independence. South Africa is scheduled to stop using Maputo for internal oil shipments in 1984, meaning it will no longer be dependent on Maputo port for any *essential* traffic. There remains strong pressure, however, from South African mine owners on their own government not to force them to reduce the use of the cheaper Maputo port.

Both sides have also begun long-term projects to reduce dependence on the other. South Africa is building a new railway through Swaziland to the port of Richard's Bay, which will reduce the economic advantages of Maputo, and make it possible to avoid Mozambique entirely if the border were closed. Similarly, Mozambique is building a new power line from Maputo to the Massingir dam, which could provide electricity if South Africa pulled out the plug.

Independence in Zimbabwe in 1980 changed the political and economic realities of the region. Now there is a continuous band of majority-ruled states stretched across Southern Africa. Within weeks of Zimbabwe's independence, they *all* agreed to join the Southern African Development Coordination Conference (SADCC) to 'liberate our economies from their dependence on the Republic of South Africa'. They included not only the Front-Line States of Angola, Botswana, Mozambique, Tanzania, Zambia and Zimbabwe, which had already taken a strong political line, but also Lesotho, Malawi and Swaziland. South Africa had counted on these last three as at least partial allies.

The key to breaking South African dominance is restructuring the regional transport and communications system, now centred on Johannesburg. Historically five of the colonies which became SADCC states had exported through Mozambique, but sanctions rerouted this traffic through South Africa. To redirect this flow, the first SADCC conference in Maputo in December 1980 proposed expenditure of £1,000 million on projects to rehabilitate transport and communications links; 40% of these are in Mozambique.

This new political alignment came as a rude shock to Pretoria. Back in 1965, with UDI (Unilateral Declaration of Independence) in Rhodesia, it had seemed to the Whites that Rhodesia, South Africa, and the Portuguese colonies of Mozambique and Angola would remain a White-ruled bastion. Independence in Mozambique put the strategy in question, but so long as Rhodesia remained under white dominance, apartheid was not at risk. In any case, Ian Smith was attacking Mozambique, so South Africa could stay on the sidelines and maintain normal trade.

Independence in Zimbabwe, after the Frelimo victory in Mozambique, gave an important psychological boost to the black freedom struggle inside South Africa. SADCC threatened South Africa's regional economic dominance, the rock on which its political hegemony was built. Inside South Africa, there was talk of a 'total onslaught' which threatened the very existence of apartheid. The military took a dominant role in government and launched a campaign of destabilization against its neighbours designed to keep them on their knees. Mozambique, both because of its Marxism and because of the strategic importance of its ports and railways, became the main target. South African aggression became the overriding problem for Frelimo, and for the Mozambican people as a whole.

South Africa moved directly against SADCC. In Mozambique it repeatedly attacked the railways, roads, oil pipeline and fuel storage depot which serve Zimbabwe and Malawi, in an effort to keep traffic moving through South Africa.

Maputo was directly attacked twice. On 30 January 1981 lorryloads of South African commandos came over the border and drove to the western suburb of Matola where they attacked two houses occupied by members of the African National Congress (ANC), and blew up a house occupied by the South African Congress of Trade Unions (SACTU). In all, 13 South African refugees and a Portuguese electricity technician were killed. The commandos left behind one dead, a British mercenary wearing a helmet painted with swastikas and the slogan 'Sieg Heil'.

A dozen South African air force planes hit Matola and another Maputo suburb, Liberdade (Liberty), on 23 May 1983. The South Africans called it Operation *Skerwe*, Afrikaans for shrapnel, and the planes strafed the two suburbs with special fragmentation rockets. Three workers at the Somopal jam factory were killed as they arrived for work. A child playing on the street was killed. An ANC man died as he washed a car, and a soldier guarding a bridge was killed. At least 40 other people, mostly women and children, were injured by the shards of shrapnel. The South Africans said they were attacking ANC bases, but there were no ANC bases to hit.

A week later, anti-aircraft fire shot down another plane as it flew lazily over the heart of Maputo. It was an Israeli-built, remote-controlled spy plane, which had been sending live close-up television pictures to South Africa. The Israelis used just this kind of plane, the Israeli Aircraft Industry 'Scout', over Lebanon before their invasion in 1982. And it is known that there are close links between the Israeli and South African militaries. Maputo is only 40 miles from the South African border, as close as Beirut is to the Israeli border. All this inevitably raised fears that Maputo could become a second Beirut.

South Africa also sends its agents into Maputo, to plant bombs, distribute leaflets, make telephone threats, and otherwise create confusion. The saddest and most dramatic event was the killing of Ruth First by a parcel bomb on 17 August 1982. She was a prominent member of the ANC and South African Communist Party (SACP), as well as being the wife of ANC and SACP leader Joe Slovo. But in Mozambique she had worked primarily as research director of the Centre of African Studies of Eduardo Mondlane University, where she moulded a team that did significant research into the most urgent problems of socialist transition. Her work influenced many of the policy changes introduced at the Frelimo Fourth Party Congress the following year.

These dramatic attacks are only a tiny sample of South Africa's destabilization of Mozambique. Primarily it works through the Mozambique National Resistance (MNR) which is causing problems in half the country. The MNR is discussed in detail in Chapter 21; and one story of its impact will do here.

'I was on my way back to school after the holiday,' said João Dedeus, a student at the Agricultural Institute in Chimoio, 'when they attacked the bus with machine-guns. It crashed, and they shot at us as we climbed out. The "bandits" stole clothes, shoes, watches – anything. I was hurt so I was slow, and they did this,' he said, pointing to his face. A big gash had been cut up the side of his face, and his eye plucked out. 'Then they set fire to the bus.' At least ten people were killed in the original machine-gunning and crash, and three more were burned to death in the bus.

Part II
Winning Control

3. Shopkeeper Colonialism – Mozambique before 1960

A bookshop in Beira still sells a colonial map of the city. It shows a cathedral by the sea, a casino, and an Avenida Salazar along the beach. None of these ever existed. The cathedral and casino were drawn on it as if they existed by Portuguese colonists, sublime in the belief that colonialism would be there long enough to build them, that it could hold out against the wave of decolonization sweeping Africa. Down to the last days the Portuguese held on to their faith. When independence came and the astounded settlers fled in disarray, they abandoned half-finished tower blocks begun only a year or two before.

The settlers were right to believe that Portuguese colonialism was different. But the reasons were poverty and fascism, not cultural superiority, as they thought. Even now, Portugal is the second poorest country in Europe; only Albania is poorer. The World Bank lists Portugal as a 'developing country'. Thus Portuguese capital was never able to exploit Mozambique effectively. This weakness, and the fascism that was so closely linked to it, both caused Portugal to hold on to its colonies longer and made a neocolonial solution impossible. The Portuguese talked romantically of 500 years of empire, but *effective* Portuguese colonialism was brief. The poorest and most underdeveloped of Europe's colonial powers left behind one of the poorest countries in Africa.

Independence came 485 years after the first Portuguese arrived to find an established trading community. Vasco da Gama reported ports filled with ships as large as his own with more sophisticated instruments and navigational charts; some port cities had multi-storey buildings. In the 16th century the Portuguese set up their own trading network and were dealing with the Monomotapa empire, builders of Great Zimbabwe. By 1629 Portugal had gained sufficient military control in Zambézia to begin land grants. These were called *prazos*, meaning limited time, as the grants were theoretically for only three generations. During that time, however, the prazo holder had unlimited feudal power in his territory. Profits were made from the ivory and gold, from taxes on the African population, and increasingly from the slave trade. By the 1820s, up to 30,000 slaves a year were being exported from Quelimane to Brazil and Cuba, representing 85% of the exports (by value) from that port. Indeed, it was so profitable that the Government tripled the export duty on slaves to raise more revenue. In 1842 the British navy began anti-slavery patrols in the Mozambique channel, but they were no more successful than those 130 years later which tried to stop oil going to Rhodesia. In the 1850s and 1860s, the trade was still 20,000 slaves per year, going to Réunion and then Madagascar and Cuba. Although the trade had often been declared illegal, a governor general in the 1880s admitted it still involved 2,000–4,000 slaves per year. And a post-independence oral history project found reports of the slave trade continuing at least until 1912. So Mozambique probably lost two million people to slavery. World War I took its toll as well; Portugal was pushed into backing Britain and up to 10,000 Mozambicans were killed fighting the Germans who controlled Tanganyika to the north. The effects of this forced depopulation are still apparent today – vast areas of Mozambique are virtually empty.

With fewer slaves and less ivory, trade in central Mozambique shifted to agricultural products. In the 1870s a free market was introduced and peasants were encouraged to produce food and oilseeds for sale. But Portugal was under growing pressure from the other colonial powers to actually occupy the territory; Britain and Germany even discussed plans to divide Mozambique between them. Without the capital to exploit Mozambique at more than a minimal level, Portugal had little choice but to lease the land and people to foreign capitalists.

In the 1870s the first tiny plantations along the Zambezi River began producing opium, as well as sugar for distillation into alcohol to be sold to Mozambicans and miners in the Transvaal. With government encouragement, more and larger plantations were established in Zambézia. John P. Hornung developed the Sena Sugar Estates into the largest plantation in the colony. Boror developed one of the biggest coconut plantations in the world. Madal and the Zambézia Company also had sizeable estates. None were Portuguese. To ensure complete control of their labour supply, these companies also took over some of the old prazos. This provoked significant migrations, as families moved from one prazo to another to find the least onerous conditions.

In 1891 one-third of the country was simply given to two chartered companies. The Mozambique Company took present-day Manica and Sofala Provinces while the Niassa Company leased Niassa and Cabo Delgado.

African lands were taken over and peasant cash cropping was curbed. At the same time, forced labour was introduced. The Native Labour Regulations of 1899 specified that 'All natives of the Portuguese overseas provinces are subject to the moral and legal obligation of attempting to obtain, through work, the means they lack for subsistence and to improve their social condition. They have full liberty to choose the method of fulfilling this obligation, but if they fail to fulfil it, the public authorities may force them to do so.' A head tax was introduced as well. All Africans had to carry cards showing their work and tax records. Traditional chiefs, known as *régulos*, were expected to ensure that men under them took wage labour and paid their taxes; those régulos who refused were simply replaced by more compliant men. This was not accepted by the Mozambicans, who fought back. The last feudal ruler in the south, Gungunhana, was beaten in 1895. But armed resistance in Zambézia continued until 1920.

The south of Mozambique was then set aside to serve the growing Rand gold fields. In 1909 an agreement was signed between the government of the Transvaal and Portugal guaranteeing mine labour. In exchange, half of all Transvaal trade would go through the new port of Lourenço Marques. Wenela (Witwatersrand Native Labour Association) was given exclusive recruiting rights south of the River Save. For the next 66 years there were normally 80,000 to 110,000 Mozambicans in South African mines, and Lourenço Marques was developed on the strength of the Rand port traffic. For the miners, life was harsh: an estimated 43,000 Mozambicans died of accidents and disease in South African mines between 1902 and 1914, while another 20,000 died in Rhodesian mines between 1900 and 1920. But the money was vital, both for Portugal and for the peasant economy. Remittances from miners and South African port and railway traffic accounted for about one-fifth of Mozambique's foreign exchange, much the most important source of revenue. In the peasant economy in the three southern provinces of Mozambique, mine money was eight times that earned by selling cash crops.

Just as Portugal's economy was dominated by British capital, so Mozambique was dominated by Britain and South Africa. More than half the colony's trade was with Britain, British colonies or South Africa. Mozambique seemed more a British than a Portuguese colony. The two biggest chartered companies, Mozambique and Niassa, were British, as was the giant Sena Sugar Estates. The ports and railways were largely developed to serve British colonies and South Africa: Lourenço Marques for the Rand, and Beira for Southern Rhodesia (Zimbabwe) and Nyasaland (Malawi). Newspapers in Beira and Lourenço Marques were partly in English. In 1931 Sena Sugar Estates was still paying most of its wages in British sterling. In 1932 a Beira hotel would not let the Portuguese colonial minister pay in Portuguese currency.

The fascist 'new state' of António Salazar which came to power as a result of a military coup in 1926 tried to change this. Industrialization in Portugal was encouraged and national capital promoted at the expense of British. Salazar tried to make more effective use of the colonies. Until then, Portugal had only earned money by leasing out Mozambican labour – to neighbouring countries and foreign-owned plantations. Salazar said the colonies should 'produce raw materials to sell to the motherland in exchange for manufactured goods' and could provide 'a logical solution to Portugal's problem of overpopulation' through resettlement in the colonies.

Earlier, Portugal had tried to encourage capitalist agriculture through the prazos and then the chartered companies, using the right to collect taxes and employ forced labour as a sweetener. But it was unsuccessful, as the prazo holders and chartered companies were undercapitalized and just lived off their taxes. So the Government decided to try to exploit the country itself. Prazos were ended in 1930 and the Niassa Company charter was not renewed in 1928. The somewhat more successful Mozambique Company continued to rule Manica and Sofala until 1941, and it continues today as part of Entreposto. So it was only in 1941 that the Government's writ ran to the whole colony.

Portuguese capital did move into tea growing and cotton ginning, for example. But it was only when World War II weakened the grip of British capital that Portuguese capital began to dominate. Thus it was not until the late 1940s that Portugal finally accounted for more than half the trade with its own colony. Portugal always remained too poor to invest very much in Mozambique, so it could only profit from increased use of cheap labour. But at the same time, Portugal's poverty meant that it could not forgo the profitable export of workers to neighbouring countries.

With 500,000 men working outside the country, and weak Portuguese capital demanding more cheap labour, the only choice was to increase the exploitation of labour and force the peasants to grow certain crops on their own land. This involved much tighter state control over the 'natives'. Soon the central role of the colonial state apparatus became the recruitment of labour, both for direct sale abroad and to the existing foreign-owned plantations, as well as to stimulate investment by Portuguese capital.

To ensure that labour was to remain cheap, it was kept migrant. This meant the employer only paid a man enough to keep him alive and pay his tax; the costs of food, clothing, housing and so on for the whole family were carried by the women at home, who maintained the family plots. Precautions were taken to ensure that peasants always had a family farm to return to: communal tenure was preserved to ensure that no group of landless workers emerged, and forced cultivation of subsistence crops was later imposed. At the same time, planters were organized into recruiting syndicates so that they did not compete for workers and push up wages.

The state needed the maximum number of workers, and the full force of fascism was put behind this. Stricter labour laws were imposed, requiring every able-bodied man to work six months each year. The minimum (and thus the normal) wage for the six months was set at just twice the annual head tax. In Zambézia this tax was paid by the employer directly to the administrator, and it became a main source of colonial government revenue. (Of course Portugal itself benefited much more from the cheap raw materials and export markets.)

Men caught avoiding work were sent to do road building, at an even lower wage or none at all. Sometimes the two were combined. Using the census, the colonial administrator compiled a list of men who had not done wage labour for six months, and sent his police to round them up. First they did two weeks of road work to punish them for their 'idleness' and then they were handed over to the recruiters. Administrators were also expected to catch men who escaped before finishing their contracts. This usually involved beating the man with a *palmatória* and sending him back to start his contract from scratch without pay for the part already served. If the man could not be found, his wife and children were arrested and forced to work. The Portuguese became very skilled and efficient at this kind of force. During the 1940s and 1950s, more than 85% of available men in Zambézia worked on contracts to plantations.

Judith Head, of the Eduardo Mondlane University, studied the increased exploitation of labour by Sena Sugar Estates, the *largest private employer* in colonial Mozambique. Workers were paid for the day only if they, or their team, finished a defined task. Between 1930 and 1950 tasks steadily increased: cane cutting rose from 3 tons per man per day to 3.85, while a team of eight labourers was expected to load four instead of three trucks with cane. A government inspector in 1956 found men working 11 hours a day without a break. Meanwhile, living conditions were so bad that workers became increasingly debilitated. At night five to eight men slept on the floor of each straw hut with only blankets to cover them. There were few latrines and no running water, so they washed, urinated and defecated in water they also had to drink.

In 1942 the company's own doctor complained of the conditions in the company flour mill at Marromeu. The men worked 12-hour shifts and the night shift was locked in. The doctor noted that, 'If by chance any worker needs to defecate, it is there that he does it using a sack to keep the excrement until he has finished his shift . . . . It is beyond understanding that a place where flour is milled, a product which is handled for human consumption, also serves as a urinal and a place for defecation.'

Food was equally bad. The men had only one meal a day and that was mainly flour which they had to cook themselves, and often ate raw because they were too tired to cook. Furthermore, they received their day's ration only if they finished the assigned task. Under international pressure, the colonial authorities introduced regulations to try to improve living standards slightly, but Sena simply ignored them. For many years Sena resisted pressure to give the workers fruit and vegetables, and Dr Head notes that, 'For 27 years Sena Sugar Estates managed to avoid the law which stipulated that workers were to receive three meals a day.'

For the plantations, a six-month term of forced labour was ideal. It covered seasonal peaks and allowed them to exhaust the man physically, then send him home to his family farm for six months to recover, while paying nothing to the cost of supporting him or his family. For Sena there was one problem: men were dropping dead on the long walk home after their contract. So the company doctor was instructed to keep in hospital those too weak to go home until they recovered sufficient strength.

Forced labour, known as *chibalo*, was not just used for plantations. Forced labourers built the roads and railways; thousands worked in the ports. They were the basis of the construction industry in Lourenço Marques, and built the cathedral. Social clubs in the capital became accustomed to using chibalo labourers for building tennis courts, cutting the grass, and so on. And the availability of chibalo workers kept African wages down; in Lourenço Marques the ratio between wages of white and black carpenters spread from three to one in 1906 to 13 to one in 1960.

Textiles are usually one of the first areas of industrialization for an underdeveloped country, and the Portuguese 'new state' was no exception. Portugal's new textile industry depended on having a monopoly market in the colonies and a secure supply of cheap cotton. The fascist state tackled this problem in the obvious way: peasants were forced to grow cotton and sell it to the state at well below world market prices.

As the men were already forced to do chibalo labour, each woman was required to grow one acre of cotton. This was enforced through sheer brutality: women who failed to grow their cotton were beaten and raped. In areas like Nampula where there was less demand for chibalo labour, men were also forced to grow cotton. To make the system easier to police, peasants were made to build roads and move their farms next to the roads. By the late 1940s, more than 600,000 peasant families were producing cotton and Portugal was getting 96% of its needs from its colonies, mostly Mozambique. Forced cropping seemed such a good idea that in areas where cotton would not grow, peasants were forced to grow rice or groundnuts.

But the double oppression of forced labour and forced cropping was finally too much. Cotton and rice are labour intensive and have exactly the same cycles as normal peasant food crops, particularly grains, beans and peanuts. And plantation labour peaks are similar to food-crop labour peaks. So with the man away and the woman forced to work on the cotton crop, the family was unable to grow enough food. Several severe famines in the 1940s were linked to forced cotton growing. The fascist answer was more force: peasants were also required to grow cassava. It is much less nutritious than other food crops but requires much less work and its season does not conflict with cotton. That, at least, staved off further famines.

Although the colony was intended to supply raw materials and markets for Portuguese industry, some industry was also built in Mozambique. Before World War II, Mozambique was already producing cement, bricks, beer, cigarettes and soap for local consumption. In the 15 years after the war, it began production of flour, clothing, shoes, furniture, nails, small machinery and glass. But more than half of all investments in manufacturing industry in those 15 years went into processing plants for the four main export crops: sugar, tea, cotton and sisal. Mozambican industry remained small and limited to areas which would feed, and not compete with, the motherland.

The unwillingness of the fascist Government to break up the big estates in Portugal was leading to increasing landlessness and migration to the cities there, which in turn was leading to unemployment and threatening unrest. Tens of thousands of Portuguese went to more developed European countries in search of work (and later to avoid military service in the colonial wars). After 1950 an attempt was made to resettle the unemployed as peasant farmers on *colonatos*, particularly the massive Limpopo valley irrigation scheme. The European population grew from 27,000 in 1940 to 48,000 in 1950 and 97,000 in 1960.

Portugal claimed to have a non-racialist policy based on civilizing the Africans and drawing them into Portuguese society. Blacks could become *assimilados*, or honorary Whites, if they spoke Portuguese, abandoned their 'traditional' way of life, acquired a certain education, and earned a sufficient income from commerce or industry. And it is true that the Portuguese were more class conscious than race conscious; an educated, well-to-do African or mixed-race person would be more acceptable in Lourenço Marques society than a barefoot, illiterate white peasant. But the 1955 census recorded only 4,500 assimilados. The other 6 million Africans were subject to pass laws, forced labour, and curfews which created an effective apartheid system, whatever the colonial rhetoric.

The Roman Catholic Church already played a strong role in Mozambique, and its position was strengthened by the 1940 concordat between Portugal and the Vatican. In exchange for strong Church support for the fascist state, the Government agreed to fund missions and religious orders, give special status to the clergy, restrict the activity of Protestant missionaries and Churches, and give the Catholic Church full control and responsibility for 'native' education. This took the form of 'rudimentary education' which was the equivalent of two years of primary school and was done in Portuguese. 'Yes, schools are necessary, but schools where we teach the native the road to human dignity and the grandeur of the nation which protects him,' explained the head of the Church, Cardinal Clemente Gouveia, in a pastoral letter in 1960. But the schools were only 'to teach the native population to read, write, and count; not to make them "doctors" but as a way to make them prisoners of the earth.' The state retained the job of teaching Whites and assimilados, using the same programme as in Portugal. But education was never a priority for the fascist 'new state', and the 1955 census showed that only one-third of the Portuguese in Mozambique could read and write.

By the end of the 1950s, then, Mozambique was different in many ways from the French and British colonies soon to come to independence. It was doubly peripheral, in that it was dependent on states that themselves had peripheral economies – Portugal and South Africa. Frelimo calls this 'shopkeeper colonialism', and this was true in three senses. First, the settlers did not have economic control; they served and managed foreign enterprises. Second, the whole colony largely served its neighbours. And third, the colonists themselves were predominantly peasant farmers and shopkeepers rather than wealthy exploiters.

The colony was also dissimilar from many in Africa because fascist Portugal continued oppression and forced labour later than many others. There was no liberal parliamentary opposition to temper fascist oppression, and Portuguese capital remained too weak to accept a neocolonial solution. It was on this basis that the independence struggle began. As we will see in the following two chapters, Portuguese colonialism changed dramatically as it tried to catch up, and Portugal tried to be the only country to hold on to its colonies.

Meanwhile, Mozambicans came to the peak of their suffering at the end of the 1950s. Even the peasant agriculture and small trading which had existed in the last century had been destroyed. There was no longer any such thing as 'subsistence agriculture'. Peasants were an integral part of the cash economy and they were expected to buy things which forced labour and forced cropping allowed them no time to grow or make. (Yet their buying power remained too small to support much local industry.) They were, in practice, no longer peasants but peasant-workers.

This left many scars, that continue to the present. The diet was permanently corrupted; after two generations of an enforced diet, primarily of cassava, peasants have become accustomed to it and accept undernourishment. They do not (and cannot) return to the more varied, nutritious mix of crops they grew generations ago. The ban on trade by Africans has left Mozambique as one of the few countries where bus and train stops are not thronged with vendors. Organizing new cooperatives and communal villages is painfully slow because of the lack of organizing experience. Decades of monocropping and overcropping have led to soil degradation and erosion that will require technical and social revolutions to redress. And hundreds of thousands of Mozambicans have spent most of their adult life working abroad, and have no jobs at home and no means to set themselves up as peasant farmers.

Mozambique is one of the poorest countries in Africa not because it lacks natural resources, nor because Portugal left it undeveloped, but rather because Portugal actively underdeveloped it. This legacy appears repeatedly throughout this book, and dogs Frelimo today.

4. Armed Struggle

Colonial Mozambique's biggest export was people. As well as the officially contracted miners, literally hundreds of thousands fled to neighbouring countries. They picked Nyasaland tea instead of Mozambican tea and cut Tanganyikan sisal instead of Mozambican sisal. They were paid a bit more. But many who talked to the History Workshop of the Centre of African Studies stressed their attempts to escape the brutality of forced labour: beatings, imprisonment, starvation and sometimes even death.

So while Portugal tried to resist the decolonization that was going on around it, its own subject people were taking part in that process. In Tanganyika, Mozambican sisal cutters joined Julius Nyerere's Tanganyika African National Union (Tanu) and participated in its meetings, discussing self-determination and the need to struggle for independence. One of the corner-stones of Tanu was the formation of cooperatives of peasant coffee and cotton producers as a basis for political organization and struggle.

On the Mueda plateau in the north of Mozambique, many people went back and forth regularly (if illegally) to Tanzania, and they brought back the ideas of Tanu and cooperatives. In 1956 a local teacher, João Namimba, went to Tanganyika to talk with Nyerere, who stressed that Mozambicans must form their own movement. So in 1957 the African Voluntary Cotton Society of Mozambique (Saavm, from the Portuguese initials) was formed on Mueda. Lázaro Nkavandame was president and Namimba vice-president. One secretary was Raimundo Pachinuapa (now state inspector), and an early member was Alberto Joaquim Chipande (now Defence Minister and a member of the Frelimo Politburo). They negotiated a licence with the colonial administrator for the cotton co-op.

There were many contradictions in the process. Cotton was intensely disliked because it was a forced crop; it had already been a focus of struggle with peasants refusing to grow it. Yet it was the only crop that would earn enough profit to make a co-op viable. Some other administrators in the region opposed Saavm because they saw, correctly, that it was a base for something more; the Mueda administrator supported it as a way to stop the flight to Tanzania and to integrate the people into the colonial economy. The co-op was highly popular because members were

23

exempt from forced labour on the sisal plantations. Although much of the work was still on individual plots, and members sold their own cotton, they did some tasks in common, like clearing land. Furthermore, the co-op monitored individual sales to ensure that the monopoly buyer did not cheat co-op members. Most important, Saavm members developed and controlled their own organization.

From 1957 to 1960 the co-op produced three times as much cotton as had been produced on Mueda from purely forced cotton growing, and the income of its more than 3,000 members rose. The existence of Saavm, and the close contacts with what was happening on the other side of the Rovuma River in Tanganyika, raised the consciousness of the people. Various demands were made to the administrator and several people were arrested. On 16 June 1960 a large crowd gathered outside the administrator's office to protest to the visiting provincial governor. The governor ordered the soldiers to fire on the crowd, and as many as 600 people were killed.

The Mueda massacre showed more clearly than any other single event that the peaceful transition to independence taking place in neighbouring Tanganyika and elsewhere on the continent was not possible in Mozambique. Several independence movements were quickly formed by exiles outside the country. On Mueda, Saavm collapsed, but Nkavandame and others continued to organize. They received permission to set up a new, smaller rice-growing co-op. They distributed cards for the Mozambique African National Union (Manu) whch had been formed in Kenya in 1961. When Frelimo was established the following year, João Namimba was sent as a delegate to its First Congress. But Portuguese oppression grew and, as more co-op members were arrested, Chipande, Nkavandame and others fled to Tanganyika to join Frelimo.

In the south there was movement, too. There were a few strikes, involving dockers, nurses and others. Protestant Churches gave covert support to Black nationalism. Multi-racial organizations were formed, most notably the Nucleus of Mozambican Secondary Students, which included Frelimo's first President, Eduardo Mondlane, three present Politburo members (Armando Guebuza, Joaquim Chissano, and Mariano Matsinhe), and the present Health Minister, Pascoal Mocumbi. In Paris, exiled intellectuals from the Portuguese colonies, including present Frelimo Politburo member Marcelino dos Santos, came together.

Inside Mozambique, the secret police (Pide) was strong and it could enforce the total ban on political activities. So the first organizations were formed outside the country in 1960 and 1961. Manu was based on the model of Tanu and Kanu, the Kenya African National Union. Udenamo was set up in Southern Rhodesia on the model of Joshua Nkomo's National Democratic Party, and was headed by the Rev. Uria Simango and Adelino Gwambe. Unami was established in Malawi.

With the independence of Tanganyika in December 1961, all three moved their headquarters to Dar es Salaam. Nyerere put pressure on them to merge. On 25 June 1962 they finally came together to form the Front for the Liberation of Mozambique (Frelimo), which held its First Congress later that year. Mondlane was elected President, Simango Vice-President, and dos Santos Secretary for External Relations. Nyerere then allowed Frelimo to use Tanganyika as a base.

Mondlane was born in 1920, the youngest child of the third wife of a régulo in Gaza Province. After completing what little education was available to Blacks in Mozambique, he taught himself English and won a scholarship to South Africa where he finally completed secondary school at age 27. His political activities earned him expulsion from South Africa and harassment from Pide. In 1951 he won a scholarship to study in the US where he eventually gained a PhD. In 1957 he started working for the Trusteeship Department of the United Nations. In that post he became friendly with Nyerere and maintained contact with a number of Mozambican nationalists. In 1961, with the protection of a UN passport, he spent three months in Mozambique talking to groups working clandestinely inside the country. He went on to Salisbury (now Harare) to talk with Udenamo and remained in contact with all three movements as he tried to organize a joint body. Mondlane himself had not joined any of the three because of his UN post, which he resigned in late 1961 to take a more active part in nationalist activity. He commented later that, 'In June 1962 I came to Dar es Salaam with the sole purpose of convincing those who were still doubtful about unity.'

Frelimo remained a very loose grouping of exile organizations which distrusted each other and were already infiltrated by Pide. The first years were marked by infighting, intrigues, purges, and defections. 'Almost immediately after the closing session of the First Congress some members of the Central Committee began manoeuvring to expel others,' Mondlane told the Second Congress. Within three years, most of those who founded Frelimo had left. But Frelimo provided the essential focus for those who, like the present President Samora Machel, were to flee Mozambique.

The defectors formed and re-formed a host of organizations. Finally, in mid-1965 the Zambian Government called a conference in an effort to reunify the movement. Mondlane attended but walked out when the others refused to rejoin Frelimo. The remaining groups formed Coremo, the Mozambique Revolutionary Committee, headed by Gwambe. Internationally Coremo was associated with Unita and the Pan Africanist Congress (PAC). Although Coremo launched a few raids into Tete Province from Zambia, it seems never to have been very effective. The failure of Coremo proved a boon to Frelimo later, because it meant that at independence, Frelimo did not face a challenge from another credible liberation movement like Zapu in Zimbabwe and Unita in Angola.

Anders Nilsson/AIM

A war veteran offers a gun he mended to President Samora Machel. April 1983, FRELIMO 4th Party Congress

First Shots

Most of Frelimo's founders were in exile in British colonies, so, despite the lesson of the Mueda massacre, they expected a struggle similar to those being waged by nationalist organizations in those colonies: demonstrations, strikes and other non-violent protests leading to negotiation and eventual independence. But Portugal refused to talk with Frelimo, and talks between Portugal and the United Nations proved fruitless.

The first shots were fired on 25 September 1964. Six years later, Frelimo's magazine *Mozambique Revolution* admitted that 'a majority of the founding members of Frelimo' was not prepared for an armed struggle. Many dropped out and joined the splinter groups. The Frelimo First Congress in September 1962 had made provision for military action, and a first group – including Machel and Chipande – were sent to Algeria in January 1963 for military training. But there were sharp divisions within Frelimo as to what the military tactics should be. Some called for an uprising in the capital. Others, influenced by the writings of Che Guevara, argued that small groups throughout the country could inspire the peasants to attack the settlers. A third group, including those trained in Algeria, called for a longer guerrilla struggle.

At first, all three lines were pushed. But an uprising in the Angolan capital, Luanda, had failed in February 1961, and the Frelimo underground network in Lourenço Marques was broken in late 1964, so the first option was never tried. The actions of September 1964 were a mix of the other two. It was intended to make raids in Tete, Zambézia, Niassa and Cabo Delgado on the same day. Only in Cabo Delgado, where Frelimo had been able to do some political organizing, was the action really successful. Activity in Tete and Zambézia had to be quickly abandoned for lack of support, and because Frelimo could not use Malawi as a rear base and thus had trouble supplying those two fronts. Thus it was already becoming clear which military line would have to be followed.

For six years after the start of the armed struggle, the internecine struggle continued with purges and assassinations. Samora Machel admitted later that between 1967 and 1969 the leadership of Frelimo was virtually 'paralysed' by the disputes. Only three members of Frelimo's first Central Committee are on the present Central Committee: dos Santos, Matsinhe and Mocumbi. But on the battlefield Frelimo was having considerable success in Cabo Delgado and Niassa. The Portuguese soon withdrew from the sparsely populated northern strip of the country; and new recruits streamed in to join the movement. Many residents of the Mueda plateau, already politicized by the cooperatives and the massacre, moved down into the bush to join Frelimo. Frelimo's internal struggles grew from its victories, especially over the issue of how to administer the new liberated zones. The disputes, which were really about what kind of country Mozambique would be after independence, have shaped Frelimo's post-independence policies.

'For us, Marxism-Leninism was not something we chose out of a book. It was in the process of the struggle that the people's interests asserted themselves and became more and more clearly demarcated from the interests of the colonial exploiter and the would-be national exploiter,' explained the Politburo in a report in 1978. 'Marxism-Leninism is a living science which is continually developing in the process of revolutionary struggles. It is not a sclerotic, dogmatic catechism; not a complete and finalized pharmacopoeia.'

As the main purpose of this book is to discuss post-independence Mozambique, the rest of this chapter will concentrate on these disputes and how they moulded Frelimo. I will largely ignore the increasingly successful armed struggle. (Barry Munslow's recent book, *Mozambique: The Revolution and Its Origins*, gives a more detailed picture of colonial history and the liberation struggle than is possible here.)

Frelimo tends retrospectively to summarize this period as a 'constant struggle between two lines'. In practice, the divisions were never so clear at the time; the 'wrong' line often drew a considerable number of adherents, and the 'wrong' side was not itself homogeneous. Nevertheless, the splits grew out of attempts to resolve real, practical problems, and often showed very clearly where the interests of the participants lay. From this troubled period emerged a leadership which was committed and able to bring about a socialist transformation in Mozambique, and which has remained remarkably unified for 15 years.

Evolving Policies

As the war gained momentum, food became a problem. Some of the peasants who went into the bush expected Frelimo to feed them, and the guerrillas had to organize them to produce food. Similarly, the guerrillas had to feed themselves, so at training camps in Tanzania and at bases inside Mozambique they had small farms. Eventually they organized people to set up collective plots to help feed the fighters.

This was done under difficult conditions, because Frelimo's hit-and-run tactics against the Portuguese often provoked retaliation against nearby peasants. Huts were bombed, crops burned, and, later, commando groups made brutal raids. Thus Frelimo was forced to provide some sort of protection and to organize people so that they could be protected. One way was to cluster houses in small groups hidden under trees; these proved to be embryos of the later communal villages.

People had to be organized to serve as porters to carry military supplies for long distances from Tanzania. The same method was used to organize a lively trade, with cashew nuts and sesame seeds being exported and consumer goods brought back. Life was harsh in the liberated zones and the workload clearly increased. It became clear that half the workforce, the women, were being effectively excluded. This led Frelimo to an increasing integration of women, first as porters and later as guerrillas.

All of this inevitably led the guerrillas into political work in the liberated zones. Furthermore, the basis of Frelimo's advance was to send political organizers out into Portuguese-held areas first to lay the groundwork and ensure that the guerrillas would be well received. Out of this evolved the tradition of regular public meetings and of living close to the people. It was also essential for Frelimo's leaders, many of whom came from bourgeois urban backgrounds, to learn from the peasants about their experiences and needs. Thus the meetings became real exchanges, and Frelimo gained support precisely because it was so open to education and criticism from the base.

This, in turn, led to two other lines which Frelimo has maintained since. First was a strict morality. Guerrillas could not abuse the peasants and especially not mistreat women; they had to be seen as better than the Portuguese and the chiefs, or they would find disgruntled peasants betraying them to the Portuguese. Second, they began sharing services with the people. For example, first aid assistants trained to treat guerrilla casualties found themselves pressed to provide health services to the people. This led Frelimo to develop a rudimentary health service in the liberated zones which served as a basis for the post-independence commitment to primary health care. Similarly, Frelimo's own efforts to teach its fighters to read led to schools in the liberated zones. The regular public meetings and the provision of alternative services evolved into an alternative system of government. The liberated zones were more than simply places where Portuguese writ no longer ran.

Racism, regionalism, and tribalism were also early problems for Frelimo. The three groups that formed Frelimo represented three different regions with different languages and cultural backgrounds. From the beginning, groups were integrated and underwent training together. Eventually Portuguese was selected as a unifying language and all fighters were expected to learn and use it. (In practice some of the older exiled leaders continued to use English, while the fighters used a mix of Portuguese and Kiswahili, reflecting the use of Tanzania as a rearbase.) Much stress was also placed on culture as a unifying force, and guerrillas learned the songs and dances of other tribes.

The struggle in the colonies became associated with the anti-fascist struggle in Portugal, which meant that from the first it was not simply a black nationalist uprising. One member of the first Central Committee, dos Santos, is of mixed race, as is Rebelo who was an early participant in the armed struggle. In 1963 a white Portuguese air force officer, Jacinto Veloso, stole a plane and flew to Tanganyika to join Frelimo. Veloso, now a member of the Politburo, was accompanied by the present white Agriculture Minister, João Ferreira. This gave a multi-racial character to Frelimo which was not present in some other liberation movements.

All of this may seem blindingly obvious now, set down in this way, but it wasn't to the participants at the time – nor has it been to many of the groups fighting for independence in Africa over the past three decades. In Frelimo, every one of these points was fought over.

For example, Frelimo initially followed the model of the British colonies and separated the political and military into the departments of interior and defence. The non-political army was to do the fighting while a new administration handled political issues. Initially, Frelimo did not worry too much about administering the newly liberated zones. As a broad anti-colonial front, it had drawn support from some of the local chiefs and traditional leaders, who tended to be left in charge with the adopted British title of 'chairmen'. The chairmen in Cabo Delgado also controlled commerce, including the Frelimo 'People's Shops', and had large farms using hired labour. Nkavandame, for example, already had one shop in the late 1950s and expanded his private business through the cotton cooperative and profits from hiring out a tractor. During the war, he used his post as head of the Provincial Cooperatives Committee for personal benefit, using Frelimo transport in Tanzania to carry goods for his shops. Thus the chairmen were a group looking for a change in government, but not in social or economic relations. For the guerrillas, and increasingly for the rest of the peasants, the war was not simply to change the colour of the exploiters. Tensions grew.

It was not until two years after the start of the armed struggle that Frelimo's Central Committee finally sorted out the question of military tactics. Although it had been most successful in Cabo Delgado, Frelimo by then was also active in significant parts of Niassa. Samora Machel took over as army commander after the death of Filipe Samual Magaia on 10 October 1966. It was clear by then that Portugal would not easily abandon its colony as some Frelimo founders had hoped. Instead Portugal was bringing in troops and foreign capital to defend the colony. Thus the October 1966 Central Committee session called for the integration of the mass of the people in a prolonged struggle. The distinction between political and military wings was ended and it was decided that everyone should undergo both military and political training.

In a paper published at independence, Frelimo summarized its military tactics. It concentrated on rural zones to which it had easy access and where the enemy was weak, enabling it to steadily liberate more territory and people. It acted like a crocodile which stayed in the water to gain maximum advantage over the enemy. Enemy bases and convoys served as targets. The idea was not to gain spectacular victories, but to accumulate small ones, destroying the small bases that protect the big one so that the Portuguese would eventually be reduced to isolated, useless islands surrounded by liberated zones.

The chairmen ignored the decision to integrate the military and political wings and also opposed the concept of a prolonged people's war. A group led by Nkavandame launched a campaign against the department of defence. They said the guerrillas were wasting time with political activities instead of fighting and were responsible for Portuguese attacks on people in the liberated zones. Eventually they urged the peasants to stop feeding the guerrillas.

Women proved another area of conflict. Women were involved in the first clandestine youth groups and served as porters and spies against the Portuguese. The October 1966 Central Committee meeting made Frelimo's first commitment to women's emancipation. This was opposed by the more conservative leaders. Nevertheless, in 1967 Frelimo created a women's detachment and sent the first women for military training at the main camp in Nachingwea, Tanzania. This provoked further opposition and required considerable explanation. It led Frelimo down the path of opposing polygamy, initiation rites and other forms of discrimination against women, in a direct confrontation with the chairmen and traditional authorities.

Some of the sharpest disputes were centred on education. Frelimo took the line that educated people must return to fight and work in the liberated zones. There was resistance to this, both out of self-interest and from the argument that with trained people so scarce it was silly to risk their being killed. Mondlane went to the United States in 1966 and 1967 in an unsuccessful effort to convince students to return when they completed their first degrees instead of studying for advanced degrees. Students in the United States and Czechoslovakia responded with public attacks on the Frelimo leadership. US students accused Mondlane of being a traitor and harassing students who might be future rivals.

José Massinga was a leader of the US student group who eventually went on to get a PhD in Geneva instead of returning to the fight. He did return in 1973, under Frelimo's policy of reconciliation. Eventually Massinga became director of staff planning in the Ministry of Foreign Affairs. In 1981 he admitted being an agent for the US Central Intelligence Agency.

Similar problems arose among secondary school students in Dar es Salaam. The use of Portuguese and the lack of international accreditation for the Frelimo Secondary School effectively cut off the avenue of study in the US and brought protests, led by Father Mateus Gwenjere in particular. He had been a mission teacher in Tete who recruited a number of his pupils for Frelimo with the promise of scholarships in America. He followed them to Dar es Salaam in 1967 and began teaching at the secondary school.

Gwenjere and others also promoted racial tensions, obliquely against President Mondlane's white American wife Janet, who headed the Mozambique Institute, and more explicitly against other Whites at the institute and secondary school. Black nationalists within Frelimo had strong support from some elements in Tanu and in the Tanzanian Government, and in January 1968 they arranged the expulsion of two white British women working for the institute.

On 5 March there was a confrontation at the secondary school over the unwillingness of students to go to the liberated zones and their desire to have courses geared to diplomas rather than the immediate needs of the struggle. Four-fifths of the students fled, according to Barry Munslow. The secondary school was closed. Frelimo lost a significant part of its trained people, particularly vitally necessary health workers. But trained health workers were of little use if they were not willing to go where they were needed, and Frelimo learned to do without them – a valuable lesson it applied seven years later when Portuguese technicians fled at independence.

Soon after, the black nationalists responded by organizing the expulsion of three white Mozambicans, two teachers at the secondary school (Veloso and Fernando Ganhão, now rector of Eduardo Mondlane University) and a doctor, Helder Martins, who became the first Health Minister.

Other disputes were also rending Frelimo. For example, on 9 May a group attacked the Frelimo offices, killing a Central Committee member. With the crisis reaching its peak, Frelimo agreed to call its Second Congress, to start on 20 July 1968. Two central issues were where the Congress was to be held, and whether the guerrillas were to be represented. The leadership wanted it in the liberated zone while their opponents wanted it on 'neutral ground' in Tanzania. Similarly, the chairmen, who had never accepted the abolition of the distinction between political and military, argued that the Congress should be for the political leadership only. They lost on both counts. The Congress was in Matchedje, in Niassa, and a Cabo Delgado delegation was headed by the provincial military commander, Raimundo Pachinuapa. These two choices made the outcome of the Congress clear, and it was boycotted by Nkavandame and some of his chairmen.

The Congress approved the line of a protracted war based on mass mobilization, and approved the setting up of administrative structures in the liberated zones which were to be alternative to both the Portuguese and the traditional chiefs. Its anti-racist line was shown by a commitment to clemency for prisoners of war. Economic development was stressed, and cooperatives promoted. Mondlane and Simango were re-elected President and Vice-President.

Reaction

Naturally Nkavandame did not accept the outcome of the Congress. He retained the support of some people inside Tanu and the Tanzanian Government, and he was able to convince the Tanzanians to close the border to prevent Frelimo from going to Cabo Delgado. Tanu organized a meeting in Mtwara in southern Tanzania but it failed to reconcile the two sides. Tanu then backed the Frelimo leadership and reopened the border. Nkavandame pushed for an independent and separate Cabo Delgado, probably on the model of Biafra, which had recently seceded from Nigeria and was backed by Tanzania. He set up his own army and killed a Frelimo official who tried to cross into Cabo Delgado. Portugal stepped up its attacks on the province and there were no guerrillas to protect the people, who were already unhappy about being exploited by Nkavandame's shops. So Nkavandame gained little support, and in April defected to the Portuguese. Another Frelimo official, external secretary Miguel Murrupa, went over to the Portuguese a few months later.

This was overshadowed by the assassination of Mondlane on 3 February 1969. He was killed by a bomb concealed in a book, almost certainly sent by Pide, but probably with help from dissidents within the Frelimo leadership. Simango, as Vice-President, tried to take Mondlane's place, but he was thwarted at a Central Committee meeting in April which named a three-man Presidential Council of Simango, Machel, and dos Santos. Outmanoeuvred, Simango later resigned and in November published a document entitled 'Gloomy Situation in Frelimo'. In it, and in a letter shortly after to the Organization of African Unity, Simango set out his very clear differences with Frelimo.

First, he accused a group from the south – Machel, Chissano, dos Santos, Guebuza and the late Mondlane – of dominating the organization. He said that after Mondlane's death they conspired with his widow Janet, who he claimed was a CIA agent, to assassinate several people including himself.

Second, he demanded that the white Janet Mondlane be replaced as director of the Mozambique Institute by 'an African', that there should not be (white) Portuguese teachers at the secondary school, and that Frelimo should not accept the dos Santos line that Whites could 'also be Mozambicans like the black masses and should not be discriminated against'.

Finally, he argued that 'we are not strong enough to fight the Portuguese and their allies and at the same time wage war against a national bourgeois class. If they [the bourgeoisie] existed we would rally them to fight with us against the common enemy.' And he said that 'the question of scientific socialism and capitalism in Mozambique should not be allowed to divide us.'

Simango's view drew the support of most Mozambicans outside the country, particularly students, who had not been part of the struggle and did not understand the transformation taking place inside Frelimo. Several Frelimo officials abroad, including the representatives in Egypt and Sweden, resigned in support of Simango. Some followed him into Coremo. (When stability was restored inside Frelimo, those who had chosen the wrong side were invited to return to the fold, and some did.)

The departure of Nkavandame and Simango represented the final disappearance of the black nationalist and bourgeois elements in Frelimo. And it finally clarified a series of central tenets, which have characterized Frelimo since:

*the revolution is socialist, anti-colonialist, and anti-fascist, not anti-White or anti-Portuguese;

*the goal is to liberate all of Mozambique, not simply one part, and Frelimo must be non-tribal and non-racial;

*the army is a political force and everyone must undergo both political and military training and take part in the struggle;

*mass health and education and collective production are viewed as important;

*the people should govern themselves, and not be ruled by traditional chiefs and traditional law;

*commerce must be controlled by the state and not private enterprise.

As will become clear in the rest of this book, these hard won goals dominate post-independence policy. For example, Frelimo never even considered giving authority to chiefs or reintroducing 'traditional courts' for some people as was done in neighbouring countries; instead, it pushed for elected councils and a unified legal system. Similarly, in 1982 as the struggle against the anti-government Mozambique National Resistance increased, many officials were sent for military training and went about their civilian jobs armed, while the army had a clear political influence on the Fourth Congress in promoting what might be called a pro-peasant line.

Several additional points should be stressed. First, Nkavandame's manipulating the cooperatives for his own benefit and his control of commerce were seen as responsible for turning the peasants against Frelimo in Cabo Delgado. They could see that Nkavandame was simply replacing the merchants who had fled and was using his authority to make the peasants carry goods for very low salaries. As much as anything else, this moulded Frelimo's commitment to socialist economics.

This made clear to Frelimo the second point: that the internal struggle had been basically a class struggle. This led it specifically to reject Nyerere's ideas of 'African socialism' based on communal traditions, which ignored the feudal roots and exploitations of those traditions. In 1978 the Central Committee stressed that while Marxism-Leninism is a tool and Frelimo must develop its own revolution, 'it is nevertheless necessary for us to always be on guard against the chauvinistic deviations of "specific socialism". We reject the idea that there can be an "African socialism" or a "Mozambican socialism".'

Third, the struggle had revealed the need for 'people's power' and mass involvement. As Machel noted in 1973, 'Our main strength, and our reason to exist, is the people. To resolve our problems we must depend on the people, following a mass line.'

Fourth, there had been a dispute over whether top officials should go into the liberated zones. When the political and military leadership was separate, political leaders did not. Nkavandame and others always argued, as had the students, that it was an unnecessary risk. Indeed, a number of liberation movements stuck to this line. But with the merging of political and military, the Second Congress said 'leaders should make frequent visits' to the liberated zones. This, too, has continued to the present. Ministers all spend time out in the provinces. These are not simply fleeting visits. For example, ministers often serve for a month as holiday replacements for governors.

Finally, Frelimo drew support from all quarters. Military training and equipment came from Algeria, Egypt, Israel (until the 1967 war), Zaire, the Soviet Union, Eastern Europe and China. There was financial and humanitarian help from Scandinavian countries and groups in Western Europe and the United States. Frelimo never forgets its early friends, and it has continued its policy of keeping its support as broadly based as possible. It still receives assistance from both China and the Soviet Union, for example.

Thus Frelimo's basic policies on democracy, commerce, contact with the base, the role of the army and women, race, and so on were moulded directly out of the necessities of waging a successful guerrilla war.

On to Victory

With Frelimo in crisis after the assassination of Mondlane and various defections, the Portuguese military commander, General Kaulza de Arriaga, launched the largest military operation of the war, with 35,000 troops. From May to August 1970 he hammered the liberated zones and demonstrated that his troops could go anywhere in the country. Frelimo divided its guerrillas into small units. It concentrated on mobilizing the people to hold out against the attacks, on protecting key points like water holes, and on hit-and-run attacks like those in the early stages of the war. It proved an expensive stalemate; Kaulza could go anywhere he wanted, but was quite unable to maintain effective control. Frelimo really had won over the people. Eventually Kaulza pulled back. Operation Gordian Knot had failed, and the Portuguese never tried anything like it again.

By 1974 the Portuguese in Cabo Delgado were restricted to the towns and isolated bases connected by dangerous dirt tracks. Journalists who went out with Portuguese troops reported that convoys could only move 10 to 15 miles a day, because they had to follow groups of black soldiers known as 'picadors' who walked in front sticking long poles into the ground to dislodge mines. Nevertheless, convoys always hit mines or were ambushed. Frelimo guerrillas came to within one mile of bases at night.

Frelimo had reopened the Tete front in 1968, following four years of clandestine political work and Zambia's agreement to provide rearbases.

During Gordian Knot it diverted some of its troops to this front, and moved south of the Zambezi River. In 1972 it moved into Manica and Sofala, and the following year it established a base in the Gorongosa mountains within 100 miles of Beira. On New Year's Day 1974 Frelimo began attacks on the Beira-Rhodesia railway and moved into white farming areas near Vila Pery (now Chimoio).

War-weary conscript troops, serving four-year stints in Mozambique, were less and less willing to fight. So the Portuguese turned to elite groups of Portuguese and Mozambican volunteers, particularly the commandos and special paratroops. Pide, fed up with the army's reluctance to fight Frelimo, set up its own elite army, the *flechas* (arrows). They responded to Frelimo's advances with some of the worst atrocities of the war. In Tete Province commandos massacred hundreds of peasants in the village of Wiriamu in December 1972 because they supported Frelimo.

At Inhaminga, a key railway junction north of Beira, Pide set up a headquarters to try to stop the Frelimo advance. In the middle of the railway yard there is still a tiny concrete bunker, almost below ground level. A railway worker who had been there in 1974 at the time of the massacre told me that people were taken into the bunker, usually at night, to be tortured. Then they were taken away and shot. 'No one left alive,' he said. A bulldozer was used to dig mass graves. Some victims were brought to the bunker in sealed railway wagons from further up the line. Pide arrested a number of railway workers. 'One day there was a Frelimo attack near here. A man was off work that day and when he came in the next day, the boss said: "Where were you? You were with Frelimo." The man said no, his child was ill. But he was taken away and never came back.'

5. Combating Frelimo – 1961–74

Faced with the rise of nationalism throughout Africa in the late 1950s, Portugal radically changed its policies. These changes were accelerated by the founding of nationalist groups in Mozambique and Angola, and especially by the start of the revolution in Angola in 1961.

The Portuguese secret police Pide was established in Mozambique and began to recruit thousands of agents to infiltrate any possible area of dissent – clubs, workplaces and so on. By the early 1960s Pide's style of arrests and torture had become well known in Mozambique, and was an important factor in forcing people to flee to join Frelimo rather than stay and organize inside the country.

And the army moved in. The US Government's most recent *Area Handbook for Mozambique* estimates that before Frelimo even fired a shot, there were 30,000 Portuguese troops in Mozambique, and this rose to 75,000 before the end of the war.

Naturally, the Church was enlisted in the battle. 'It is acting against nature to want independence and to take part in movements for it,' said the Archbishop of Lourenço Marques, Custódio Alvim Pereira, in August 1961. 'The native people of Africa must thank the so-called colonizers for the benefits they have received. Those with more education must dispel illusions of independence from the less educated.' As the war progressed, the Church used its radio stations to broadcast propaganda against Frelimo 'terrorists' and to stress that the Portuguese should not negotiate with Frelimo. Archbishop Pereira dismissed the reports of the Wiriamu massacre as 'pure imagination'. Priests who tried to speak out were arrested and tortured by Pide; Church leaders who protested, such as the present Bishop of Nampula, Vieira Pinto, were expelled from the country. The Protestant Churches were more sympathetic to Frelimo. Rev. Zedequias Manganhela was killed by Pide for his support of Frelimo, and there is now a street in Maputo named after him.

It was not all force, however. The Portuguese Government also made a host of concessions, especially in 1961–64. Forced labour and forced crops were officially abolished and 'natives' no longer had to carry passes.

A major programme to build schools and health posts was undertaken.

As always, the reality was somewhat different. Administrators and private cotton companies continued to force peasants to grow cotton until 1969. Forced labour for private companies did decline, but it did not disappear, and the state continued to use forced labour for road work until 1973. School building slowed down in the face of rising military expenditure and the scarcity of teachers; in 1966 there were 425 government primary schools but only 341 were in use due to lack of staff. At independence, only 10 to 15% of adults could read and write, one of the lowest levels in Africa; of 4,500 students at the university in Lourenço Marques in 1974, only 72 were Black.

Much greater stress was placed on subsidized white immigration. The 1959–64 development plan explained that 'we must people Africa with Europeans who can assure the stability of our sovereignty and promote the "Portuguesation" of the native population.' The European population jumped from 97,000 in 1960 to over 200,000 in 1970. Some settled on new colonato farms, but most stayed in the cities.

Despite the official lifting of restrictions on Mozambicans, there was strict racial discrimination in favour of the new immigrants. Permanent housing in the cities was reserved for Whites, with separate small areas for Asians, mixed race, and assimilados. Most Blacks were not allowed to build permanent houses and were forced to live in shanty towns on the edge of the cities. Similarly, virtually all skilled and semi-skilled jobs were held by Portuguese, in sharp contrast to the British and French colonies. Of 350 train drivers at independence, only one was black. Of 750 staff at the Cifel iron and steel foundry in Lourenço Marques, 100 were Portuguese. Until shortly before independence, Africans could rarely get licences to open shops.

Mozambique had the fourth largest white population in sub-Saharan Africa, after South Africa, Angola and Rhodesia. But it was not a permanent settler population. As the 1969 US *Area Handbook for Mozambique* commented, the 'Europeans in the modern sector are predominantly persons of Portuguese background who do not plan to remain in Mozambique throughout their lifetime. They come to the province on a tour of duty in the civil service or in hope of making money. Their sentiments and ties remain with Portugal', and they expect to return home, at least to retire. At independence, 90% of them did.

Increased settlement and the steady decrease in forced cropping and forced labour slowly changed agriculture, and did improve life for many Mozambican peasants. In the Limpopo valley immigrant Portuguese peasants had settled and were producing high-quality foodstuffs for the growing capital – rice, potatoes, vegetables, meat, eggs and dairy products. They largely used family labour, and were dependent on forced labour for additional help, as they could not compete with mine wages.

As chibalo labour was slowly ended in the early 1960s, they continued to use concealed forced labour and also drew on children and those too old to go to the mines. Eventually, they began to mechanize. Similarly, the plantations in central Mozambique continued to hire labour from the traditional recruiting areas. Compulsion and brutality dropped away only slowly and men still had to pay taxes. But wages went up and plantations, too, were forced to mechanize.

The final end to forced cropping came in the late 1960s as part of the settlement policy. Thousands of hectares of the best peasant land was given to new settlers – demobbed soldiers, shopkeepers, and even agricultural extension agents – to grow cotton and grain. The Cotton Institute and Cereals Institute were set up to provide technical support, loans, tractors, pesticides, and sometimes infrastructure like wells. The old system under which individual companies had monopoly cotton marketing concessions was abolished, with the result that cotton became potentially profitable for settlers for the first time. In general, no fertilizers were used, which meant soils were exhausted by independence. Even so, the new settlers found cotton only marginally profitable.

In an effort to create a class of better-off black peasant farmers who would support the Government, the Cotton and Cereals Institutes provided services to some better-off Mozambicans – a radical change from the policy of exploitation that had gone on for so long.

But there was always a defined limit to black advancement. In 1966 General Kaulza de Arriaga set out what he called Portugal's Strategic Problem: 'We can only maintain white rule in Angola and Mozambique if we people them with Whites at a rate that accompanies or slightly surpasses the production of evolved Negroes. [Thus] we must lightly restrain the promotion of Negro people, after having convinced them that they are being promoted at an adequate rate.'

Many black Mozambicans were convinced. They saw themselves as a new black bourgeoisie – an elite better than other Blacks and equal to the Whites. A few received technical training, were allowed to open businesses, and even joined the fascist party ANP. A few black artists were invited to intellectual cocktail parties. There was even a token Mozambican Black in the Portuguese Assembly. With social acceptance and increasing economic power, this group felt its demands had largely been won. More than 100,000 Mozambicans began to collaborate with the Portuguese against Frelimo 'terrorists', serving as secret police agents, militiamen, or members of elite military units (see Chapter 16). It was in this changing climate that Nkavandame and Murrupa defected to the Portuguese. And it was because of this much wider local base, as much as Frelimo's weaknesses, that Kaulza de Arriaga launched his unsuccessful Gordian Knot operation in 1970.

Industrialization was seen as a way of encouraging Portuguese settlement. Some settler capital was mobilized and the big Portuguese monopoly groups like Espirito Santo, CUF, and Banco Nacional Ultramarino did invest. But it was not enough and Portugal again allowed foreign investment; in 1965 entirely foreign-owned companies were permitted.

The 1960s were boom years, with substantial industrial growth, particularly in the intermediate goods sector (that is, goods to produce goods). A petroleum refinery was opened and then expanded. Light engineering, iron founding, steel rolling, and railway wagon construction began. Factories were built to produce paint, electrical wire, fertilizer, and chemicals.

The late 1960s saw a sharp increase in production of local consumer goods such as tinned foods, radios, ceramics, wine bottling, and plastics. Rigid laws protected the Portuguese textile industry and only one mill had been permitted in Mozambique in the 1950s. But in 1966 this law was repealed and Portuguese and local capital was encouraged to invest in textiles; several mills were started, but this occurred quite late and only one had opened by independence. The main cities expanded rapidly and high-rise blocks of flats became an important form of local investment and speculation. Cement production expanded rapidly and decorative iron work and reinforcing bars became a major product of the iron and steel industry.

Cashew nuts, a peasant crop whose season does not conflict with grain or cotton, increased substantially in the 1960s and there was extensive South African investment in cashew processing. Here there was some integration: the tins for the nuts and the industrial gases required to cure them are made locally. By independence, Mozambique was the world's largest producer of cashews.

By the end of the colonial period, Mozambique had become the eighth largest industrial producer in Africa (according to possibly inflated Portuguese statistics). It had 4% of the continent's industrial production compared to only 2% of the continent's population. About 40% of production was for export, and most of the rest for the white population.

As pressure from Frelimo grew, Portugal tried to increase its ties to the white minority regimes in Rhodesia and South Africa. In 1964 South African investment was given favoured treatment. The giant Cahora Bassa dam was begun, largely with foreign capital, with the intention of selling electricity to South Africa at just the cost of production; Portugal would gain no profits, but would make South Africa dependent on its colony. Subsidized facilities brought hundreds of thousands of white Rhodesian and South African tourists to Mozambique's beaches.

In exchange, South Africa provided military and financial help for the war against Frelimo, although it avoided being drawn in too deeply. But the new favourable treatment meant that South Africa benefited hugely from the 1960s boom in Mozambique. It increasingly supplied technical services, raw materials and consumer goods. By 1973, South Africa had finally passed Portugal as Mozambique's main supplier.

Although it may not have been obvious to the residents of the gleaming white, new blocks of flats, Mozambique's boom was built on sand. Although investment flowed in, consumer goods flowed in faster; virtually all the new industries not geared to export were dependent on imported raw materials. The Portuguese, concentrated in the cities, could not feed themselves, despite the rural settlement schemes. Grain imports rose steadily (see Appendix 5). Maize, vegetables such as potatoes and onions, and fish – all of which could easily have been grown or caught in Mozambique – were imported from South Africa.

Mozambique had always been a service economy, with mine remittances and port and railway revenues covering a permanent trade deficit. But they were not enough. By the late 1960s, exports did not cover even half of imports and the balance of payments deficit was over £20 million per year. This deficit was entirely with Portugal, which demanded payment in gold (which had, in turn, come from mine wages). When Mozambique ran out of gold, Portugal cut the link between the two currencies, and the Mozambican escudo became non-convertible. Portuguese in Mozambique found it difficult to obtain Portuguese escudos to go home on holiday. In 1971, major import restrictions were imposed.

Thus Frelimo was to inherit an already bankrupt economy which exported only half as much as it imported and could not feed itself – this must be remembered when reading about various traumas in following chapters. A South African journalist, Kerry Swift, visited Mozambique in February 1974. With the war at its height, he described some of the problems of the collapsing economy. 'Outside our hotel every morning we were met by former Portuguese servicemen trying to exchange Mozambican escudos for South African rands. The Mozambican currency has become worthless outside the territory.' The soldiers could not get home unless they had hard currency. As for the famous Lourenço Marques prawn boats, an engineer told him, 'The engines are stuck together with string and chewing gum. There's a fortune to be made reservicing them, but I can't do a thing until they buy the spares. They can't buy spares because nobody will accept Mozambican escudos.'

Some settlers began to leave in the early 1970s. Most, however, remained oblivious of the intensifying war and deteriorating economy, and believed that cosmetic changes could solve the problem. Indeed, when Frelimo in January 1974 finally moved into the white farming area 100 miles west of Beira and began attacking the Beira–Rhodesia railway, it came as a shock to many in Beira that Frelimo was now in the white heartlands. Rigid press censorship, and their own desire to ignore reality, had kept the white community in the dark. Beira Whites reacted on 18

January by rioting and storming the officers' mess, blaming the soldiers for failing to keep Frelimo away.

The Portuguese Government sent in a new military commander, and flew 10,000 more troops from Angola to back up the 65,000 already in Mozambique.

There was talk of minor concessions. The Beira city council noted that the water system allowed only 5 gallons of water a day for each Black, 10 gallons for each Asian or person of mixed race, and 58 gallons for each White. Not racist, you understand, just that a European needs 40 gallons of water for a bath and a Black needs only one. Nevertheless, it was reluctantly decided to install 70 new public taps in the shanty towns where Beira Blacks were forced to live.

But more troops and extra bathwater did not stop the revolution.

6. Reluctant Handover – 1974

The 25 April 1974 coup toppled Marcelo Caetano and ended nearly 60 years of fascism in Portugal. It was carried out by young army officers who formed the Armed Forces Movement (MFA). They were wearied by 15 years of colonial war that had cost Portugal £3,000 million and 5,000 dead; they had also been radicalized by the liberation movements – often by reading captured Frelimo and MPLA documents. Because of the splits in the Angolan liberation movements, Portugal might have held out a little longer there. But it was already heading for a widely recognized defeat in Mozambique. As a (London) *Guardian* leader commented, 'It was, in the last analysis, Frelimo which brought down the Caetano government.'

Yet the colonial wars went on. The new President of Portugal, António de Spínola, only offered Frelimo a cease-fire. He proposed a long process leading to 'self-determination', which he stressed should not be 'confused' with independence. There would eventually be an independence referendum, but it would not be 'fair' to have it yet as people were not sufficiently educated to decide their own future. When they were, he was sure they would choose to remain Portuguese.

In practice, Spínola's line was hardly surprising. He had fought under Hitler and on Franco's side in Spain, and moved on to be military commander in Guinea-Bissau. But in a book published in early 1974 he had the temerity to suggest that Portugal could not hold its empire through military means alone and should allow its overseas territories limited autonomy as part of a 'Lusitanian community'. Caetano dismissed him in March, but Spínola was not part of the coup. On the night of the coup, Caetano suggested he would be willing to hand over to Spínola, and this was accepted.

Frelimo was fighting for independence, and rejected Spínola's offer out of hand. Both sides stepped up the fighting. In May 1974 the Portuguese army increased its bombing of Frelimo bases and pro-Frelimo villages in the liberated areas. Frelimo increased raids in white farming areas west of Beira and repeatedly attacked the two railways from Beira. In July it opened a new front in Zambézia Province.

The MFA had been active in Mozambique before the coup, and many officers knew about it two weeks before. Indeed, a right-wing Italian journalist working in South Africa, Giancarlo Coccia, was phoned by military friends in Mozambique a week before and he flew to Nampula to be there when the coup took place.

The idea behind the coup had hardly been to continue the colonial wars, and the MFA quickly cut back on Portuguese attacks against Frelimo. By June in many areas there were instructions not to launch new raids and to only fire if fired on. Local cease-fires were arranged, with the encouragement of both Frelimo and the MFA. Army morale and discipline deteriorated rapidly. Thousands of Mozambicans in the Portuguese army simply deserted. In July at Boane Barracks, near Lourenço Marques, more than 2,000 soldiers and officers said they would not go north to fight. By the time Frelimo moved into Zambézia, it faced little resistance.

Meanwhile, confusion reigned. Spínola appointed a new governor to Mozambique and then sacked him three months later. Government disintegrated, along with law and order. There were right-wing bomb attacks and beatings of known leftists. Thousands of workers went on strike, and the Government ordered wage increases and prize freezes in order to keep the peace. Black demonstrators were killed by police or commandos at the Sena Sugar Estates, the Ressano Garcia border post, and elsewhere.

At the same time, there was a political explosion. The coup ended press censorship and the ban on political parties. Dozens of parties were formed, but two had a head start.

One was the Mozambique Democrats, which included a number of clandestine Frelimo militants in Lourenço Marques such as the present Information Minister, José Cabaço. Underground Frelimo supporters already worked on the weekly magazine *Tempo* and took control of the daily newspapers. With the Democrats they tried to explain what Frelimo really was to a white population who knew nothing of it except 10 years of propaganda about bloodthirsty terrorists who would nationalize babies and massacre Whites.

The other was Gumo, the most important anti-Frelimo party. It had been formed in 1973 by white politicians and businessmen who saw that they might need a black government they could control. Although the party was officially illegal, it had the tacit approval of Caetano, so Pide turned a blind eye to it. Thus it was able to organize mass rallies soon after the coup. But the leaders fell out, and Gumo collapsed. Only in August did the anti-Frelimo forces finally unite into the National Coalition Party, which included Nkavandame, Simango, and Gwenjere. By then it was too late.

The MFA had made early contacts with Frelimo and the new Portuguese Government. On 5 and 6 July Machel met with Foreign Minister Mario Soares in Lusaka (Zambia), but nothing came of the meeting as Soares only had a mandate to negotiate a cease-fire, not a handover of power. There were further contacts between Frelimo and an MFA delegation led by Melo Antunes in Rome and then in Dar es Salaam. The

Portuguese Government shifted left, and the MFA finally overrode Spínola and agreed to independence. On 7 September in Lusaka, Soares and Machel signed an agreement calling for: a cease-fire, a Frelimo-dominated Transitional Government to take office on 25 September, and full independence under Frelimo on 25 June 1975. Ten years of war ended.

In Lourenço Marques, angry white settlers rebelled and took over the radio station. They said they had been sold out by Portugal and called for a Rhodesia-style UDI. Later Simango and Gwenjere came on the radio and supported the call. Whites took over the newspaper, the radio in Nampula, and the telephone exchange, and freed 200 arrested Pide agents from prison. Coccia reports that some of those involved were from the sixth commando unit, which had carried out the Wiriamu massacre. Whites in jeeps drove through the black townships raking houses with machine-gun fire. The black community responded by setting up road-blocks and burning cars. Samora Machel came on the radio from Dar es Salaam and made an impassioned plea for calm. 'Frelimo once again declares firmly and clearly that it will not tolerate any racial conflict,' he said. 'To the white population, made up essentially of honest workers, we repeat what we have always said: our struggle is your struggle, it is a struggle against exploitation, a struggle to build a new country and establish a people's democracy.' In the black suburbs, Frelimo organizers moved quickly and successfully to calm the backlash. On 9 September, realizing that the white population was not supporting the UDI call and that a racial explosion was inevitable if it was not stopped, the Government ordered Portuguese troops to the radio station, and the rebels left peacefully. Some Whites had been killed, but many fewer than the more than 100 Blacks murdered and 500 wounded. That week Frelimo guerrillas urgently flown in from Tanzania began to patrol the townships to prevent further anti-White outbursts. On 25 September, the Transitional Government headed by Joaquim Chissano took office, and a tense calm reigned.

Just a month later, on 21 October, a group of white Portuguese commandos in downtown Lourenço Marques killed several Frelimo soldiers. This time there was an explosion. In the townships Blacks blocked all the main roads out of the city. They stopped cars and pulled white people out and killed them, or even burned them in their cars. Again Frelimo went out into the suburbs. Sebastião Mabote, a member of the Transitional Military Commission and now Deputy Defence Minister, went out and addressed meetings, calling for calm. It was over the same day. Several dozen Whites were killed – fewer than the Blacks massacred the month before, but enough to step up the white exodus.

Frelimo stressed that Whites still had a place in Mozambique, and there were no other serious racial clashes. But ten years of propaganda counted for too much, and by independence in June, more than half the Whites had fled.

7. Taking Power – 1975–76

Independence came on 25 June 1975. A month later law, medicine, education and funeral services were nationalized. Frelimo made clear that the dual systems that existed before independence and which were perpetuated in many independent African countries would not be permitted in Mozambique. There was to be no private or mission medicine or education. There would be no private lawyers and no separate 'tribal' or 'customary' law system.

The rank discrimination which had marked all of these areas before independence meant that the nationalizations were greeted with enthusiasm, and they formed the basis for Frelimo's popularity in the areas that had not been affected by the war. Use of services jumped. For example, in one year primary school enrolment doubled.

Land had been nationalized on 25 June and rented property was nationalized on 3 February 1976 (the same day that Lourenço Marques was renamed Maputo). People retained the right to occupy land they were using productively. Individuals could still own both their own house and a holiday home (and private houses are still bought and sold).

Although social services were nationalized, the means of production and financial institutions were not. Initially there seemed no intention to do so. Nevertheless, the nationalizations that did take place hit the urban settlers hard. Many professionals lost the means to high incomes; not only had doctors and lawyers earned high fees, but in the previous two decades they had invested in the tower blocks that gave Lourenço Marques and Beira such a dramatic and unexpected skyline. Even working-class Whites and assimilados had invested in property, either in small blocks on the edge of the 'cement city', or tin shacks for Blacks in the suburbs. And the end of privileged access to health and education meant a drop in standards for a minority.

This accelerated the flight of the Portuguese. Perhaps half had already left by independence, and most of the rest departed in the following year. In Maputo, there were shipping crates in front of many buildings. Abandoned dogs, once pampered pets but now sad and hungry strays, wandered the streets in packs. In rural areas, too, the Whites fled; peasant farmers killed their cattle and destroyed their machinery before they went.

Families were divided. Husbands went and wives stayed; parents went and children stayed. Several high Frelimo officials are the only members of their families who stayed; parents, brothers, and uncles all went to South Africa or Portugal. Often this created bitter antagonisms within the divided family. Typical was the case of Cisbela Ferrão. On 15 October 1976 her parents published her photo in the daily *Noticias* saying she had disappeared from home. Five days later she replied with a letter to the newspaper: 'I would like the Mozambican people to know of the problems affecting a large number of Mozambican youth with foreign parents. Because of my age, my parents have bestowed Portuguese nationality on me, and want me to accompany them to Portugal. Just because my parents have lived all their years in a colonial-fascist system and are unable to go along with the revolutionary process in Mozambique, I do not see that they have the right to hamper or prevent my participation in Mozambican life and development,' she wrote. 'I was born here in Mozambique and have lived here all my 17 years. This is my country and Frelimo is my Party.'

The period just before and just after independence was also one of intrigue and retribution which created considerable confusion. The case of Jorge Costa only came fully to light when he defected to South Africa in 1982. The son of a small-time Lourenço Marques transport owner, Costa developed a very large chip on his shoulder because of the class discrimination he suffered in his school days at the hands of the sons of the middle class. When he went to Portugal to study law in the early 1970s, he joined Frelimo (and also joined a Maoist party in Portugal after the coup there) and returned to Mozambique to help establish the new police and security services. He got his own back for imagined and real slights by harassing middle-class Whites (despite being white himself) and fomenting persecution of Whites. His actions, and those of others like him, made life unpleasant for many settlers, especially after the racial conflicts of September and October 1974.

The flight created dramatic economic problems. Tens of thousands of domestic servants were suddenly dismissed. The building boom stopped with the Lusaka agreement, and thousands of workers in the construction and building materials industries found themselves unemployed. Tourism was halted, throwing more thousands out of work.

Most dramatic was the abandoning of businesses, sometimes built up over many years. Suddenly, one day, the owner would be gone, leaving behind a workforce without a clue as to how to manage the business. For example, waiters who had never been allowed to handle money or place wholesale orders found themselves running restaurants.

Frelimo introduced the concept of 'intervention', a kind of bankruptcy procedure, in which the state took over the running of an abandoned or sabotaged business, but allowed the former owner to reclaim it later under certain circumstances. By the end of 1976, more than 300 businesses had been 'intervened'; most were small.

Nor did the owners leave empty handed. They usually took as much as they could. There were many cases of 'orders' for imported supplies that never arrived, and which were really transfers of money abroad. One of the most dramatic was Boror, which ran one of the world's largest palm plantations. They loaded the entire 1975 copra crop, worth £2 million, on to four ships and sailed away, never to return.

To some of those who left, independence provided a unique opportunity to make a killing. With the end of colonial currency controls and close government supervision, it was possible to sneak huge amounts of money out of the country. In 1975 and 1976, perhaps £150 million was illegally exported.

Some were cunning, like the owner of a Lourenço Marques light aircraft company. He generously 'gave' his company to the state, and his offer to stay and continue to run it 'for Frelimo' was accepted. He knew Frelimo had no way of monitoring him, and by the time he finally fled five years later, he had stashed away hundreds of thousands of pounds in foreign bank accounts.

Often departing owners and technicians destroyed or paralysed machinery, sometimes simply removing a few vital parts. Usually they destroyed all the records and repair manuals. Peter Sketchley, a British engineer who worked at the Cifel foundry in Maputo after independence, told how the formulas for mixing the sand used for castings had been destroyed, along with all the maintenance handbooks for the machinery and all the records of where they had been bought. What made all this more serious was the very strict division of labour by which anything technical or semi-skilled had been done by a settler. Thus the remaining workers had only the vaguest ideas of what the Portuguese had done to keep the foundry running.

The flight of the settlers seems to have surprised Frelimo. It had not nationalized the means of production or private wealth (except for land and rented property), and thus it expected many capitalists to stay. Some did, and still live very well. But most didn't. The nationalization of social services, and the loss of privilege that implies, was just too much.

The settler flight shattered the economy. Should Frelimo have tried harder to keep the Whites, as Robert Mugabe did five years later in Zimbabwe? Undoubtedly Frelimo could have stopped some of the provocations against the Whites, but this would probably have made little difference. Mozambican settlers did not have the kind of integrated economic control that their Rhodesian counterparts had; as I have noted, they were professionals and managers rather than capitalists. To keep them would have meant protecting their life styles and consumption patterns in a way that would have permanently distorted the economy. I agree with Information Minister Cabaço: 'Clearly we made many errors, but allowing the Portuguese to leave was not one of them. Keeping industry going by maintaining privilege was too high a price, and we could not accept it.'

Furthermore, if a large number of settlers had stayed, they would have blocked a socialist transition, as they have in Zimbabwe. It is clear in health (see Chapter 8), where the transition has been most successful, that such radical changes would have been impossible if more Portuguese doctors had stayed.

It was not just industry that was collapsing. The whole organization of colonial society was crumbling as doctors, lawyers, civil servants, shop-keepers and so on disappeared. Frelimo's answer was Dynamizing Groups (*Grupos Dinamizadores* – GDs). These were ad hoc committees of eight to ten people set up in villages, urban neighbourhoods, and workplaces, starting in late 1974. At first they were largely defensive. In black suburbs their function was to prevent anti-white outbursts like those in September and October. In factories, it was to prevent sabotage by the remaining settlers. They were highly successful on both counts. The violence, sabotage, and flight of capital would have been much worse had it not been for the GDs, and the very real vigilance of the workers.

Frelimo militants sometimes comment that independence came too soon, because it meant that few areas had been liberated, and thus the bulk of the population had no experience of Frelimo's policies and way of doing things. It had few cadres to spread over a very wide area. The GDs were the means to spread its control. As the name implies, they were intended to 'dynamize' people – to motivate them to take action them-selves. The GDs held regular community and workplace meetings, and served both to explain Frelimo policies and to act as an instrument of some sort of popular democracy. The vast majority of people in GDs had had no contact with Frelimo before independence, and the GDs were carried along on the spirit of independence: this is our country now and we can run it ourselves.

The GDs took over more and more official functions from the steadily collapsing colonial apparatus. In a form of workers' control, they ran abandoned factories. In villages and neighbourhoods, they served as councils, courts, police and social workers. In rural areas, they replaced the Portuguese-appointed régulos. In the 'cement cities' they tried to monitor and reassign abandoned flats in a coherent way. Night-time patrols were set up to prevent robberies. They encouraged people to dig latrines and plant collective gardens.

More than anything else, it was the GDs that introduced Mozambique to Frelimo and to 'people's democracy', and it was the GDs that kept the country running.

This was also a period of intense political struggle and high mobility. The Portuguese had never prepared a group of Blacks to 'Africanize' the administration, and many of those who had remained abroad linked themselves to Coremo or other opponents of Frelimo. Thus there was no organized succession. Furthermore, the settlers tended to just disappear, rather than hand over power in an orderly way.

Nor was it only jobs that were becoming vacant. Thousands of Blacks who had been living in the suburbs around the cities moved into flats vacated by departing settlers. This shift was particularly strong because of the extreme housing discrimination in colonial times. Urban Blacks had been largely prevented from building permanent housing by rules that required permanent homes to be of a particularly high standard. Thus there was a 'cement city' of tower blocks and substantial concrete houses, and a suburban 'cane city' of temporary houses made of reeds, metal sheeting, etc. (There were a few isolated neighbourhoods with concrete houses for better-off Blacks and Coloureds.) Unlike Rhodesia and South Africa, Blacks were not pushed off into isolated 'townships'. Instead, in Beira, Nampula and Maputo the cane city comes right up to the edge of the cement city, and it was easy for people to move.

Inevitably it was those who had some degree of privilege in colonial times and thus had been able to gain some education who were most likely to move into the higher-level jobs and cement city flats, as well as to take high positions in the GDs. For this group, independence meant direct gains – they were taking the place of the settlers. For some, the only goal was a life style like that enjoyed by the colonists. Others supported Frelimo and socialism. Most knew little about Frelimo and had mixed motives, and one of the continuing issues has been educating and motivating this group.

Some Whites and many Asians did stay on at first, seeing a chance to move into positions of power and income that had been inaccessible during colonial times because of class, race, their own lack of education and so on. Jorge Costa is an extreme example of this.

Thus the GDs took very varying forms. Sometimes they would be militant and carry out Frelimo guidelines well. Others would fall under the control of middle-class members, because they were the ones with the skills and experience. Former agents of Pide and members of the fascist ANP infiltrated the GDs. Thus Frelimo frequently had to purge and reorganize the GDs. During this period there were many examples of people gaining power in GDs, manipulating them, being caught by Frelimo, and then leaving for Portugal – the confusing sight of people chanting 'Long Live Frelimo' one day and abandoning the country the next.

Frelimo inherited a bankrupt economy with a chronic balance of payments deficit. Yet 1975 and 1976 saw modest balance of payments surpluses, cushioning the economic crisis caused by the flight of the Portuguese. Partly this was self-generating: industry was dependent on imported raw materials, so the collapse of industry meant a sharp fall in imports. Also, it was the departing Portuguese who had imported most consumer goods.

But Mozambique unexpectedly gained extra money and jobs from the South African mines. An air crash which killed Malawian miners caused President Banda suddenly to cut off mine labour from his country to South Africa. Mozambique took up some of the slack, and in 1975 the number of miners rose to 115,000. Furthermore, due to a series of strikes in the early 1970s, their wages went up significantly. Finally, they were paid in gold at the official price which Mozambique could resell at the free market rate. This system had initially represented a South African subsidy to the Portuguese war against Frelimo, and had not been very large in any case. But by 1974 the price of gold had risen to three times the official price, so this subsidy alone was worth more than £50 million a year to Frelimo.

In 1976 the crunch hit. South Africa cut the number of miners to less than 40,000. In 1978 it stopped paying in official price gold. This caused both cash and unemployment problems.

On 3 March 1976, Mozambique closed the border and imposed United Nations-sponsored sanctions against Southern Rhodesia. In part, it had no choice. It is hard to see how Mozambique could have survived virtually surrounded by hostile neighbours. Indeed, Rhodesia had already launched military attacks on Mozambican villages in February. But sanctions were far more expensive than Frelimo expected. The final cost, according to UN estimates, was about £250 million. Western countries had promosed aid to compensate for the losses, but little was actually given. And Rhodesia retaliated with stepped-up military attacks on Mozambique, which were later to disrupt the economy severely. There were air and ground attacks on border areas, and on 9 August 1976 the Rhodesians massacred 875 people in the refugee camp at Nyazónia in northern Manica Province. Probably as serious as the financial cost was the cost in time. Top officials were forced to spend increasing amounts of time on the war with Rhodesia that would have been better spent in solving economic problems.

But these clouds were only dimly seen on the horizon. In 1976 Frelimo and Mozambique were carried forward on a wave of enthusiasm. They had beaten the Portuguese and they had kept the country going, despite the exodus and sabotage. Anything seemed possible. The eighth session of the Central Committee in February 1976, the first co-ops seminar in October, the Second Conference of the Mozambican Women's Organization (OMM) in November, and especially the Frelimo Third Party Congress in February 1977 set out an optimistic blueprint for a transition to socialism.

Part III
Transformation

8. What Kind of Health Care?

The crowd fills the porch of Quissico hospital and spills off into the yard under the trees. More than 100 patients are waiting to be seen this morning; some have walked 10 miles or more. The nurse is giving a talk about TB symptoms and treatments – part of a daily routine in which patients are given preventive health talks while they wait. The talk ends with the singing of Frelimo songs and shouts of 'Viva Frelimo' and 'Viva health'. It is a scene which is repeated daily at hundreds of hospitals and health centres throughout the country. And the cheers are heartfelt, because health is seen as one of the biggest victories of the revolution.

'In the Mozambique of the colonists and capitalists, there are only hospitals where there are settlers, there are only doctors and nurses where there are people who can pay for them. In the city of Lourenço Marques alone there are more hospital beds, more doctors, more nurses, and more laboratories than in the rest of the country. Does this mean it is only in Lourenço Marques that there are sick people?' asked Samora Machel four years before independence.

Since independence, this has been radically transformed. Health care has been nationalized and socialized. There is no private medicine, health care is essentially free, and services have been significantly expanded, especially in rural areas. This means that millions of people have access to at least rudimentary health care for the first time.

And Mozambique has been in the forefront internationally, often one step ahead of the World Health Organization (WHO). An emphasis on 'primary health care' was adopted as national policy a year before WHO's big meeting in Alma Ata, USSR, in 1978 to promote the idea. Mozambique adopted a restricted medicines list before WHO published its list, and became one of the first countries to ban imports of drugs not on the list. And Mozambique was one of the first countries to ban the import of breastmilk substitutes produced by multinational companies, and instead to distribute its own brand with labels stressing that breastmilk is much better.

Frelimo pays special attention to health. 'The hospital is the only contact many people have with the state,' commented President Machel. And it 'touches their most sensitive point: health, well-being, and their very life.' And health has been used by Frelimo as a vehicle for introducing national policy changes, particularly with respect to management. Perhaps this is because the leadership understands the issues of health care more clearly; during colonial times, Machel himself was a nurse in what is now Maputo Central Hospital. But health also reflects all of Frelimo's problems in implementing a radical policy: the lack of skilled people, class pressures, and conflicting urban and rural demands.

As in most other aspects of Portuguese colonialism, health care in Mozambique fell behind even the little that was provided in British and French colonies. Neighbouring Tanganyika came to independence in 1961 with 441 ante-natal clinics; 10 years later colonial Mozambique still had only six. There was no system: the state, private clinics, and factories and railways all provided medical treatment, which was graded both by race and price. More than two-thirds of the country's doctors were in Lourenço Marques. Faced with the growing threat of Frelimo, Portugal did begin building rural health posts in the late 1960s – as usual, too late to do much good.

Even before independence, doctors saw the writing on the wall and returned to Portugal in large numbers. The nationalization of health put the rest to flight. From 500 doctors in 1970, the number dropped to 80 in 1976 (and some of those have left since). With them went many of the technicians who maintained the expensive equipment in Lourenço Marques hospitals and clinics. Health care temporarily collapsed.

But if they had to do it again, few would call for a different policy. The exodus cleared the decks of reactionary doctors who oppose change. Most who remained supported Frelimo and its radical changes; some did not, but they kept their peace.

Health services were nationalized a month after independence. The following year, Frelimo launched a national vaccination campaign. In two and a half years, smallpox vaccination was given to a remarkable 95% of the population. Measles, tuberculosis, and tetanus immunizations were also given to susceptible groups. Indeed, Frelimo vaccinated one million more people than the Portuguese 1970 census said existed in the country, and the campaign provided a highly accurate forecast for the 1980 census. In addition to the obvious health benefits, the campaign was politically important: it showed people that Frelimo was doing something, it stressed prevention, and it gave a reason to contact and mobilize everyone in the country (many of whom had had no contact with Frelimo before independence, and only knew of it as the 'terrorists' of Portuguese propaganda).

Fees were charged until the socialization of medicine in 1977. Since then, there has been only a token charge of 7½ meticais (MT) (12p), after which all treatment is free. Medicines are free to inpatients; for outpatients there is a sliding scale, ranging from nothing up to the wholesale price of the drug, depending on the type of medicine and the patient's salary.

Mozambique's new constitution called on the Government 'to organise a health service to benefit all the people'. But after the nationalisation of health in 1975, it took two years to pull together the pieces, bring in sympathetic foreign doctors, and define a new health policy. The Frelimo Third Party Congress in 1977 declared that 'priority is to be given to preventive medicine', especially environmental sanitation, mother and child health, combating preventable diseases, and organising health programmes in schools and workplaces. In terms of curative medicine, emphasis was given to the establishment of rural health posts. Together, this is commonly known as 'primary health care'.

There are two essential elements to primary health care: the use of paramedical workers with limited training, and the involvement of the community. Frelimo's interest in primary health care grew out of its experience in the armed struggle. In 1966 it began training nurses to care for the wounded, but they quickly began to treat local people in the newly liberated zones as well, and the demand was too great. So Frelimo also began to train as 'first aid assistants' both guerrillas and villagers chosen by the people themselves in local meetings. The latter usually returned to their own villages. By 1972 in Cabo Delgado province there were more than 300 health personnel. Local people were directly involved: in building the health posts, in feeding the health workers, and in carrying wounded guerrillas to health posts and sometimes on to hospitals in Tanzania. It soon became apparent, though, that staff and medicines were too limited to provide an adequate curative service, and that it is more efficient to prevent disease in the first place. Thus health education played an increasing role. Nurses at health posts gave regular talks, and Mozambican students in Tanzania toured the liberated areas during holidays to give instructions on environmental health. In some areas, people clearly responded, for example by building and using latrines. An outbreak of smallpox in the liberated zone led to the vaccination of 10,000 people in the immediate area, which prompted other vaccination campaigns.

Primary health care is not just for developing countries. What Frelimo learned in the bush was becoming equally clear in an industrialised world faced with the unacceptable costs of 'modern' medicine. Expensive high-technology health care is usually unnecessary and inappropriate: both in industrialised and developing countries, 80 to 90% of illnesses and injuries do not need doctors and can be treated by paramedical workers with a small range of drugs and simple equipment. Indeed, any GP will admit this after a typical surgery session of colds, headaches and sprains. Paramedics are now being trained in countries as diverse as the United States and China.

Industrialised countries may be able to waste money on 'modern' medicine; Mozambique cannot. Health expenditure has jumped fourfold since independence, to more than £3 per peson. This is significantly above expenditure in other countries as poor as Mozambique, and it represents 11% of the national budget. Yet is is only 3% of the per capita health expenditure in Britain, so the money must be carefully used.

Expanding Coverage

Mozambique has established a five-tier system. At the primary level, every village and urban neighbourhood should have a health post with a paramedic. For each group of health posts, there is a health centre which should provide virtually all the services needed. The centre should be headed by a doctor or nurse, and have a midwife and maternity beds, a pharmacy, a laboratory, and a preventive health and vaccination team. Frelimo stresses that primary health care is not just for rural areas. The bulk of Mozambique's urban population lives in shanty towns which had no health facilities in colonial times, so health centres are being opened there too.

Up one level are urban general, and rural hospitals, with provincial hospitals on the higher tier. At the top are the three central hospitals. At each level only the most difficult cases are referred up; those which cannot be treated in Maputo are sometimes sent abroad.

Priority is given to training paramedical workers for the lower levels. Of more than 4,500 people trained between independence and 1982, only 100 are doctors. More than 1,000 are nurses and specialised 'technicians' and 'agents' who have two or three years' training. Finally, 1,200 village health workers have been trained; they have four years of primary school and attend a six-month course, before they return to their village.

Frelimo has succeeded in extending coverage. More than half the people have access to preventive help, and over one-third to some form of curative care. Although low, this is good compared to much of Africa; in Kenya, which has been independent for more than twice as long, curative care still reaches only a fifth of the people. The number of births in Mozambican health units is triple what it was before independence. In 1982, WHO conducted a survey of mothers and children between one and two years old in randomly selected rural areas and urban neighbourhoods. The WHO team had been warned that the rural health network was still underdeveloped; but they saw 'extensive contact by mothers and their young children with primary health care services'. They found that 81% of rural children had been seen at least oncc by a health worker and that 62% had been vaccinated against tuberculosis. More than half their mothers had been immunized against tetanus during that pregnancy.

One of the most striking outcomes of the WHO survey concerns oral rehydration. Diarrhoea is one of the big killers of babies in the Third

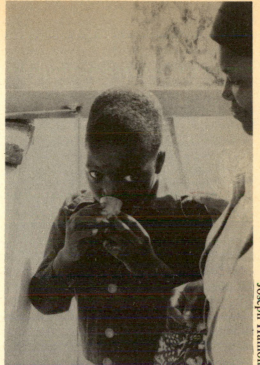

Joseph Hanlon

Drinking piperazine for round worms; Machava Health Centre pharmacy

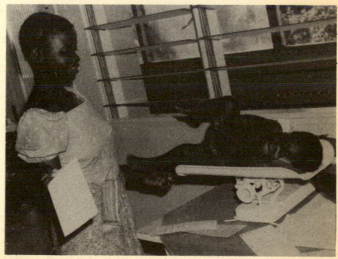

Joseph Hanlon

Mother and child care routine; Machava Health Centre

World. It has been found that it kills through dehydration. To save lives, what is needed is not expensive drugs, but simply giving the baby clean water containing a few essential salts – known in medical jargon as 'oral rehydration'. It is an excellent example of primary health care, because it costs almost nothing and can be done by anyone. Mozambique has opened a factory to make packets of oral rehydration salts and they are widely distributed to health centres and posts. Health workers have been given special short courses on this treatment. Although it was unknown in colonial times, the WHO team found that 41% of rural mothers now know about oral rehydration salts and their use.

One reason for the high use of health services by mothers and children is community involvement. The Ministry of Health has signed a formal contract with the Mozambican Women's Organization (OMM), under which local women's groups encourage mothers to attend ante-natal and well baby clinics, talk to women about family planning and nutrition, and assist in setting up and running creches.

A similar technique is being used to develop a new target area: health and safety at work. Farm and industrial workers are only a small group (150,000 people), but they are economically vital, and the working class is seen as the central political force in the socialist state. Lacking resources, the Health Ministry has signed a contract with the national association of workers' councils. In the factory, the workers pick a health and safety representative who is trained by the Health Ministry. The reps then try to prevent accidents and identify occupational hazards, ensure that affected workers take their tuberculosis and leprosy medicines, and give first aid. Working with the OMM, they encourage pregnant workers to attend ante-natal clinics, help to organize and supervise creches, and remind mothers of their legal right to a half-hour off work, morning and afternoon, to breastfeed young babies.

This kind of co-ordination and motivation of local political bodies can be effective. For example, when the doctor at a Maputo suburban health centre visited a local cashew-nut processing factory, she found that half the children in the creche were underweight, compared to 10% nationwide. The doctor then visited the creche once a month, meeting with and motivating the creche staff and mothers. She also met with the factory management, and reminded them to give mothers time to breastfeed. Four months later, only 17% of the children were underweight.

Another dramatic success for Mozambique's health policy is medicines. Basic drugs are available in the most remote rural health posts. In an era of rising prices, Mozambique is importing more drugs than before independence, but is only spending the same amount of money as a decade ago.

In most countries of the world, more than 10,000 different kinds of drugs are available. Some are dangerous; many are useless; some are

Cholera vaccination in front of Central Market, Maputo

Joseph Hanlon

Pharmacist (Machava Health Centre) hands and explains medicines to patients

Joseph Hanlon

pointless combinations of other drugs; and most are simply cheaper drugs in more expensive packets with brand names and heavy advertising. Britain tries to ban dangerous drugs, and the US tries to control useless ones as well, not always successfully. In practice, though, a few hundred drugs are sufficient for all illnesses. WHO has published an 'essential drugs list' of 200 medicines which, it says, cover the health needs of most people.

Before independence, 13,000 drugs were allowed in Mozambique, and there were almost no controls. Multinational drug companies dumped items they were no longer allowed to sell in industrialised countries with tighter regulations, and ubiquitous drug salesmen convinced doctors and nurses to prescribe drugs for conditions for which they were not effective (and could not be promoted in Britain) and were sometimes even dangerous.

Since independence, a Therapeutics Commission has carved this down to a basic list of 343 drugs, following a policy of good medicine at the lowest price. The commission studies the medical journals, choosing enough effective drugs to cover the entire spectrum of illnesses. Where two drugs are equally effective, it chooses the cheapest. All drugs are then purchased by international bidding, using the chemical (generic) name rather than the trade name. Over 200 companies bid each year, and drugs are bought both from Western multinationals and from socialist countries. Finally, there are no fancy packets. Children at a health centre drink their worm medicine on the spot; adults take away their pills wrapped in bits of paper.

Some drugs now cost Mozambique only one-tenth of what they did before independence. A particularly stark example was Reserpine, an antihypertensive drug: in 1978 bids were received from 19 companies in 13 countries, and prices ranged from 50p to £10 per thousand tablets. In chemist shops in 1982, aspirin, vitamins, and many antibiotics cost less than one-third of their price only three years earlier. And in marked contrast to colonial times, the ten drugs on which the most foreign exchange is spent are all basic drugs: aspirin, chloroquine (for malaria), antibiotics, tuberculosis drugs, and a schistosomiasis drug. The result is clear: village health posts I have visited in quite remote areas have basic drugs in stock.

Clearly there are problems. A few expensive but effective drugs are not on the list, or are ordered in very small quantities – Mozambique simply cannot afford them. And it is taking a long time to break prescribing habits created by years of advertising. For example, because of heavy promotion in colonial times, many nurses still prescribe chloramphenicol for diarrhoea in children. Not only is it unnecessary, because it has no effect on the cause of most diarrhoea, but it is positively dangerous, first because nurses may use it instead of oral rehydration, the correct treatment, and second, because chloramphenicol has nasty side-effects, including fatal aplastic anaemia. But it has to be kept on the restricted drugs list, because it is still the best drug for typhoid, despite the dangers. To help retrain the nurses, the Therapeutics Commission has now published a prescribing guide, which, for example, makes clear that chloramphenicol is only for typhoid. But it is still misused.

Still Unhealthy

Despite the gains, Mozambique remains a very unhealthy place. Children are not named until they are about two months old, as their chance of survival is so limited until then. The Government estimates that 40% of children never reach their fifth birthday. With few birth and death records, it is hard to be sure, but if anything, it's an underestimate. A doctor friend took me around the maternity section of a rural health centre near Caia, and we talked to the women. All had lost at least half of their previous children. Most die from respiratory infections or diarrhoeal diseases. Tuberculosis and measles are also important causes of death. And this is compounded by malnutrition. With so many children dying, women bear ten or more children; repeated childbirth affects their health, and one woman dies in childbirth for every 300 babies born. This is further compounded by tropical diseases: more than half of all Mozambicans are affected by malaria, and most by schistosomiasis (bilharzia or snail fever).

'Raising the level of people's health depends essentially on economic development,' explains Health Minister Pascoal Mocumbi. And he points out that the sharp drop in infant mortality and tuberculosis mortality in England was caused by economic development, long before medicines were available or there was any organized health service. Nevertheless, he believes that even in an underdeveloped country health care can have some effect, and indeed that improved health can actually assist the country's economic development. Thus the Ministry has targeted three areas: vaccination, mother and child health, and workers' health and safety.

But underdevelopment and lack of resources impose harsh limitations. For example, the Government cannot afford to pay the village health workers. The idea is that the village health worker is a local peasant chosen by the villagers for training and is supported by the village when he or she returns. Sometimes this works, as in Napala, a village of 364 families in Nampula Province. Armando Muachicarro has been village health worker there for four years. He has a wattle-and-daub health post built by local people; when I visited the village they were bringing bundles of grass to repair the roof. Armando is regarded as a member of the cooperative farm; he is in his health post four mornings a week, the same as other members work on the farm, and he receives an equal share at the end of the season. In addition he is expected to be around for emergencies, so he has been assigned a family plot close to the village where he can be found easily. In other villages in the area, the health workers are supported in this way, or else there are periodic whip-rounds to collect food and money to compensate for the time the health worker cannot spend on his farm.

But in many villages, health workers have abandoned their posts. Some were badly chosen; sometimes the only person in the village with four years of primary school was a young single man who preferred the bright lights of the city to village life. But the most common reason is lack of support. Health workers are only trained for villages that promise to support them, but many villages are simply too poor or too disorganized to carry out the promise. And some object, saying that the state pays the village schoolteacher and ought to pay the health worker, too. Of the first 1,000 village health workers trained, about one-third have abandoned their posts in communal villages. Another third still work in villages. The final third work for state farms or other businesses that pay them for the time they spend on health work.

Economic and organizational limitations are also clear in the towns. There are dozens of people waiting outside my neighbourhood health post before it even opens, and the queue does not diminish until noon. People see the health service as theirs, and they are using it in increasing numbers. Staff are undertrained and overstretched. Part of the primary health care system is triage; patients are given an initial screening in which they see a nurse or other health worker who treats the simplest cases, frequently requiring only aspirin or chloroquine or an explanation of oral rehydration. Only the serious cases are passed on to the doctor; even so, the patient gets only a few minutes with the doctor.

And the sheer workload makes the primary health care centres much more curative and much less preventive than intended. A study by British researcher Diana Jelley of a health centre in Machava, in suburban Maputo, found that there was only one person for all preventive work: vaccinations, health education, environmental hygiene, control of water supplies, and so on. It was simply impossible. He had no time to organize effective community participation and could only vaccinate those who attended the health centre, rather than go out into the neighbourhoods.

Nationally, the vaccination programme has proved much more diffi-cult than the original mass campaign. It is planned to immunize every baby against tuberculosis, measles, polio, diphtheria, whooping cough and tetanus. But the WHO survey found that only 8% of rural one-year-olds had received them all; even in Maputo, only one-third were fully immunized. The failure was shown by a measles outbreak in Maputo in late 1981: 1,283 children were hospitalized and 151 died. The problem is that the system is just too complex for Mozambique now. Babies must be vaccinated at five different times during their first year. But visits of vaccination teams in rural areas are irregular, mothers receive insuf-ficient warning, and there is not enough encouragement and education to ensure that children receive all the shots. It would probably have been better to concentrate at first on only the most essential immunizations, rather than trying to give so many.

Another problem is that, despite the expansion of the health services, the 'inverse care law' still applies – people who most need the services have the least access to them. The Machava study showed that non-users of preventive services had higher mortality rates and thus were more in need of them; the percentage of women with high-risk pregnancies who regularly attend ante-natal clinics is lower than that of women with normal pregnancies, and the babies brought to well baby clinics are already the healthier ones. Three factors seem responsible: lack of time, lack of training and an unnecessary split between curative and preventive medicine (usually there is no link between well and ill baby sections of the health centre).

The vast majority of health workers were trained in colonial times, and recycling courses have been insufficient to retrain them. Thus the nurses who do triage have no special diagnostic training and often get the diagnosis wrong; further, their prescribing skills are weak and they sometimes make mistakes with simple things like the correct dosage of chloroquine. Even worse is a continuing colonial mentality. Health was one of the few areas where black Mozambicans could advance during colonial times. Becoming a nurse, the highest position available, gave a Mozambican a privileged social position. Even though they were always inferior to the colonial bourgeoisie, they adopted the ideology of that group, and looked down on other Mozambicans – according to President Machel, who, as an ex-nurse, ought to know. Diana Jelley found that in Machava the nurses looked down on the mothers of low-weight children and on pregnant women who attended ante-natal clinics irregularly, perhaps because these women were usually of a lower socio-economic class. The attitude was punitive rather than supportive. Low baby weight, for example, was simply seen as the fault of the mother, and no extra time or help was given to the women who particularly needed it.

Struggle for Resources

Frelimo is justifiably proud of its progress since independence. The health service is radically improved. But that progress pales somewhat when you realize that in most ways Mozambique has only caught up with other developing countries. For example, Mozambique has one health unit bed per thousand people, a typical figure for poor countries. And the average Mozambican sees a health worker only once every two years, compared to four times a year in neighbouring Tanzania. Furthermore, despite its apparent priority to the rural areas, Mozambique shows the same urban-rural maldistribution as most developing countries. In 1981, only 15% of doctors practised in rural areas, while half (180 of 365) were in the capital; this is similar to the proportions seen elsewhere in Africa. The Maputo Central Hospital has nearly 2,000 staff: 15% of the country's entire health workforce, and more than any one of Mozambique's ten provinces. Staff accounts for 56% of the entire health budget, so it is a good measure of distribution of resources. In 1979, the only year such a calculation was made, expenditure on staff was £7 for each resident of the city of Maputo, and only 40p for each rural resident.

The Vice-Minister of Health, Dr Fernando Vaz, criticized me for raising this. 'This is a populist way of looking at things. You are asking the wrong question. How many doctors were there in Maputo in colonial times? More than 400! You should ask how many doctors there were in rural areas in colonial times.' And in one sense he is right; even 15% of doctors in rural areas is an improvement. Furthermore, there are clear indications of change. Between 1979 and 1981 the number of rural doctors increased by 56% (from 36 to 56), the number of health centres and posts by 20%, and the number of rural maternity beds by 17%. In general, these are new resources; the extra doctors in rural areas are new doctors and there has been no change in the number in the capital. This, Dr Vaz argues, is how it should be. 'We have here the minimum personnel necessary for the Central Hospital to function. If you give this to the rural zones, you paralyse the Central Hospital. If we did that, it would be pure populism and leftism.'

Not everyone agrees. A joint study committee of Unicef and WHO, in a 1981 report on 'National Decision-making for Primary Health Care', noted that Mozambique's 'concentration on developed urban health centres slowed down the expansion of rural coverage. . . . An approach to primary health care which was in many respects textbook in conception was being insufficiently translated into reality.'

In other words, there is a struggle going on for resources. There are intertwined conflicts between urban and rural, curative and preventive, professional and lay control of health, and between classes. As Vaz says, 'What happens in the city of Maputo today has a different effect from what happens elsewhere, because the Government is here.' City residents queuing outside the health centre know that they are not being treated as the colonial bourgeoisie was, and as they themselves now expect to be treated. So they put pressure on the Government, often through the Party, as peasants never can. The problem was articulated in terms of the poor quality of curative care, and President Machel responded to this pressure in a speech to health workers on 4 December 1979. Where the Third Congress had given 'priority . . . to preventive medicine', the President said that, 'On a par with preventive action it is necessary to develop our curative capacity.' Primary health care has an important curative component, and this is what the general public sensed was inadequate. But this was confused by some health workers, probably intentionally, with high-level hospital care. So instead of recycling nurses so that they could better perform triage, it was decided to improve hospital services; a few specialists are being trained, and closed heart surgery has begun.

Much was made in the debate about 'quality'. Vaz, for example, told me that 'the quality of health care given in colonial times was good'. For Vaz, who had been a successful surgeon in Lourenço Marques, colonial care is still the bench-mark. This is what he means when he goes on to say that in addition to expanding rural coverage, Frelimo also committed itself to 'maintain and increase the quality of medicine provided in the hospitals'. The medical elite that defines 'quality' may be more sympathetic than those who fled at independence, but they are still hospital doctors trained in the same Portuguese medical schools. The Ministry of Health's own submission to the Alma Ata primary heath care conference was scathing about just this sort of doctor: medical students are taught an elitist, 'academicist' mentality of sophisticated medicine that cannot be understood by the lay person. 'Medicine becomes a religion and the professors are the clergy.'

In these conditions, 'quality' becomes synonymous with 'difficult' and 'theoretical'. Medical students in Maputo are still given a highly theoretical course with a stress on the technical and curative; more attention is paid to obscure illness than to community medicine. Paramedical courses, too, are highly theoretical. But the response to complaints in 1979 about poor curative care was simply to raise the entrance standards (admittedly only to six years of primary school) for paramedical courses instead of making them more practical.

The power of doctors is part of an increasingly bitter class struggle. The Maputo Central Hospital has seen one of the most successful transformations since independence. Samora Machel had visited it several times, and in 1976 he appointed a restructuring committee to develop a system of workers' councils in wards and various departments. In many areas of the hospital they functioned well, and they seemed a real success of 'people's power'.

Thus it came as a surprise when the President in his 1979 health speech made no mention of the workers' councils. Instead he stressed the need for hierarchies in which everyone knew their place, and the power of directors. 'It is the director who decides,' Machel noted. Orders came from the top. Water, he said, does not run up the mountain. In the hospitals, Machel continued, 'there is total confusion'. People are afraid to give orders and subordinates refuse to carry them out. Hospitals are dirty and disorganised. He told horror stories about orderlies refusing to sweep and demanding to know why doctors had written particular prescriptions. 'Populism and ultra-democracy have been installed in the hospitals. People's power has been confused with populism.' No one knows who is in charge; 'there are no pyramids, no hierarchies.' And he went on to talk of 'liberalism and absolute egalitarianism [which] provoke indiscipline', adding that 'liberalism is a virus that causes epidemics.' The President repeatedly stressed the overriding authority of directors, doctors and teachers. 'Students debate with doctors, with teachers. Here in Mozambique we cannot permit this.'

A gruelling eight-day meeting of health workers and the Party followed to analyse the speech and to prepare guidelines for the health services to carry out. The meetings were chaired by the two top Party officials, Jorge Rebelo and Marcelino dos Santos. And it was clear that Samora Machel had gone too far. The final report stressed that the workers' council is 'one of the essential pillars of people's power' and 'a fulcrum in the class struggle in the hospitals'. Thus workers' councils had to be strengthened. And it spelled out clearly the careful balance, which was to be frequently stressed later, of 'combining a strong individual director with collective work methods'. The department head is automatically head of the workers' council in the department and he or she takes the decisions; there are no votes in the meetings. But the director 'must study their opinions' and the implication is that he or she must have good reasons to override them.

On the issue of curative medicine, the report stressed the importance of curative care as a way of 'mobilising people to accept preventive measures'.

However, while the speech was published and widely discussed, the report of the Party and health workers was never published. Thus 'wrong' interpretations of the President's speech remained unchallenged.

It is clear in retrospect that certain groups had seized the opportunity to regain lost status and privilege. Many of the doctors who stayed in Mozambique after independence, as well as those who qualified soon after, did not actively oppose Frelimo's health policies; but they were not happy with them. They came from middle-class backgrounds and had begun medical school expecting to enter highly paid private practices. At the very least, they now wanted powerful, prestigious posts in the Central Hospital. They were not pleased to be sent to the provinces, or, if still in the Central Hospital, to be kept in check by workers' councils.

And hospital workers did control the abuses of the more reactionary doctors, sometimes in simple ways, like suggesting that doctors need not be arrogant with patients and staff, or that Central Hospital doctors might make ward rounds instead of having patients brought to their office outside the ward. But it was with Frelimo Party membership that hospital workers showed what the doctors considered unacceptable strength. When Frelimo became a 'vanguard Party' instead of a mass Party in 1978, it followed the unusual system of requiring candidates for Party membership to be approved by mass meetings of their co-workers. In the Maputo Central Hospital, the workers rejected two of the five doctors put forward – on good grounds, my medical friends tell me. Party membership is obviously important for any advancement in Mozambique, and the doctors expected to be approved automatically. One of the rejected doctors put himself forward again in the Ministry of Health, where he was approved by a less militant workforce.

When opinion was being canvassed in preparation for the President's health speech, the Central Hospital restructuring committee, which the President had personally appointed and which had so successfully introduced workers' councils, was mysteriously not asked to comment. Doctors outside Maputo, however, were asked their views.

Some of the unfounded horror stories given to Machel reportedly came from Dr Bernadino Costa, then provincial health director in Gaza and a surgeon in Xai-Xai hospital. Hard working and conscientious as a doctor, he was also arrogant and elitist. He was known for his outspoken complaints about 'cheeky orderlies' and used his post as provincial director to transfer away from Xai-Xai a social worker who had opposed his admission to the Party. Three years later Bernadino Costa left for Portugal just days before his brother Jorge, a high security official, defected to South Africa.

This clique convinced the President that curative care had been neglected, and the problem could be solved only if they were given more power. Clearly this same group had a vested interest in not distributing the report of the Party and health workers. The result was that, despite the report, workers' councils fell into disuse, often because they were ignored by doctors who never liked them anyway.

The critics won other victories as well. A few weeks later, the Health Minister, Dr Helder Martins, was dismissed. Many doctors in the provinces were recalled to Maputo, ostensibly for more training. And there were minor gains. A continuing complaint of the urban middle classes had been that the restricted drugs list had deprived them of patent medicines. After the health speech, Eno Salts, Essential Balm and a few other items reappeared in chemist shops. This may seem trivial, but it cost scarce foreign exchange at a time when the Government did not have money to import enough basic drugs, and when I saw the vaccination campaign grinding to a halt in many rural areas because there were no inner tubes for the vaccinators' motor bikes.

But their own health, and especially that of their family, is the area where people are least willing to be egalitarian. It is, as Machel admits, 'the most sensitive point'. And people are clearly willing to use whatever rank or power they have to obtain what they see as better health care.

Inevitably a minister's child is more likely to be sent abroad for treatment than the child of a peasant. 'The people like to see their leaders well treated, because they know the power they represent is the power that corresponds to their aspirations,' Machel explained in the health speech. And he went on in the speech to call for special privileges, including special hospital rooms, for officials. 'Is it right for a director to be in the same ward as his subordinate? Is it right for the wife of a minister to be in the same ward as the wife of a cook?' he asked.

People clearly expect to see officials better treated. After centuries of feudal and colonial rule, Mozambicans assume it is one of the perquisites of power. And with the new stress on hierarchies, the middle classes and city dwellers also assume that they have a right to better health care than the peasants. In its report to the Alma Ata primary health care conference, the Mozambican Government warned of the need 'to repudiate the false idea that primary health care is for rural people and that there is a system of high technical level for city dwellers'. Has that warning been dismissed along with Martins, the man responsible for the report?

So far, it appears not. In the end, the critics did not win. Rather, Frelimo effectively institutionalized the continuing class struggle. The new Health Minister is Dr Pascoal Mocumbi, a long-time Frelimo militant whose medical training (as an obstetrician) was not in Portugal, and whose bias is towards primary health care. He was previously provincial health director in Sofala, where he insisted on continuing to practise medicine for a few hours a week, and instead of working in the Beira Central Hospital, he chose to work in a suburban health centre. However, Frelimo also created the new post of Vice-Minister of Health and appointed Dr Vaz, previously head of the Maputo Central Hospital and a chief proponent of high quality curative care.

After his appointment, Mocumbi travelled around the country and talked to health workers, not just in city hospitals but in rural areas, too; and he pushed ahead with primary health care. In particular, a new programme of integrated mother and child care was begun. Mocumbi also succeeded in bypassing the medical elite's demands. He got around the ruling that new trainees had to have at least six years' schooling by introducing a recycling programme for orderlies with four years' schooling plus several years' work experience, in which they are trained as paramedics. Mocumbi went one step further and appointed three provincial directors who were not doctors but 'technicians', with nine years' primary school plus a three-year course. One is not even a medical technician but a social-work technician. That is a highly appropriate choice, as a provincial director should concentrate on primary health care. These moves have been followed up by the appointment of a number of 'agents' (with six years' primary school plus a two-year course) as district health directors, even in some districts where there is a doctor.

But can Mocumbi and Frelimo resist the siren call of professionalism and high technology medicine? The Ministry of Health has already approved the start of open heart surgery in 1985. Each step to more sophisticated medicine can be justified by the rhetoric of primary health care: specialists are needed for teaching and for treatment of officials, heart surgery is not very expensive, and so on.

Most doctors in rural areas are still foreigners; the ones responsible for the President's 1979 speech won their return tickets to Maputo. The plan for 1990 calls for 450 Mozambican doctors (half the total) in rural areas.

Yet newly qualified Mozambican doctors still treat rural service as a form of penance, and cling to the ruling that they need only spend two years out there. The two policies are clearly in conflict, and the pressure for more specialists and more doctors in Maputo will be great.

9. Halting Economic Collapse

Putting health workers in the countryside proved much easier than transforming the bankrupt, distorted, sabotaged economy which Frelimo inherited. Production was falling rapidly. The rural marketing network collapsed, as Portuguese and Asian traders either fled to Portugal or moved to the cities to take over businesses there. Peasants could not sell their surpluses or buy consumer goods, so peasant production plummeted. Most Portuguese settlers abandoned their farms, usually killing their cattle and destroying the tractors or driving them over the border. Industrial production dived as owners and skilled workers left, machinery was damaged, and no spares or raw materials were imported.

By the time of the Frelimo Third Congress in 1977 the worst of the collapse had been halted, and the Congress turned its attention to the 'long and difficult battle for the effective conquest of economic power'. This involved first recovery, with an implicit goal of returning to 1973 production levels (the peak colonial year) by 1980. Second, the Congress set down general guidelines for the socialist transformation of the economy, changing both the nature of the products and the relations of production.

For the short term, the Third Congress stressed satisfying basic needs and restructuring the existing means of production. In agriculture, 'priority must be given to producing the main foods the people lack, notably maize, peanuts, rice, vegetables, fruit, meat, and eggs.' In its report to the Congress, the Central Committee argued that 'state-owned enterprises are the quickest means of responding to the country's food requirements because of the size of the area they cover, their rational organisation of human and material resources, and the immediate availability of machinery.

'In industry, the principal objective will be to increase and diversify the production of the main goods the people need, particularly cloth, clothing, shoes, and basic food products.' The short-term 'target is to increase production from existing industrial capacity' and there is an 'urgent' need to 'convert sectors producing . . . for the luxury consumption of the colonial elites' to produce instead for 'the real needs of the working masses'. Individual industries should be reorganized and reoriented to increase linkages between them. 'Direction units' were to be established by the state for each industrial sector to plan and control production by both state and private firms. Small units, particularly in the metal-working sector, were to be reorganized and merged into larger units.

In commerce, the Congress admitted the need was very basic: 'to organise an operating commercial network'. Consumer cooperatives were seen as the long-term socialist answer, but in the shorter term there would continue to be private shops and a chain of state-run People's Shops. The state should pay more attention to control of the wholesale trade and the establishment and enforcement of fixed prices.

For long-term development, agriculture was seen as the 'base', industry the 'dynamising factor', and heavy industry the 'decisive factor'. The Third Congress argued that 'the building of socialism demands that the economy be centrally planned and directed by the state', and ordered that a National Planning Commission be set up that year. Although a role remained for private capital, the Congress declared: 'The establishment of state-owned firms is a priority objective, . . . all the strategic sectors of the economy must be under state control, [and] the state-owned sector of the economy will tend to be the principal source of state finance.'

Note was taken of the 'low level of class consciousness among many workers', which meant that 'a fundamental task for the Party and state is to speed up the transformation of labour relations.'

With respect to agriculture, Frelimo came to independence with reasonably clear ideas about rural development, which is not surprising since it fought the armed struggle in rural areas. The policy was 'socialization of the countryside', involving state and cooperative farms, with people living in new villages. This is the central issue of economic transformation, as 85% of the population live in rural areas, and it is discussed in detail in Chapters 12 and 13.

With respect to industry and commerce, however, Frelimo had no firm ideas and little economic experience. These were not discussed at the eighth session of the Central Committee in February 1976 which defined most of Frelimo's policies for the transition to socialism. The Third Congress dealt with rural development, but did not consider long-term industrial policy. It only mentioned two scientific projects, an agricultural implements factory and a forest industries complex; it left long-term industrialisation to be set out in a special plan to be submitted in 1980 (which was eventually expanded to be the ten-year plan).

Yet Frelimo inherited a sizeable industrial base. If Portuguese statistics are to be believed, Mozambique was the eighth most industrialized country in Africa. It had heavy industry and even built railway wagons. The cashew-nut industry is a good example. Traditionally the nuts were processed by hand or sent to India for hand processing. But several firms, including Anglo-American Corporation of South Africa, invested in cashew-processing machinery. And the South African subsidiary of the British firm Metal Box set up small factories to assemble tins for cashew nuts.

It was not, however, the kind of industrialization that Frelimo wanted. There were few mass consumption goods and few linkages between industries. Instead, Mozambique largely manufactured exports and luxury consumer goods, and was highly dependent on imported raw materials. Industry divided sharply into three categories:

*Processing *local agricultural products for export*: 30% of industrial production. This included tea, cotton, copra, sisal, sugar and cashew nuts.

*Processing *local agricultural products for local use*: 30% of industrial production. This was largely rice milling, meat, dairy products and so on, for settler consumption, with a few mass consumption items like cotton textiles and soap.

*Processing *imported raw materials for local use*: 33%. Beer alone accounted for 4% of Mozambique's total industrial production. Clothing, synthetic textiles and printing were also important. Included in this group are most intermediate goods (that is, goods to make other goods): iron and steel products, paints, chemicals and fertilizers. These were largely quality consumer goods or intermediate goods to make luxury consumer items.

The remainder is accounted for by two important industries, the oil refinery and cement. The latter went mainly to the Cahora Bassa dam and high-rise blocks in the cities. (More details are given in Appendix 5.)

To satisfy its goals, Frelimo had to restructure and expand industry significantly. Some efforts were made to change the nature of production. Cifel, the Maputo iron and steel foundry, had produced reinforcing bars for concrete high-rise buildings, as well as some decorative iron work, neither of which were any longer needed. So they began casting giant rollers for sugar-cane crushing; these had previously been imported. Some efforts were also made to use more local raw materials, for example substituting cotton for imported synthetic fibres.

In general, however, Mozambican industry proved extremely fragile. It was difficult to co-ordinate it, change its production, or even keep it running. In particular, colonial industry was undercapitalized; much machinery was old, often imported second hand. And it was highly inefficient, cosseted for many years by starvation wages and protected markets. The country's largest textile mill, Textáfrica in Chimoio, produced at only half capacity in colonial times; many of its looms had been acquired second hand in Portugal in 1951 and its finishing equipment was old, varied and badly maintained.

On paper, colonial Mozambique had a large industrial workforce (100,000 people), but the skilled workers were all Portuguese who left. There were skilled Mozambicans, but they were all in South African mines and factories, and it proved difficult to slot them in to replace departing Portuguese.

Most firms were tiny, controlled by one or two people who did all the ordering, selling and often the repairs. When they left, the workers had no idea what to do. Maintenance was deferred and machinery began to break down.

Falling agricultural production meant fewer raw materials.

Importing proved a nightmare. Dynamizing Groups and Frelimo-appointed managers had no experience of importing raw materials and spares. Efforts to centralize this into state import agencies proved a disaster: a quote would be obtained, usually valid for three months, but the Mozambican bureaucracy could not move quickly enough to place the order in time. So another quote had to be obtained, and so on.

Central planning and the National Planning Commission were supposed to rationalize and reorganize the economy. But unrealistic targets set in Maputo offices made a nonsense of the whole process. No one could produce more than half their target under the best of circumstances. When what they were producing was an input for someone else, their shortfalls set off a chain reaction. The growing foreign exchange crisis, exacerbated by agricultural exports falling far short of unrealistic plans, meant that imports of essential spares and raw materials were delayed.

Transport and other linkages proved a major bottleneck. In colonial times individual factory managers had placed orders and set up deliveries in person or on the telephone, usually with individual transport owners and wholesalers acting as intermediaries. It was inefficient but it worked. But most of these people fled, and Frelimo has never been able to make central planning as effective.

Reluctant Nationalization

Although the Third Congress argued that 'all strategic sectors of the economy must be under state control', only three nationalizations can be considered 'political' in the sense that they were not strictly necessary to keep a business operating. In January 1977, just before the Third Congress, the insurance industry was nationalized. In May the Portuguese- and French-owned oil refinery was taken over. And at the end of 1977 most banks were nationalized and integrated into the Bank of Mozambique and the new People's Development Bank. But even that was not entirely political; the private banks had been involved in the illegal export of capital. And one private bank, the Portuguese- and British-owned Standard Totta, was not nationalized and still operates. Restrictions were imposed, however, prohibiting anyone but the Bank of Mozambique from dealing in foreign currency. Similarly the Government set up a series of state firms which largely took over importing and exporting.

Otherwise, Mozambique was extremely reluctant to take over anything that was actually running. Thus it only 'intervened' in companies that were abandoned or sabotaged. For example, it finally took over the coal-mines in 1978 after 250 miners had been killed in two accidents in the previous 18 months as a result of inadequate safety precautions. The Moatize mine had been owned jointly by the Entreposto group (a descendant of the old Mozambique Company) and Iscor, the South African iron and steel corporation.

Later that year, the state took over the Mozambique Shipping Company from CUF, a Portuguese group by then controlled by the Portuguese state as a result of nationalizations there in 1975. The Mozambique firm had bought a large ship from its Portuguese parent company and 'leased' it back without charge, had failed to insure its ships, and had run up large debts to the Bank of Mozambique.

The British-owned Sena Sugar Estates was finally taken over in 1978 when production had fallen to less than one-third of pre-independence levels, and it owed £25 million to the Bank of Mozambique and more than £2 million to foreign creditors. Curiously, towards the end of the colonial period the owners had ordered the construction of one of Africa's largest sugar mills, which would probably have been uneconomic even if the company had continued. It was due for completion by 1976. But when the firm was 'intervened' in 1978 it was still unfinished, while Sena had already closed down the old factory it was to replace. 'A long-term sabotage plan' commented the weekly magazine *Tempo*.

Increasingly firms were 'intervened' when the foreign owners refused to make repairs, ran up debts to the Bank of Mozambique, and continued to try to sneak money out of the country. In 1979 the Government 'intervened' the cement company, a steel pipe factory, the glass company, and four small mining companies. In 1980 the largest miller and the breweries were taken over. In 1981 Anglo-American Corporation of South Africa abandoned its cashew-nut processing factories in Mozambique.

The Ministry of Industry gives this breakdown of percentage ownership of industry:

	1977	1982
State	1	25
'Intervened'	5	37
Mixed state/private	9	11
Private	85	27

Some areas, like textiles and clothing, involve all four categories. There are still private sugar, tea, and sisal plantations. It makes co-ordination extremely difficult, and has made the 'direction units' less effective than they might have been.

Frelimo repeatedly stated that there was a place for private enterprise. Whatever the theoretical considerations, Frelimo simply did not have the management capacity, especially for the host of small businesses. In 1978 the President told the Central Committee, 'Our state cannot waste its energies selling needles and razor blades or running tea rooms and barber shops.' Considerable effort was needed to keep these tiny 'intervened' firms going, often without success. The state-run chain of People's Shops was a particular disaster; the shelves were empty while the shop managers gave themselves and their friends high salaries and sat around waiting for the state to give them goods to sell. Finally in 1980 the state began to sell off most of its small businesses, including the People's Shops. This not only reflected the state's own lack of management capacity. It also showed that there were local capitalists with enough money and confidence in Frelimo's promises to want to expand and take over firms which had been abandoned only four or five years before.

There were also repeated efforts to attract private foreign capital to develop new industries. Generally the deal offered was that the foreign firm would provide all the capital, technology and imported raw materials; it would have to earn the money to repay its costs and provide profits by exporting some of the production. On this basis Mozambique promised to be generous in allowing foreign investors considerable control and the right to significant profits. The hope was that Mozambique would gain industrial development, skills, and some products at relatively little cost to itself. This has not been successful so far, in part because up to the time of writing (mid-1983) Mozambique has apparently never allowed a private company to repatriate profits, and in part because of the world recession. The only significant investment on this basis is the 1983 agreement by Shell and Exxon to spend £40 million for onshore oil exploration in Cabo Delgado.

Mozambique also looked for mixed ventures and management contracts. Here it had better results. A model frequently cited by Mozambique is Mabor Tyre. Construction started in 1972 and stopped after the coup in Portugal. The new Frelimo Government renegotiated the agreement with the Portuguese Mabor and its US parent, General Tire. The state owns 87% and General Tire most of the rest. Mabor and General manage the firm and earn their income in management fees and from the supply of raw materials, rather than from repatriated profits. Production is high and of good quality and Mozambicans are being trained.

A similar but much less successful project is Texmoque, a textile mill in Nampula. Again the project was started before independence but only got off the ground afterwards. Textáfrica, the Portuguese-owned textile mill in Chimoio, owns 43% and the state owns 38%. But Textáfrica's contribution was entirely second (or third) hand machinery, largely from its factory in Chimoio; it brought in no new capital from abroad. Much of this machinery is old and worn, and was sent to Nampula lacking essential components. A major part was 132 looms which had been imported, second hand, by Textáfrica in 1951. Equipment which had to be imported was purchased on supplier credits guaranteed by the Bank of Mozambique, so Textáfrica took no risk, but this equipment was purchased by Textáfrica's owners and agents. The price of the project and especially of imported equipment rose rapidly during the early phase. There were allegations (never proven) that the prices had been inflated so that the private investors could illegally transfer capital out of Mozambique. The private investors also supplied highly paid Portuguese technicians, many of whom were criticized as incompetent and who failed to train Mozambicans to take their places. Four years after opening, Texmoque was still operating at only 10% of capacity.

Dollars

Mozambique (and other Third World countries) came to independence as suppliers of raw materials and importers of manufactured goods, their economies tied entirely to the industrialized world. As we have already seen, two-thirds of Mozambique's industry was tied to the developed countries (and much of the rest served settlers). Clearly a Third World country's demand for imported consumer goods will always exceed its ability to export low-priced agricultural products in exchange. Thus some choice must always be made about what to import.

Most Third World countries impose some controls on imports and currency, often in the face of opposition from the developed world and the International Monetary Fund (IMF). In Mozambique (and in many planned economies) all imports and other expenditures abroad must be approved by the central bank, to make sure that the limited exports are being traded for the goods most needed by the country. This control is imposed in two ways. First by requiring import licences, and second by making the local currency non-convertible. Mozambican banknotes cannot be taken out of the country and can only be exchanged for other currencies at the Bank of Mozambique. But a Mozambican firm cannot simply go to the bank and exchange Mozambican meticais for British pounds. This is possible only for a previously authorized import.

The Bank of Mozambique quotes an exchange rate which it uses for these transactions, and which I use in this book. By definition it is an artificial exchange rate. But in terms of wages and prices, it seems roughly correct. The minimum agricultural wage is £1 per day while skilled workers earn more than £75 per month. Bread costs 3p for a half-pound loaf, simple cotton dresses cost around £25, my rent (based on my higher income) for a two-bedroom flat is £28 per month, and the air fare to the north of the country is £88.

But it is really necessary to think in terms of two separate currencies, meticais for internal commerce and dollars for foreign trade. All of Mozambique's exports are priced on the world market in US dollars, as are all of its imports (even from the socialist bloc). Thus a 'devaluation' would have little direct effect, since it does not affect the real price of Mozambique's imports or exports.

Because so much is imported, the overriding constraint to development is foreign currency – dollars. It makes no difference if a firm is profitable in meticais if the foreign exchange does not exist to import raw materials, spare parts and technical expertise.

Even seemingly local industries have a significant dollar cost. For example, textiles made from local cotton still have one-sixth of their cost in foreign currency for chemicals and spare parts. The development process aims at producing more of those imports locally, but it will take some years. Furthermore, Mozambique's ambitious development plan assumes considerable imports of machinery.

Mozambique pays for its imports by exporting agricultural products, prawns and coal; from port and railway traffic and miners' wages; and from foreign aid and loans. Even before independence, Mozambique was effectively bankrupt, importing more than it exported. Portugal had already made the Mozambican currency non-convertible, which caused shortages of imported goods in the colony in the years just before independence. Afterwards, South Africa cut the number of miners to one-third and steadily reduced port traffic, significantly reducing Mozambique's earnings. Sanctions against Rhodesia cost Mozambique £250 million in lost port, railway and other earnings; they also increased defence expenditures. Furthermore, the international terms of trade turned against Mozambique: raw material prices fell while those of manufactured goods rose. Five tons of cotton would 'pay' for a lorry in 1975, but in 1980 a lorry 'cost' 13 tons of cotton. Overall, the average price of exports rose 40% while the average price of non-oil imports rose 60% and oil prices rose fourfold.

Just after independence, Mozambique was cushioned. The number of miners stayed high and they were paid in gold at the official price. The value of prawns and cashew nuts, which are luxury goods, held up better than other commodities. And Mozambique's imports fell dramatically as abandoned firms failed to import raw materials. Thus in 1975 and 1976 Mozambique had its first balance of payments surpluses in many years; the deficit only became large in 1978. This meant that at first Mozambique did not pay much attention to foreign exchange constraints, and it still does not usually take into account the quite high dollar cost of locally produced products. But this factor is often lurking in the background. One of the major causes of low industrial production is the inability to import essential raw materials and spare parts.

The failure to take this into account can have serious consequences. Mozambique's first and most prestigious post-independence development project is the Ifloma forest industries complex in Chimoio, completed in 1983 with more than £15 million in Swedish aid and credits. It includes a sophisticated sawmill plus a particle board (chipboard) factory. Particle board is made from the wood chips left over at the sawmill, and is used for furniture and building in many countries, although it is not common in Mozambique where hardwoods are used instead. The argument for the project was that if particle board was used for Mozambican furniture and building, the hardwoods thus saved could be exported, earning foreign exchange. The economics seem clear. The factory would produce enough particle board to release £4 million in hardwood per year for export, yet its foreign exchange cost would be only £2 million per year (half depreciation and half for chemicals), a clear foreign currency profit of £2 million annually.

In fact, this calculation is spurious. The hardwoods could be exported whether or not particle board is produced; the decision will never be whether or not to export wood, but rather whether or not to build furniture for local consumption; furniture making has already been curtailed to increase wood exports. Once it is in full production, the particle board factory will require £1 million annually for glues and chemicals alone – 1.5% of Mozambique's entire imports. Since the particle board factory is making a product entirely for local consumption and not for export, it will have to take its place in the queue with all other firms pleading for scarce imported raw materials. It is highly unlikely that the government will ever authorize so much hard currency for that single project. Thus Mozambique's first prestige development project is producing what will be considered a luxury item largely dependent on imported raw materials, little different from colonial industries. And shortages of foreign exchange ensure that it will run at a tiny fraction of capacity.

The Meticais Mountain

Hard currency may be in short supply, but there is no lack of Mozambican meticais. Salaries rose dramatically just before independence, up to five-fold or more for skilled workers. In some cases these resulted from the real victories of strikes towards the end of the colonial period. But all too often they were a form of economic sabotage: workers were given massive increases to keep them quiet while the managers packed their bags and took money out of the country. In 1980 Frelimo raised the minimum wage by 50%, granting a wage increase to 170,000 low-paid workers and adding £17 million to the annual wage bill (at the same time, it reduced starting salaries for the higher paid, in an effort to close differentials). Prices rose, but not nearly as much as salaries, in part because food and basic consumer goods are subsidized at the rate of more than £60 million per year. State-owned companies received massive subsidies. The Fourth Congress was told that the annual wage bill was £160 million above the total value of goods on sale. Furthermore, the nationalizations sharply cut expenditure: health and education are free, and urban rents do not even cover maintenance costs.

In the cities, spending power rose dramatically during the transitional period and shortly after independence, and many people had a sudden taste of the life style of the colonists, eating meat every day instead of once a week, and buying luxury goods like wine. But Frelimo could not hope to maintain this standard – which caused some discontent later in the cities – nor did it want to. Imports of luxury items like cars and refrigerators for private sale were stopped completely (although they are still imported in small quantities for high state officials). And the import of raw materials for locally packed goods like toothpaste was cut back. What foreign currency was available (itself reduced by the economic crisis) was diverted away from the importing of consumer goods and raw materials to that of producer goods like tractors and other machinery to develop the country. This meant that the volume of consumer goods never returned to 1973 levels and the newly created demand was never met.

Price and rent subsidies largely benefit city people and were intended as support to the working class. Producer prices for farmers doubled, but the terms of trade still went against the peasants. This was inevitable. Frelimo made it clear that agriculture was to be the base of development. It is the only possible internal source of accumulation, which means the money for industrial development can only come from the rural areas or from abroad. For Mozambique, capital means dollars, so it is really in terms of foreign exchange that the peasants were squeezed. The combination of a lack of consumer goods and a continued weak marketing network meant that peasants were able to buy goods worth only about half the meticais value of the produce they were selling (effectively nullifying the doubling of producer prices). Thus peasants built up large stocks of meticais they could not spend.

Although there were opportunities for savings and for investment, especially in the 1980 sale of government-owned small businesses, there was still too much money chasing too few goods: it was largely taken up by black-market traders. With the price of basic foodstuffs rigidly controlled, inflation showed up in less strictly controlled goods. Clothing and restaurant meals, for example, tripled in price in the eight years after independence. Goods transport, still largely in private hands, became vastly expensive. A black market grew up in consumer goods and hard-to-control items like fish. The price of scarce goods which were no longer easily imported, like stereos and car parts, jumped to 10 to 15 times their value at the official exchange rate. Thefts increased. One morning I came out of my house to find the windscreen had been stolen from my car.

10. The Rise and Fall of the Ten-Year Plan

'We refuse to remain eternally suppliers of raw materials. We refuse to allow the old colonial relations to remain, even under a new guise. We refuse to participate in the international division of labour in a subordinate position, paying more and more for finished products and selling our labour power for less and less. We refuse to sell the ore and be left only with the holes,' President Machel told the People's Assembly in 1979. By the following year the National Planning Commission was to submit a ten-year plan for the 'radical transformation of our country'.

The potential is there; Mozambique is a rich country. Although the British drew the boundaries very carefully when Africa was carved up in the last century, and most of the best land and mineral deposits are in what is now South Africa and Zimbabwe, Mozambique still has more potential than many African countries. It has all the essentials for development: land, water, energy and minerals. The Portuguese never tapped these resources. They never even did a complete geological survey of the country.

Mozambique is a net energy exporter. The energy value of the coal it exports is similar to that of the imported oil it uses, and the electricity from Cabora Bassa sold to South Africa is equivalent to three times that much energy. The generating capacity of the Cabora Bassa dam could be doubled and several other dams built. Mozambique has vast coal reserves and production could be increased 20-fold. There are untapped gas reserves (which the Portuguese had intended to pipe directly to South Africa and not even use in Mozambique) and possibly oil.

In colonial times, small quantities of marble, asbestos, semi-precious stones, graphite, copper, gold and tantalite were mined. In fact, the tantalite reserves are some of the largest in the world, and there is titanium as well, which could be a small but significant export. But it is the reserves of iron ore and nepheline-syenite that are significant for industrial development. Using its own iron ore and coal, Mozambique could produce steel. Nepheline-syenite is an alternative to bauxite as a source for aluminium, and with Cabora Bassa electricity Mozambique might develop its own aluminium industry.

Mozambique has the same surface area as Britain and France combined, but a population of only 13 million. Most of the arable land is still unused and there is enormous potential for agricultural development for both food and tropical export crops like citrus and bananas. Weather is highly variable, so irrigation is needed, but two of the region's largest rivers, the Limpopo and Zambezi, flow through Mozambique, as do a number of smaller ones.

Faced with such potential, it is not surprising that Mozambique thought it could get outsiders to put up the cash and that there would be enough profit for both sides. 'We need technology. We need finance. But we have the resources, labour capacity, organization and geographic location,' Machel said. 'We do not fear cooperation with private firms from other countries, so long as it is mutually advantageous. Above all, we are aware of what we want and how to get it.'

Romania took on a one-million-acre cotton project in the north, paying all the foreign exchange costs for an opportunity to grow cotton it could no longer buy from the Soviet Union. Few others went that far, but there was a lot of soft credit available in the early years. Countries involved in agricultural projects, either on a commercial basis or in assistance programmes, included: the Soviet Union, China, East Germany, Bulgaria, Romania, Sweden, Brazil, Italy, Algeria, North Korea, France, Portugal and Kuwait. There was a major expansion of irrigated cropland in the Limpopo valley and of highland farming in Angonia (Tete). New projects were opened in Lioma (Zambézia) and in Niassa, as well as the million-acre cotton scheme.

Two textile mills were started, a blanket factory in Pemba and one of Southern Africa's largest mills in Mocuba, Zambézia.

Two major electrification projects were also begun. One involved Italian, French, Swedish and East German help for more than 1,000 miles of power line linking the Cahora Bassa dam to Mocuba, Quelimane, Nampula and Nacala. Another is a 250-mile line from a new power station on the Massingir dam in the Limpopo valley to Xai-Xai and Maputo.

In colonial times transport links had all gone east-west to serve the interior. Portugal only started to build a paved road linking the north and south of the country in the late 1960s when it became a military necessity. So independent Mozambique began to fill that gap.

Equally important, Frelimo had taken effective control of the economy. Production was rising. Thousands of people had been trained and were growing into their new jobs, albeit with the inevitable problems of inexperience. For example, the ports and railways lost 7,000 skilled and semi-skilled workers at independence. It wasn't just managers and technicians who were Portuguese, but fork-lift truck drivers and ticket collectors, too. There was only one black engine driver before independence. The railways responded by training thousands of people, with the help of only a few hundred foreign technicians, largely from East Germany and India. The trains run and the ports function – not, perhaps, to

European standards, but very well by Third World standards and vastly better than could have been expected.

Frelimo may have taken control of the economy, but it admittedly had not transformed its structure from the one left by Portuguese colonialism. This was the next step.

By 1980, with many projects already under way, the economy recovering, and peace and independence in Zimbabwe, the wildest dreams seemed possible. They were incorporated in the ten-year plan for 1981–90, approved in 1981. It called for unprecedented growth rates, so that Mozambique could win 'victory over underdevelopment' in just one decade. Gross National Product (GNP) was to rise at 17% per year throughout the decade; construction would grow at 40% per year in the first half of the decade; agricultural production would increase fivefold by the end of the decade.

There was to be a massive increase in exports and a 'rapid increase' in local production to substitute for imports. The link between industry and agriculture was also stressed, with heavy industry providing the tractors and other machinery needed for farming.

The stress was on 'big projects' costing more than £5,000 million during the decade. There was to be 'accelerated development of state farms on a basis of large areas and mechanization' involving more than 2.5 million acres. Production was to start of iron and steel, aluminium, paper, chemicals and fertilizers from gas, and heavy engineering, plus two lorry factories and bus and tractor assembly plants. There would be textile mills in every province plus large soap and oil factories. Mozambique would begin manufacturing pharmaceuticals.

The big project mentality swept all before it. The ten-year plan called for all peasants to live in communal villages and work on co-ops or state farms by 1990, but only one-quarter of agricultural investment was planned for co-ops. There was no support for small, local industries; all consumer goods were to come from the biggest, most modern factories.

The mood had already been set with the establishment in 1979 of the State Secretariat for the *Accelerated* Development of the Limpopo and Incomati Regions. It seemed possible to accelerate development and concentrate it into one decade.

It was a lovely dream and a rude awakening. Investors did not flood in with money in suitcases. Even in the best of times the necessary money would not have been available, but with a worsening world recession there was no hope. Despite brave Third World talk of a 'new international economic order', foreign investment was not going to countries which were serious about breaking the old colonial relations. Superprofits were still the name of the game, and if Mozambique would not play, neither would international capital.

For its part, Mozambique lacked the planning capacity, trained people, and infrastructure to carry out a plan that required building new cities and railways, moving literally millions of peasants, and virtually transforming the countryside in a few years. The big projects which had already started fell further and further behind. And peace was brief: South Africa began its attacks.

Finally, despite Frelimo's increasing control over the economy, it failed to rebuild the crucial links between city and country. It proved impossible to plan marketing in the same way as industrial and agricultural projects. So the initial collapse of the trading system was compounded by the lack of consumer goods for peasants, and by war, reducing the flow of food and industrial raw materials to the cities. This was an essential component in a growing economic crisis.

The ten-year plan had been due in June 1980, but was not finally approved by the People's Assembly until October 1981. It was never published. Even delegates to the People's Assembly were only allowed to see a summary which they had to return at the end of the session. The National Planning Commission refused to talk to me (or any foreign journalist) about it. And with good reason. The ten-year plan was a dead letter the day it was approved. Work had already begun on a three-year plan for 1982–85 with investment and development goals only one-third as much as those of the ten-year plan for the same period.

11. Postponing Development

Surveying the wreckage of the economy, Frelimo's Political Economy Secretary Marcelino dos Santos admitted to the Fourth Congress that economic collapse had wiped out many of the gains since independence, and that things were unlikely to improve in the near future. It was necessary 'to adopt less rapid growth rates and to postpone implementation of some expected new investment', he said. 'The growth rates now proposed will lead to an insignificant increase in our country's Gross National Product by 1985.'

The economy had recovered in 1978 and 1979. In 1980 the worsening foreign exchange crisis meant cuts in imported raw materials and spares, leading to a fall in overall industrial production. But 1981 saw a rise again, this time without increased imports because of a programme to make better use of local raw materials. Overall, for the period 1977–81 the economy had at least grown as fast as the population, even if it had not returned to pre-independence levels. But in 1982 there was a precipitous 7% fall in GNP. Dos Santos gave these figures for percentage growth rates of GNP to the Congress (more details in the Appendix):

| | Percentage growth rates | | |
	77–81	82	= 77–82
Agriculture	9	− 2	6
Industry	14	−16	− 2
Transport	15	− 7	8
Building	25	+ 4	30
Retail	0	− 4	− 4
Overall GNP	*12*	*− 7*	*4*

Population growth during the 1977–82 period was about 14%, so living standards clearly fell. The data showed that, as people complained, the shops *were* emptier than ever before.

Dos Santos called for a GNP increase of 10 to 12% by 1985. This would give the same per capita GNP as in 1977, probably the worst year in the early post-independence period.

It was a grim picture indeed that dos Santos painted. And the People's

Assembly in its meeting the month before the Fourth Congress had admitted that 'our difficulties in large measure result from internal factors'. I have tried to analyse some of these internal factors in previous chapters, and will talk more of them later. And it is clear that Frelimo must shoulder much of the blame for the crisis. Nevertheless, it was outside factors that tipped the balance, hammering an economy that was just getting on its feet.

Frelimo might have pulled it off: built the textile mills fast enough to supply cloth to the peasants before they became too upset at having money they could not spend; increased exports fast enough to pay rising debts; and improved the productivity of state farms. In the event, it was like kicking a juggler who was already off balance – you never know if he would have been able to keep all the balls in the air.

Weather, war and world recession made a total nonsense not only of Frelimo's grand plans, but of many possible reforms. The worst drought on record hit Southern Africa. In the south of Mozambique, rainfall in 1982 and 1983 was only half normal. Thus the 1982 crop was smaller than usual and the 1983 crop was minuscule. The 'great grey green greasy' Limpopo River was reduced to a trickle. Upstream, irrigation was limited, while towards the coast irrigation became impossible as sea water penetrated far upstream. The South African-backed Mozambique National Resistance (MNR, see Chapter 21) was disrupting traffic and attacking economic targets in a third of the country. Armed bands destroyed 1,000 rural shops, 20 sawmills, cotton gins, and tea factories. Hundreds of cars and trucks and more than 20 locomotives were also destroyed. More than 40 foreign technicians were kidnapped and four killed. Sweden was forced to abandon the showpiece Ifloma forest industries complex after it was built, leaving it paralysed due to lack of operating staff. Hundreds of villages were burned. Crops were burned in the fields and in peasant grain stores, and agricultural marketing lorries and farm machinery were destroyed; an estimated one-quarter of the normally marketed grain was lost due to MNR action.

The war and weather combined with lower peasant sales resulting from Frelimo's own policies (see Chapter 12) to cause a dramatic fall in exports. Cashew nuts, sugar, and copra fell to record low levels, while cotton and prawns (also affected by the weather) both dropped significantly. Because the MNR had kept the railway closed, a full year's coal production was stockpiled at the Moatize mine.

The world recession hit Mozambique directly. In 1982 the average price of its exports fell 11% compared to 1981 while the average price of its imports rose 3%. Interest rates on foreign debt rose and it became increasingly difficult to obtain credit or aid. And debts incurred in the late 1970s began to fall due, without the planned jumps in production that were intended to repay them.

One result was a financial crisis. Mozambique had been able to spend some of its own foreign currency reserves to get projects started and to pay for items not funded from abroad. Thus in 1980 it was able to carry out 80% of its capital budget. The foreign exchange squeeze made this impossible in later years. Only 60% of the 1981 capital budget was implemented. In 1982 the Government did not even publish a capital budget; it privately admitted that it could only build new projects entirely paid for by foreign finance.

Mozambique had developed a reputation for hard negotiating, playing off various firms and countries against each other and extracting reasonable deals. Its performance collapsed as credit became the only issue. Prices well above the odds were agreed simply because payment could be deferred for two or three years. Finished goods were bought on credit while factories making those goods remained paralysed for lack of cash to buy raw materials; in 1982 Mozambique imported 15,000 bicycles from India, while its bicycle factory produced at only a fraction of capacity because it was not allowed to import kits to assemble bicycles.

Mozambique has developed a compulsive secrecy about financial matters, and publishes fewer details about trade, foreign debts and balance of payments than almost any other country. It justifies this on the almost Victorian boast that it always paid its debts on time, so no one has a right to ask any questions. Even the US Government had to admit at the end of 1982 that Mozambique 'has honoured all of its credit commitments since independence'.

But in 1983 that boast began to look slightly frayed. Delays of up to five months in paying foreign debts were reported; this is short by the standards of Zambia and many other African countries, but since punctuality had been a point of pride, it was obvious that the coffers were empty. Imports of even essentials were cut. Foreign travel by government officials was sharply curbed. Some foreign technicians paid by Mozambique in hard currency were abruptly dismissed.

Internal financial controls were also crumbling. The Government had invariably underspent its budget because of shortages of goods, building materials and so on. But in 1983 it simply did not publish a national budget, a clear sign that it had been overwhelmed by the crisis and was living hand to mouth.

The crisis affected the whole economy. Production in heavy industry held steady or rose, with increases in 1982 in items ranging from cement to railway wagons to bicycles. But there were sharp falls in consumer goods production, including textiles, clothing, soap, cooking oil, beverages, and dry cell batteries. All but the last two were a direct result of falling agricultural production, but all were also affected by cuts in raw material imports. In addition, imports of consumer goods were sharply cut; this only increased black marketeering and peasant withdrawal from the official cash economy.

In some provinces, including Gaza, it was admitted that more than half the peasant surplus was going into the black market, known as *candonga*. In a speech in February 1983 in Gaza, a frustrated Samora Machel exclaimed: 'The shops are empty, but everything is available on candonga.'

Frelimo had steadfastly maintained, at least in public, that candonga was purely the result of evil businessmen, the 'internal enemy', trying to sabotage the economy. But the governor of the Bank of Mozambique, Prakash Ratilal, admitted to the People's Assembly in March 1983 that 'when there is more money than products, candonga finds fertile ground in which to grow'. He commented on people with large amounts of money in their hands and nothing to spend it on, and admitted that 'the metical has become devalued and is no longer accepted as a means of exchange', recognition that a barter economy had grown up in many areas.

The economy dominated the Frelimo Fourth Party Congress in April 1983, and there was a candid admission of errors: 'Mistakes were made. Some of them could have been avoided, even though our capacity to respond to problems is conditioned by the weakness of our economic management system which has not yet accumulated sufficient experience.' In addition to the criticisms of agriculture mentioned in the next chapter, the Central Committee admitted:

*'We have not managed to involve the enthusiasm and creativity of our people sufficiently in the effort to develop our economy. Decisions have been excessively centralised.'

*'Difficulties in giving investment priority to rehabilitation has meant that today our industrial and transport infrastructure has serious maintenance problems.'

*'The quality of production has been deteriorating, particularly in products that supply the people.'

*'Investments . . . have not been accompanied by efficient organisation of maintenance nor by adequate supplies of spare parts.'

Two examples will show the results of these mistakes. The weekly magazine *Tempo* on 3 July 1983 told the tale of a cotton gin in Montepuez, Cabo Delgado. In 1982, 380 tons of cotton had been ruined because it had been left out in the rain. This occurred because: 1) a high pressure safety valve broke and had to be sent to Maputo for repair, paralyzing the factory for two months; 2) burlap sacking for family cotton producers arrived in September instead of July so marketing was not complete when the rains started; and 3) there was no space in the warehouse anyway, because 1,100 tons of cottonseed had not been removed by an oil and soap company, and hundreds of tons of cotton from two years before had still not been collected by the state export agency. It would have been much worse had not peasant cotton production fallen to half the previous year's level because there were no consumer goods, particularly cotton cloth, to buy with the money the peasants earned when they sold their cotton.

The other example comes from a 1981 survey of the shoe industry. It had still not recovered from the departure of the old managers, who had taken all the documentation and 'know-how' with them. Production was less than 20% of capacity, and output was of low quality. Leather quality was poor, due to lack of care in the slaughterhouses, poor initial conservation of skins, and lack of imported chemicals for tanning. Cutters wasted leather because they did not position pieces well in the hides and were forced to cut leather with hack saws because they did not have files to sharpen their knives. Production was also reduced by the inability to import key items: nails, glues, dies, thread and inner soles. Machinery was not maintained, and sometimes not even oiled, so that one-third of it (including some sophisticated, modern equipment) had been out of order for several years.

The Congress adopted three goals for the 1983–85 period: to 'overcome the most basic signs of hunger', to defeat the MNR and the black marketeers, and to 'consolidate the basis for more rapid development in the second half of the decade'.

To achieve these goals, 'resources must be allocated with priority to small-scale projects which have an immediate effect on people's living standards' and which use local raw materials. In addition, maximum use should be made of installed capacity, rehabilitating where necessary. Finally, no new projects were to be started (except a much delayed farm implements factory) but work on existing projects should be speeded up.

Stress was placed on decentralization of planning. Individual districts are to have considerably more control and the National Planning Commission less. Plans should be tailored to existing realities. It was suggested, for example, that 'levels of coal production be adjusted to available transport capacity' instead of simply increasing production and stockpiling it in order to meet ever higher plan targets.

One of the most dramatic changes of line at the Fourth Congress was much stronger support for the private sector. Private business had always been allowed, and the Party Programme approved at the Third Congress in 1977 stressed that 'small and medium agricultural proprietors' and 'artisans and small property owners' should be supported by the Party and state to the extent that they supplied the people.

But the Fourth Congress called for additional support to the private sector. Small and local industries should be supported whether ço-ops or private. 'The state must encourage the most dynamic businessmen,' according to the economic directives of the Fourth Congress.

The view on retail trade was more mixed. Private shops were to be encouraged and would even be permitted to expand into communal villages and liberated zones where they had been restricted previously. But district administrators and the local people would be given more power to monitor private shops. In Maputo, for example, each neighbourhood has a commission composed of members of the Dynamizing Group and the women's organization which has the right to inspect private shops. The wholesalers should tell the commission what goods have been given to the local merchant so that it can make sure that a few boxes don't fall off the back of the lorry on the way to the shop. Similarly, consumer goods factories, like the brewery, set up workers' committees to check distribution lists to make sure goods were not being diverted.

On the productive side, increased support for private businessmen was to be matched by tighter control. For example, the economic directives call for private farmers to be required to sell produce to the state in proportion to the support they receive. But with food shortages growing more serious during the 1983 drought, any food was an improvement, so that few restrictions were imposed on private farmers.

Indeed, the directives recognized that 'the objective possibilities for black marketeering come from the enormous imbalance between the money in people's pockets and the goods or other expenses that must be paid by the population.' Thus the key is increased production.

In many ways, Frelimo had gone full circle with the Fourth Congress. Small projects and local initiative had been promoted in the early years of independence, only to be overwhelmed by the big projects. Soap is a good example. In 1978 President Machel reported that 'the Central Committee has given prominence to the necessity of the Party and state to motivate . . . people's solutions such as local brickmaking, artisanal soap making, and using animal traction and bicycles.'

Two years later at a press conference, when asked about local soap making, Machel replied: 'We do not think of village soap production. We think of factories making Lux and Lifebuoy.' This was the line of the ten-year plan. But only three years later, the Fourth Congress called for a programme 'to install small industries producing cooking oil and soap at local level'. If the 1978 Central Committee orientation had been carried out, would there have been more soap in the shops at the time of the Fourth Congress?

Part IV
Socialization of the Countryside

12. Agriculture: The Base for Development

Agriculture Minister Joaquim de Carvalho was dismissed in August 1978 because he 'scorned the family sector, the principal source of agricultural production in our country', according to the President's office. He was also expelled from the Central Committee, which pointed to the 'need to reinforce the support for family agriculture which still occupies a predominant place in our economy'.

Five years, and three agriculture ministers later, the Central Committee looked back on its 1978 declaration and admitted that since then 'little had been done. In practice, almost no support was given to the family sector.' Indeed, 'the family sector was pushed to one side while state farms grew to excessive size', the Central Committee told the Fourth Party Congress. Shortly after, Carvalho returned to the Government as Foreign Trade Minister, perhaps an admission that it had been wrong to put the blame on one man.

The dispute is not about more or less socialism, but rather about which route to socialism. Agricultural policy is central and has been marked by continuing struggle, producing sharp shifts in balance between big state farms on one side and peasant cooperatives and family farms on the other:

*The Third Party Congress in February 1977 ruled that the state farm sector must be 'dominant and determinant' and that 'technical resources must be concentrated on state production units'. Co-ops were to be 'actively supported', but clearly ran a poor second. Family farming was ignored.

*Only 18 months later, the Central Committee dismissed Carvalho and stressed 'the great importance of family production'.

*The ten-year plan approved in 1981 saw family farming only as something to be eliminated by the end of the decade. Co-ops had an important social and political role but priority was to go to 'accelerated development of the state sector'.

*The Fourth Congress in 1983 again put the stress on the family sector.

The level of struggle between these lines was graphically shown in the Limpopo River valley in Gaza Province, where there is competition for the best river valley and irrigated land. Much of the land had been assigned to state farms under Serli, the State Secretariat for the Accelerated Development of the Limpopo and Incomati Regions. In 1982 in Chibuto district, the provincial government took 40,000 acres away from Serli (which had been unable to use it) and distributed it instead to peasant and private farmers. But at the same time, just 50 miles upstream, Serli was pushing peasants off their land to expand state farm tobacco production, while 25 miles downstream from Chibuto, peasants were resisting Serli efforts to push them off rich valley land to expand state banana production.

To understand this seemingly intractable contradiction, it is necessary to look at what Frelimo inherited from the Portuguese, and how it intends to transform that inheritance to socialist agriculture. It is also essential to remember that 85% of Mozambicans are rural, and that Frelimo has accepted that agriculture will remain the base of the economy for years to come. Thus agriculture, more than industry, is at the core of any transition to socialism.

Commercialized agriculture at the time of independence was divided roughly into thirds, as this table from Marc Wuyts of the Centre of African Studies (CEA) of Eduardo Mondlane University, shows:

| | Percentages of Marketed Output | | | |
	South	*Centre*	*North*	*Total*
Peasant	4	11	16	31
Plantation	1	33	1	35
Settler	14	14	6	34
Total	*19*	*58*	*23*	*100*

Plantations, largely in the centre of the country, grew tea, sugar, copra and sisal for export.

Settler farmers grew higher-value crops, particularly tobacco and food for the settlers in the cities: rice, meat, dairy products and vegetables. Some settler farmers had been in Mozambique for two generations. They tended to have farms in the higher, more temperate zones, which were also larger than average, although still small by Rhodesian settler standards. Most settler farmers, however, were Portuguese peasants with small family farms who arrived barefoot from Portugal, typically after 1950, for one of the government-sponsored *colonato* resettlement schemes. The largest colonato was of irrigated small holdings in the Limpopo valley. Generally the settlers depended on family labour with forced 'native' labour at peak seasons. The more recent settlers, especially on the colonatos, still thought of Portugal as home; and they simply went home at independence. Fearing retribution from the Blacks whom they had brutalized so recently, they fled in panic, usually destroying machinery and killing cattle before they left.

Peasants produced a third of marketed crops, including most of the cashew nuts and cotton, Mozambique's two main exports. They also sold food for plantation and city workers. As they largely fed themselves as well, peasants accounted for three-quarters of all agricultural production. Nevertheless, the vast majority of peasants follow the traditional bush-fallow system of agriculture: they farm a small area with only basic hand tools, using the land until it is tired, and then clear new land nearby.

The central feature of peasant life was the colonial state's tight control over, and super-exploitation of, labour. In central Mozambique, all men were forced to work half the year on plantations (which dominate the economy of that region). In the south all men worked in the mines, and, as the table shows, neither peasant nor plantation agriculture was very important. In half the country, peasants were also forced to grow cotton or rice. This was most common in the north, which explains why peasant agriculture predominated in that region.

The capitalist enterprises were dependent on cheap labour for their profitability, either working directly in mines or on plantations, or working on their own farms to produce cotton. Capital was equally dependent on a backward family agricultural sector to sustain the migrant and cash-cropping labour force, so that the enterprises did not have to pay any of the costs of reproduction of the workforce.

The policy of exploiting labour in this way meant that the Portuguese ensured that every family always had a farm for the worker to go back to, and that rich peasants never emerged to push poor peasants off the land and compete with settlers for labour. This has important implications, because it means that two factors which play major roles in socialist transformation elsewhere are not significant here: there are no landless labourers so there is no need for a traditional land reform, and there is no important group of rich peasants to try to block socialization. This is discussed further in Chapter 17. Clearly there is competition for good land, as in the Limpopo valley, and some peasants are richer than others. Nevertheless, in Mozambique these issues are much less important than elsewhere.

Thus the two essential tasks for a socialist transformation of Mozambican agriculture must be a fundamental shift in the relations between state and peasant, and a rapid modernization of peasant agriculture.

Independence, however, brought a host of special problems. The flight of the settlers cut the supply of food to the cities. Peasants, through wage labour and cash cropping, were deeply embedded in a cash economy entirely controlled by the settlers. Thus the flight of the Portuguese shopkeepers and traders also caused a collapse of the marketing network which provoked a crisis in the peasant sector as well. Furthermore, South Africa's sudden decision in 1976 to cut the number of Mozambican miners to only one-third caused major unemployment in the south, deepening the peasant crisis. Finally, many foreign owners steadily bled and abandoned their plantations, cutting exports. The peasant crisis and marketing collapse also meant less cotton and cashew nuts, and fewer marketed food crops.

So on top of the two essential tasks for socialist transformation, there are four urgent and interconnected crises: urban food, export crops, agricultural marketing and rural unemployment.

Frelimo faced what the CEA's Bridget O'Laughlin calls 'the classical task of a socialist revolution confronting the heritage of a capitalist economy: how to reorder class relations while maintaining a productive base. The task is particularly arduous in Mozambique . . . because of the pervasive involvement of the state in labour recruiting in the colonial period.' This means that 'the state cannot abandon its responsibility . . . for assuring labour supplies in major sectors of the economy.'

Agriculture must be the main source of capital accumulation for industrial development, and the bulk of Mozambicans will depend on agriculture for their livelihood for decades to come. Thus, according to Samora Machel, 'socialisation of the countryside is the backbone of our development and the decisive factor for the victory of socialism.' Socialization of the countryside has three components: state farms, cooperative farms and 'communal' villages.

State farms must lead the transformation of the country's backward agriculture: they must become the most productive and technologically advanced sector. There seems no other sensible way to run the abandoned large plantations. There are choices as to how to run abandoned smaller settler farms, but as state farms they can become models for development.

But state farms will employ fewer than 400,000 people by the end of the decade, leaving more than six million adults on their own land. Cooperativization is the only way to make rapid technical jumps in their productivity. Both state farms and co-ops are to be commercial farms, largely producing crops for sale. Although they should also produce some food for workers and members, it is assumed that all rural people will retain at least large gardens to produce much of their own food.

Most important is the political transformation that comes only through production: state farms can create a rural working class to lead the revolution, while co-ops should instil a spirit of cooperative work to improve people's own lives. Central to this economic and political transformation must be a social transformation which breaks the rural-urban divide and makes country life sufficiently attractive to stop migration to the cities. This is to be done through villagization. Mozambique is sparsely populated and most of the 10 million peasants still live on widely scattered family plots, both because traditional farming methods require large tracts of land, and because peasants fled further and further into the bush to escape forced labour and taxation. If they remain dispersed, there can be no cooperative farming. Only with villages nearby can state farms build up a permanent instead of a migrant workforce. Also, only in villages is it possible to make the necessary investments to raise the peasants' living standard – a school, health post, shop and water supply – and to organize social and cultural activities. Villagization is hardly a new idea. Tanzania has implemented it, and the colonial authorities moved peasants into fortified villages and along 'cotton roads' where they could better control them. But Frelimo's 'communal villages' also have a central political point: only in a village can country people organize politically and create viable democratic institutions.

Within this generally agreed programme of socialization of the countryside, it has proved impossible to strike a balance in the allocation of resources. This has been the focus of struggle within the Ministry of Agriculture and within the Frelimo Party itself. In the rest of this chapter, I will look at the state/co-op/family farm imbroglio. In the following chapter I will look at communal villages, which ought to be an integral part of rural development, but have so far been treated separately.

It is essential to remember the total inexperience of everyone trying to carry out socialization of the countryside. There was a general commitment to change, but only the vaguest notions of how it was to come about. Even the high-level policy makers were feeling their way.

At lower levels the differences with neighbouring countries came into play starkly. Before independence, most black Mozambicans had been barred from running businesses of their own and from organizing co-operatives; indeed from gaining experience of organizing anything at all. The guerrillas had gained some organizing experience in the liberation war, but it was often not applicable, and there were not enough experienced cadres to work everywhere in the country. The appalling illiteracy rate meant that many villages had no one at all who could write or keep any kind of records of a co-op.

The peasants who formed themselves into cooperatives, the new district administrators, and the new state farm managers simply had no idea what to do. Productivity gains from co-ops and state farms come largely through improved work organization and improved technology, but few of those involved had enough experience with either to provide useful guidance. Similar problems plagued those who tried to re-establish the commercial networks.

Typical is the tale of the cotton agents, told by the CEA after a study in Lugela district in Zambézia. During colonial times the Government used *capatazes* (black overseers) to administer the system of forced cotton growing and to ensure that people worked the requisite time on their cotton plots. They were kept on after independence to distribute cotton-seed and encourage cotton cultivation. But they had little technical knowledge, and many did not know what they were supposed to do now that they could no longer beat the people.

State Farms: The Quickest Way?

'We must dedicate special attention to supplying the urban centres,' the Third Party Congress said in 1977. And it claimed that 'State-owned enterprises are the quickest way of responding to the country's food needs because of the size of the areas they cover, their rational organization of human and material resources, and the immediate availability of machinery.'

It was more a hope than a reality, because the first state farm crops were only harvested later that year. The new state farms had been formed the year before by grouping together the most accessible of the abandoned settler farms; isolated and less accessible ones were left for co-ops. Machinery, as the Congress noted, is essential for higher production. Unfortunately, it was not immediately available, so in the four years after the Congress, Mozambique imported £50 million in agricultural machinery, including 3,000 tractors and 300 combine harvesters. During the last decade of the colonial period, 700 tractors a year were imported. So the new large importation only served to replace those wearing out naturally and those destroyed or driven over the border by fleeing settlers. But as part of a quest for modernization, the new tractors tended to be larger and more powerful than the ones they replaced. And the combine harvesters were new; the colonists had depended on semi-forced seasonal labour for their harvests.

The state sector expanded rapidly with new projects and extensions of existing farms, and as abandoned plantations fell under state control. In combination with a decline in peasant production due to the continued marketing crisis, the state came to dominate production of marketed crops. This table gives a rough comparison between 1970 and 1980 of percentages of marketed production:

| | 1970 | | 1980 | | |
	Private	Peasant	State	Private	Peasant
Total	69	31	52	10	38
Cotton	35	65	45	10	45
Sugar	100	—	85	15	—
Cashew	10	90	—	—	100
Tea	100	—	90	10	—
Sisal	100	—	30	70	—
Copra	80	20	20	40	40
Rice	60	40	80	—	20
Tobacco	80	20	55	40	5

By 1981 state farms covered 350,000 acres and the National Planning Commission was pushing hard for further rapid expansion. The ten-year plan approved in that year called for 2.5 million acres of new state farms to be developed by 1990 at a cost of £2,000 million.

Just two years later, the Fourth Congress called a temporary halt; the period up to 1985 was to be one of consolidation and reorganization. Frelimo admitted that Mozambique had neither the managerial nor technical expertise to run giant state farms.

It was hardly surprising and should have been obvious from the beginning, considering the colonial policy of not training black Mozambicans and not allowing them to run businesses. Furthermore, settler farms had usually been quite basic. It was the white farmer himself who did the ploughing and maintained the tractor, usually without any kind of proper workshop. Big state farms have large amounts of sophisticated machinery requiring specialist workshops and mechanical training. Furthermore, running modern farms requires a higher degree of organization than that possessed by the settlers when they had run those farms; ploughing, planting, spraying and weeding must be done at exactly the right time, which means that machinery, inputs and staff must all be available on schedule.

Speaking at the Fourth Congress, Marcelino dos Santos stressed that 'our tractor driver must understand the machine and keep it operating. The problem does not lie in introducing new and more advanced technologies into our cultural realities. It is how to introduce them in a way that they can be taken up, understood, and used effectively. Where we neglected this consideration is where we find the machine stopped, the lorry seized up, and the tractor misused.' Earlier that year, Agriculture Minister Sergio Vieira remarked on the 'gigantism' of state farms which simply 'multiplied the inefficiency and disorder of their administration'.

But what dos Santos and Vieira ruefully admitted in 1983 had been manifestly clear for several years. In 1981, the same year that the ten-year plan was finalized, the Ministry of Agriculture admitted that not one state farm was profitable. Arnaldo Ribeiro, director of the Agricultural Direction Unit, told a technical meeting in January 1981 that 'we have not sufficiently dominated the technologies we use.' Equipment imported just a year or two before was already out of action because of accidents caused by drunken driving, failure to clean machinery and store it properly at the end of the season, and ignoring the most elementary maintenance procedures like checking the oil and water. Later that year Ribeiro commented that, although state farms had greatly expanded and now had huge fields of grain and many more tractors and combine harvesters, 'this growth has not been accompanied by the creation of an infrastructure to maintain and repair this equipment.'

Furthermore, the Ministry had done its sums and found that with its high degree of mechanization, it needed very high productivity to make a profit. For example, Ribeiro said that to break even, state farms need to produce two tons of maize per acre. This is less than is produced in neighbouring Zimbabwe or on modern European farms, where yields go up to 3.5 tons, but in 1981 Mozambican state farms were producing only a half-ton per acre.

It was clear then that the state farms were not to be the quick way to solve the country's food needs, nor were they proving to be a way to accumulate capital. More than four-fifths of state farm costs are in foreign exchange, for machinery, fuel, fertilizer and pesticides. This means that when state farms lose money, it would actually be cheaper to import the grain than produce it (see Appendix 1 for more details).

The biggest and least efficient state farm is Cail, the Limpopo Agro-Industrial Complex, which is part of the equally disastrous Serli. By 1983 Cail had run up debts to the Bank of Mozambique of more than £10 million, not including costs of machinery, which Cail used with spectacular inefficiency; expensive combine harvesters collected only 500 tons of rice during their lifetime, compared to ten times that amount in Europe. This is both because they last such a short time and because they are used on fewer acres each season.

Mozambicans will inevitably take time to learn to use new machinery and new techniques, and this hard currency subsidy to state farm grain is really the price of that education. Back in 1978, the head of Cail, Jorge Tembe, told me that 'such problems are natural when you are growing – a child falls down, and then gets up.' Mozambique's state farms are now seven years old, and still falling down.

One reason is that state farm managers have not turned to the one group that could best help them walk: the workers. However untrained they are, many state farm labourers have worked on those farms for decades. They knew, for example, that they were being asked to plant potatoes in land where they would not grow. They knew where to find returned miners with mechanical skills who could have helped maintain the tractors.

But they were never asked. Workers were supposd to be drawn into planning and management through production councils, but they rarely were. Instead they were told forcefully to 'carry out the plan', so they planted the potatoes and let unskilled mechanics botch the job. State farms are largely run in the same way as their capitalist predecessors; the only difference is that the new managers have less experience and expertise than the colonial ones. Thus the state farms have manifestly failed to change the relationship between state and peasant and build a rural working class, which was one of the central justifications of state farms.

After the Fourth Congress, Serli was abolished. Its big state farms, including Cail, were broken into smaller units, and much of the under-used land was given to peasants and larger private farmers. Tembe was finally transferred. A new Agriculture Minister, João Ferreira, was appointed, and in a visit to the Limpopo region lasting several days he gave the workers more opportunity to use their initiative to solve problems.

But it is clear that Frelimo does not expect much improvement. The Fourth Congress set a state farm maize productivity target for 1985 of only 1 ton per acre, half that needed for profitability, which implies subsidies for years to come.

Co-ops to 'Liberate Creative Initiative'

In the liberated zones, peasants formed collective plots to grow food for the guerrillas. At independence, Frelimo urged peasants throughout the country to set up similar collective plots as a basis for future cooperatives and thousands were formed for the 1975–76 season. Similarly, many abandoned settler farms were spontaneously taken over as co-ops. Peasants were anxious to try new and better ways.

Yet the cooperative movement never took off. Interest in the collective plots flagged and they were largely abandoned. There were 180 co-ops in 1977, but this only grew to 375 in 1981; co-op membership was 25,000 in 1977 and 37,000 in 1981. The land they cultivated never exceeded 30,000 acres and actually began to fall in 1982. Production fell by half from 1979 to 1981.

Analysing the problem in 1981, the Frelimo Political Economy Department noted that 'peasants work their family farm for personal interest, out of necessity to feed and clothe themselves and their family. They work with enthusiasm on the family farm whether they are the most reactionary peasant or a Party member.' By contrast, 'Cooperative members today do not work on the cooperative with the same interest that they dig their family plot.' Too often they look on work on the cooperative farm as a civic duty like participation in work parties to clean the village or open a new road.

The problem is that in the vast majority of cooperatives, members earn less per hour of work than they would from cash crops on their family farm. As the Party report commented, 'The most effective motivation will be higher profits from the cooperative than the family farm.'

The first national cooperatives seminar, in October 1976, set out the general policy. Co-ops will 'produce more and better with the same effort' because they will 'liberate the creative initiative of their members'. Nevertheless, State support in providing infrastructure, inputs, and training was seen as 'fundamental'.

The seminar also argued that co-ops must depend primarily on the efforts of their members. Machinery should be used only as a complement to human labour, not as a substitute, and should be employed only when the best use is already being made of manual labour. Further, animal traction should be used before machinery is introduced.

The collapse of the co-op movement was largely because of the difficulties involved in carrying out this sensible policy and maintaining some sort of balance. In practice, it is much harder to run a co-op than a family farm. Work must be organized, records kept, decisions made about what crops to grow and whether to hire a tractor. Yet hardly anyone knew what a co-op was or how to establish one. In most zones the peasants had been barred by the colonial authorities from forming or running any kind of organization, so they had little idea what to do. The new administrators were at least literate, but they also had no experience with co-ops.

Three trends emerged. In one, the slogan 'depend on our own efforts' was used, implying that no state support was needed and that peasants would miraculously increase production simply by working together. Or sometimes peasants were showered with assistance far beyond their ability to assimilate it. Third, and most often, peasants were encouraged to join co-ops with the promise of a tractor and other help which was not available and never arrived.

The problems are really complex. Often it is possible to make a jump in production simply through common effort, for example by building a small dam and growing irrigated vegetables. But even that requires initial help from an agricultural extension worker. Improved seeds, fertilizer and new crops are often cited as ways co-ops can increase productivity, but they too require outside inputs. Ploughing is usually the most labour-intensive part of the farming cycle, and thus the question of tractors is dominant. Most co-ops were based on abandoned settler farms, which had usually been tractor ploughed, and it was silly ever to expect co-ops to dig that land by hand. Indeed, the colonial state, through the cereals and cotton institutes, provided a great deal of help to small farmers, and it was hardly realistic to believe that the new co-ops could run with less assistance.

Much depended on district administrators and provincial agriculture departments. In the early days, inexperienced administrators took widely varying approaches to co-ops. In Zambézia Province one co-op had its tractor taken away and given to a state farm. In neighbouring Nampula Province, co-ops were sold tractors at bargain prices. Inevitably, too, the results of cooperatives varied widely. Samora Machel Communal Village in Nampula made national newspaper headlines in 1977 with its cotton profit of £15,000, while others nearby could not even pay the cost of their inputs and ran into debt.

Faced with growing pressure on all sides (not just from co-ops) and their own limitations of time and experience, district and provincial administrators usually tried to find easier short-term solutions. In particular, rather than starting the long process of training illiterate co-op members, they took authority over the co-ops themselves. By 1977 the Ministry of Agriculture was talking of the need for provincial departments of agriculture to take control of the co-ops, making plans which were only later to be approved by the members. This only compounded the problem, because the plans were unrealistic and responded more to pressures from above to set high targets than to the reality on the ground. Sometimes the tractors would come and plough and plant more land than the co-op had members to weed and harvest. More often the plan included tractors or seeds which never arrived or came much too late, or crops that members did not want to grow.

Officials would make fleeting visits to the co-ops, complain that the peasants were lazy and just sitting around waiting for the tractors, and then rush off.

The 1976 co-op seminar said that it was essential that a special agency be established to support co-ops. One was set up but it was never more than a shell with a handful of people. In any case, the growing bias towards state farms led to a compromise policy that state farms must support the cooperatives in their area. Since state farm managers could not operate their own farms and meet their inflated targets, they never had any resources to spare for the co-ops. In 1982 the Council of Ministers ruefully admitted that Mozambique did not yet understand how to put into practice the policy of links between state and cooperative sectors. 'We have maintained the erroneous view that cooperatives will develop by themselves.'

The ten-year plan called for co-ops to receive only 25% of agricultural investment, and the state farms the other 75%. (With this much smaller investment, by the end of the decade the co-ops were expected to farm seven times as much land and produce twice the value of crops as the state sector – a remarkable admission that even the planners expected co-ops to make much better use of their investment.) But from 1977 to 1981, only 2% of agricultural investments were in co-ops.

Even in areas where little investment was required, there was little progress. From the first co-ops seminar through to the Fourth Congress, public figures and the press kept asking why nothing was being done to encourage animal traction, to sort out bank credit for co-ops, and to adjust price structures to give special benefits to co-ops.

Looking at the crumbled cooperative programme in 1982, the Ministry of Agriculture concluded that the problems were not simply incompetence and inexperience, but that there was an element of sabotage involved: 'The cooperative process encountered its first obstacle in the class position of state officials, which manifested itself in the form of subtle opposition to cooperativization, and through paternalism.' Analysing that report, the Council of Ministers went further and said that 'these elements' block and delay the distribution of necessary inputs to the co-ops 'with the intention of undermining the cooperative process'.

Lack of state support for co-ops was one of the issues raised by peasants during the preparations for the Fourth Congress. The Economic and Social Directives of the Congress stress the need for the state to 'ensure the necessary agro-technical support' to existing co-ops. 'In this way we can guarantee an increase in the cooperative members' returns so that they see from results the real advantages of cooperation and become a model and an example for other peasants.'

Yet there remains an overriding paternalism towards co-ops that could torpedo the planned assistance. At the Fourth Congress, the president of the Mozambican Heroes' Co-op was a delegate and speaker. Raimundo Valõi was already a member of the Central Committee and his is a model cooperative, proudly shown off to journalists and other visitors. He was clearly well versed in the issues and stressed basic problems. Only one of the seven pumps worked because there were no spare parts available. They had only one truck; the acquisition of a pickup truck would help with marketing. When he finished, Samora Machel responded with a bravura performance. He made the Minister of Public Works stand up, and ordered him to give the cooperative roofing sheets to build houses. He made the head of Serli stand up and ordered him to electrify the co-op immediately. He said Valõi was wrong to ask simply for a pickup truck: he should have a lorry. It was, however, exactly the wrong answer. The point Valõi was making, and which was being made throughout the Congress, was that co-ops needed just a little more state help, with pump spares and the like; then they could depend on their own efforts. By showering Valõi with assistance, the President was not only playing the benevolent father, he was also wreaking havoc with any kind of planning and any attempt to distribute resources rationally.

If cooperatives policy seems confusing to the reader, it seems a lot worse to the peasants trying to form co-ops. To show the contrasting impact of these problems, it is worth looking at three co-ops.

Necheche and Napala are two communal villages just a few miles apart in Nampula Province, and they provide a striking contrast between unsuccessful and successful cooperatives. I visited both in November 1982. Necheche had been a model village and received considerable government help. Work brigades from the city were mobilized to help build the village and to help with the weeding and cotton harvest on the co-op. The district provides the tractor and a lorry. At first the co-op was highly successful. After the 1979–80 season it made a profit of £6,000. The 88 members went on a binge, giving parties and running up £1,500 in unpaid bills at the consumer co-op (which was run by the co-op farm). The next year, membership tripled but only the same amount of land was farmed and overall profits fell to £1,000, so each member collected less money. For 1981–82, the tractor ploughed more land, but by now the co-op was supposedly well established so no work brigades came from the city to help. The cooperative members could not get it together to weed the cotton, so production was very low. But then they failed to harvest even that. By contrast, cotton production on the family farms had been good. Co-op officials told me that they had lost money, but had no idea how much, or how to deal with the loss. They had no records. When I visited, the fields had been tractor ploughed for the coming season, but the remaining co-op members had decided they would not plant cotton – only maize, sorghum and beans. With me was a shocked worker from the provincial communal villages commission, who told me – and them – that the tractor had been provided only because the co-op had committed itself in the national plan to grow 250 acres of cotton. In any case, grain was not profitable enough to pay for the tractor. Nor was it clear how good the crop would be – the rains had already begun when I visited, but planting had not yet started. Last year the co-op maize had failed because it was planted too late; members apparently waited until after they had planted their family plots. The village, too, was a shambles. Buildings were falling down as the villagers waited for brigades to come back and repair them; the schoolteacher had moved his classes to a neighbouring town because the villagers failed to repair his collapsing school. The health worker, too, had left. I met with village officials in the crumbling meeting hall, and asked if residents were moving out of the village. There was embarrassed shuffling and a few officials mumbled, 'No.' Then the secretary of the women's organization, Rosa Natala, spoke up: 'Many people are leaving; 17 families so far this year.'

In Napala 54 new families had moved into the village that year. The main street was clean and the houses in good repair; the villagers were building a new school. Napala had never been a model village; it was far off any good road and largely 'depending on its own efforts'. Co-op officials had a school notebook with neat records showing how many days each member had worked (profits are distributed on this basis) and what the expenses and profits were. The co-op had started with 150 members on an abandoned settler farm, and also made £6,000 in its first season (1976–77), which it used to buy a tractor and set up a consumer co-op. Membership rose steadily to 200 for the 1979–80 season. But the area declined, and as happened in many co-ops the days worked also increased. In part this was because people seem to work less hard on the co-op than on their own farms, and in part because members attend more regularly in seasons when they have more free time. Unfortunately they have more free time when there is less work to do on the family farm and also less work on the co-op; the co-op was too inexperienced to control this, so they credited members with a day's work just for showing up. As a result the overall profit was only £3,000 for more total days worked, and so people earned much less. In 1980, the tractor broke down, and the co-op faced a crisis. Yet the members seemed committed to the idea of co-operative farming, and for the following two years continued to grow cotton and maize entirely by hand. Membership only fell to 135. When I arrived, the tractor had finally returned from the workshop, and the co-op members were hoping for a better year. Because Napala had not been drowned in help, it had been able to build a more solid base. Yet it was clear that a minimum of state help was needed. Why did it take two years to get the tractor fixed, for example? Most serious, when I was there the rains had already started, yet the Government had still not collected the co-op's cotton which was stored outside and under the eaves of the consumer co-op building. Will Napala not be paid for that cotton, and will that be the final blow?

One of the most successful cooperatives is Chinhamancungo in Manica Province, near the border with Zimbabwe. Based on an abandoned settler farm, it has many natural advantages: rich land, a 75-acre orchard, a dam and a main tarred road alongside. It started in 1975 with no equipment; members were better-off peasants who used their own oxen and ploughs on the co-op. It faced many problems and the number of members dwindled from 168 to 58 by 1978. After that, life on the co-op picked up. Vegetables sold at the roadside provided a regular income and the co-op acquired a tractor.

The members have shown considerable imagination. For example, to reduce wear and tear on the tractor, it is used only for heavy work, particularly ploughing, while oxen are used for lighter tasks. A large part of the production is not sold, but is distributed directly to members. Recently they built a canteen and each person receives a hot lunch after working on the co-op for the morning. The co-op grows wheat and has its own bakery, with bread distributed only to members. Thus, although the cash income from the co-op (about 1,000 MT per month) is only half what members would earn in wage labour, the overall benefits make life very good for them. With increasing success, many of those who dropped out wanted to rejoin, but the remaining co-op members said no. The co-op president, Zeca Lampião, was elected to the Central Committee at the Fourth Congress. He told the Congress: 'We are building socialism because what we produce is not for someone else – for António or for João – but for ourselves.'

Three factors have clearly made this co-op work: natural advantages, imagination and hard work, and a good relationship with the state. The co-op had state support for a tractor and spares, and to maintain a pump. The co-op received permission from the province to keep the wheat they grow to make bread (often co-ops are required to sell wheat to the state). And they had the sense to stand up to the state; the 1980–81 plan sent by the Ministry of Agriculture required them to grow soya beans, but they grew other beans instead. 'We don't eat soya,' noted Lampião.

These examples show the need for a slow and steady build-up by the co-ops. A dispute which has bubbled on since independence is how rapidly cooperativization can take place, and if there is a need for some kind of pre-cooperatives.

In the liberated areas, peasants were organized in a variety of ways, including collective plots to feed the guerrillas, mutual aid societies, and simply by grouping plots together to be more easily protected by the guerrillas.

At the first national cooperatives meeting in Quelimane in October 1976, representatives from East Germany and Bulgaria stressed that their experience was that cooperativization must be gradual. Both countries started with associations of peasants for mutual assistance and to obtain credit, and it took 20 years to cooperativize fully. Germany even had three levels of co-ops; in the lowest, peasants kept their own land and only ploughed their fields jointly; the next level involved shared machinery, and only the most advanced included common land.

In his closing speech to the conference, the Minister of Agriculture said he accepted the point of the foreign visitors that cooperativization 'is a prolonged struggle'. Then in June 1978 he suggested 'the progressive substitution of dispersed, disorganized family farms with farms in blocks that will make possible increased productivity. This will permit the introduction of elementary technologies that require little capital but increase the productivity of human labour.' This was adopted as Ministry of Agriculture policy for the new communal villages.

João Ferreira, then provincial agriculture director in Cabo Delgado (and in 1983 named the fourth Agriculture Minister), began such an experiment with sets of 20 families grouping their farms together into blocks. The families themselves stressed that they could not simply abandon their old farms, so it was agreed that they would open up 2.5 acres a year within the blocks, until they were cultivating completely in blocks after four years. Ferreira stressed that it was not simply farming side by side in the old way. Instead, the peasants would learn better techniques together and would share new equipment. In this way 'we arrive at cooperativization gradually', he said.

Then Carvalho was sacked as Agriculture Minister. In February 1979 the Cabo Delgado provincial government slammed the idea of blocks as 'reactionary' and based on the false premise that 'African peasants are individualistic by nature and thus are not ready to begin a socialist transformation of the countryside.' Indeed, the provincial government declared that peasants had already shown 'massive support for immediate cooperativization'. At the time, there were only 19 co-ops in the entire province, one of the lowest rates in the country; by 1982 the number had risen only to 21. Nationally, cooperative participation also remained minimal.

Carvalho's replacement as Agriculture Minister, Mario Machungo, was in turn replaced by Sergio Vieira. His first report on socialization of the countryside, in April 1982, recognized 'that gradual cooperativization is indispensable'. In particular, Vieira proposed the formation of peasant associations for the sale of produce and purchase of inputs, which would permit them to learn improved methods of production and 'initiate them into collective habits'. The Central Committee report to the Fourth Congress confirmed this policy, and the formation of peasant associations began. There were also renewed experiments with block farming.

Family Farming Remains the Base

Family farmers produce three-quarters of all crops in Mozambique. Although they consume most of it themselves, they still grow one-third of marketed crops, including all of the cashew nuts, traditionally Mozambique's largest export, and half the cotton, another key export. Yet family farming collapsed into crisis because of a total lack of government support.

Mozambican peasants are not 'subsistence farmers' in the sense of being able to survive entirely on their own. They depend on selling surplus to buy the means of production and essential consumer goods they do not produce themselves. Thus they were badly hit by the collapse of the marketing system at independence. With its lack of marketing experience, it was not surprising that Frelimo had difficulty rebuilding the commercial network, or that the state-run People's Shops were such a disaster. But the overriding problem was the complete failure to appreciate the importance of marketing to family farmers.

It was not as if people did not notice. The same Central Committee session in 1978 that expelled Joaquim de Carvalho stressed the importance of 'stimulating individual production while collective patterns are being organized'. A year later Samora Machel noted that, 'Stimulating the family farmer requires a commercial network to supply the farmer and his family with indispensable articles and to acquire his surplus production.'

But there was strong opposition to this by those who argued that it was necessary to squeeze the peasants in order to extract from them as much surplus as possible to fund the big industrial and agricultural projects that were to be the basis of development. Marcelo de Andrade, national director of planning, stressed that, 'The 1980s are not a decade of consumption, but of sacrifice.'

There was also a problem of supplying the wrong goods. In 1983 Frelimo's Political Economy Secretary Marcelino dos Santos admitted to the Fourth Congress: 'We are not bothering about manufacturing the hoe because we are awaiting the arrival of the tractor we must import. We are distributing tinned beans, that cost foreign exchange, in a communal village that produces beans and from which no one has bothered to collect surplus production. We overload the peasant with items he does not use, but do not provide him with a lamp, cloth, a file, or a hammer. None the less, we expect him to exchange his production for goods he does not need.'

Most peasants use only the most basic hand tools: hoe, machete and axe. In colonial times Mozambique produced about 700,000 hoes a year and imported others. After independence production fell to less than half and imports were stopped. Hoes only last about five years, so the impact was soon felt. In July 1977 Agriculture Minister Carvalho visited Nampula Province and *Tempo* reported that he was told in one village: 'We would like to produce more, but for this we need the hoes, machetes, knives, and axes that we cannot get.' It was more a lack of interest than lack of money; the Scandinavian countries had just provided money for 300,000 hand tools, but it was only spent much later – on other things.

Frelimo had encouraged private shopkeepers to return to rural areas, and many did. Furthermore, the state established marketing brigades to go to more remote rural areas to buy peasant and co-op surplus. So by 1981 the state had set up a reasonable rural commercialization system. But it gave the shopkeepers and brigades little to sell to the peasants in exchange. Zambézia is Mozambique's richest agricultural province. Yet when I visited it in 1982, the shops were empty except for salt, tea, curry powder, a few men's clothes and the ubiquitous tinned beans. It had been three years since anyone had seen bicycle parts.

Goods to rural areas simply came at the bottom of the list. Imports were cut repeatedly, yet local production could not meet demand. And there was always the bias towards the urban areas. When I visited Mocuba district in Zambézia, each person was able to buy less than one-twentieth of the soap and sugar guaranteed to each Maputo resident. *Capulanas*, the brightly coloured cloths used by women for everything from skirts to baby slings, were a particular focus of discontent: each woman must have at least two a year, but in Mocuba that year there was only one capulana for every three women.

Despite all the statements about the need to provide consumer goods for the peasants, the total supply of goods fell by a quarter from 1980 to 1982, largely due to a drop in textile imports. Imports of machinery and capital goods for the big projects were always a higher priority than consumer goods. By some estimates, peasants in 1982 were being expected to sell twice as much in crops as they could buy with the money they received. Peasants already had huge amounts of money in their hands from previous seasons and nothing to spend it on. Indeed, in many rural areas there was an effective barter system operating; peasants brought goods to market and sold them only if there was something else to buy. This was acknowledged, and encouraged, by a ruling in 1982 that consumer goods should be sold only to peasants who brought crops to sell. It recognized the reality that peasants could buy the available goods several times over, but it was in direct violation of the private commerce law passed only three years before which prohibited links between sales and purchases. The following year the Central Committee admitted that there was a need 'to re-establish the market economy'.

Inevitably, production of peasant surplus fell dramatically. Cashew-nut sales dropped to half the colonial peak, as peasants ate the nuts themselves and abandoned the trees more distant from their homes. The Ministry of Agriculture admitted that in Cabo Delgado less cashew was being sold in 1982 than was exported from the liberated zones there during the war! Cotton production fell, too. But most important was the drop in the sale of food crops. Plantations traditionally bought maize, cassava, beans and other crops from peasants to feed their workers, and food for workers in the cities came from peasants as well. Plantations, in turn, had even more trouble keeping workers who were unable to buy food with their wages.

The inevitable effect of too much money chasing too few goods was a vastly expanded black market. My visit to Zambézia in 1982 and reports from other provinces suggested that at least half of the peasant-marketed surplus was being sold through the black market. Not only does the state not control commerce, but it only knows about half of it. (And thus agricultural statistics, like those I reproduce at the end of this book, must be treated as highly suspect.)

In Zambézia the black market was, ironically, run largely by the state itself, as the army, schools, and the sugar, tea, and cotton plantations went to villages and paid double the official price to buy maize, beans and cassava. Such trading was explicitly banned, but continued anyway; plantations had to feed their workers and the official state wholesaler, Agricom, could not buy enough at the official price.

A second aspect of the black market also flourished, as private traders came from the cities bringing dried fish (an important part of the diet in many parts of the country which is ignored by the state trading system) and illegally obtained soap, sugar and batteries. Private traders made massive profits out of the black market and established an entirely parallel supply system for the cities.

Two essential lessons come out of this: first, how important the family sector continues to be; and second, how intimately connected that sector is to the market, and how sensitive it is to market forces. Peasants clearly do respond to the stimuli of higher prices and consumer goods, whether they are provided legally or not. In my view, the overriding issue is consumer goods, and I am convinced that peasants would produce significantly more in exchange for more consumer goods, even if the prices of those goods were increased substantially – so long as they were the items which peasants really wanted, such as capulanas and bicycle parts.

On the other hand, peasants do sell for money, even without goods to buy, if the price is right. Thus the plantations can buy maize without trading consumer goods by paying double the price. In areas around Mocuba, a growing industrial town in Zambézia, there was a crackdown on cassava prices which was successful in that peasants were no longer able to get high prices for their crop. They responded by leaving the cassava in the ground, and there was hunger in Mocuba. Finally, peasants do switch to more profitable crops. There has been a general switch from cotton to sunflower and, where the black-market price is good, from maize to cassava; both require less work to earn the same profit, and their peak work demands are different from those of subsistence food crops, which allows a more balanced workload.

Despite the lip-service paid to the family sector since independence, it was 1982 before Frelimo really began to appreciate the significance of the peasant crisis, by which time it had become so deep as to require measures that may be beyond Frelimo's economic or political means.

Action was then taken. In Gaza, there was a major land redistribution, with 40,000 acres of unused land being redistributed to individual farmers. Literally millions of hand tools were imported in 1983. The Fourth Congress talked repeatedly about the family sector. The importance of marketing, both in actually collecting produce and in providing consumer goods, was recognized both with respect to family farms and to co-ops as well; there is no point in working on a co-op if no one comes to buy what you grow, and if they do, there is still nothing to buy with the profits.

In 1982 both producer and consumer prices of maize, cassava and some other products were raised by 50% – a useful shift in the city-country balance. A joint meeting of the Agriculture and Internal Commerce Ministries in March 1983 noted that state marketing bodies tended to buy only those products included in the official state plan and to sell only consumer goods that come from big factories or abroad. Dried fish, fruit, coconuts, sweet potatoes, bricks, furniture and pottery are all in demand in areas where they are not produced, and can be exchanged for the products like maize that are in the official state plan. The Fourth Congress also stressed the importance of local small industry, to make oil, soap, building materials and so on.

Nevertheless, Frelimo does not seem to have very high hopes for family farms. The Congress called for an increase in purchases from the family sector of 40–45% by 1985, compared to 1982. This amount is less than is already being sold by peasants on the black market and thus represents no real increase in production. Furthermore, the stock of consumer goods is to be increased only by 20–23% in that period. Priority for the extra goods is to go to workers, which suggests there will not be a large enough increase in consumer goods in the countryside to meet even the small expected increase in peasant sales.

The 1983 state plan called for the 'goods supplied to the family sector to be, at the minimum, equal to the value of the produce sold'. But that is a faint hope, as the same plan promised little increase in consumer goods. In a few areas, there were to be significant increases: bicycle production was to be five times that of 1981, £3 million is to be spent on importing haberdashery for the countryside, and more sugar will be kept inside the country instead of being exported. Capulana production is to double, but still only to just over one capulana per woman. Planned production of oil, soap, cigarettes and matches for 1983 was close to 1981 levels, and below colonial production levels, when the population was one-third smaller.

Indeed, Frelimo seems to be placing its highest hopes on the one sector that has nothing to do with socialization of the countryside: the private sector. It is never exactly clear what constitutes a 'private' farmer, but the term seems to mean those Portuguese who stayed on and those Mozambicans who have their own capital to invest in farming, such as returned miners, shopkeepers and professionals like nurses. It seems specifically to exclude peasants who earn their livelihood entirely from their own farms, and thus contrasts sharply with agricultural support schemes which try to identify 'progressive peasant farmers' – schemes like those run by the cereals and cotton institutes shortly before independence, and those supported by aid agencies in many countries.

Private farmers have received increasing support with credit, inputs, and the opportunity to buy and hire tractors. Sometimes this support filled a real gap, and allowed Portuguese farmers who stayed an opportunity to return to pre-independence levels of production. In other cases, private farmers were allowed to take over abandoned farms, particularly in the green zones around the cities, which had never been used for co-ops or state farms.

Forgotten Linkages

The continued massive deficits of state farms, the stagnation of co-operativization, and the collapse of the family sector combine to spell a crisis in agriculture that has not been affected by repeated changes of Minister.

War and weather have made matters worse. On the other hand, the spread of the MNR was made easier by peasants disaffected by Frelimo's agricultural policy. And as this part of Africa has highly variable weather, a country as large as Mozambique must expect, and plan for, an agricultural disaster somewhere every season.

One could also argue, as does Michael Ellman of Amsterdam University, that big socialist farms do not work because 'agriculture is fundamentally different from industry'. There are fewer economies of scale because large farms simply require too much management. Even in the advanced capitalist countries of America and Western Europe smaller farms are proportionately more important than smaller industrial units, and large capitalist farms depend to a great extent for their profitability on low paid and migrant farm workers, which should be unacceptable in a socialist country. It is hard to know if this is applicable to Mozambique, but Mozambique does fit Ellman's comment that, 'Each new state socialist country has been surprised to discover that large-scale socialist agriculture suffers from serious problems.'

External factors may have made Mozambique's agricultural crisis worse, but they did not cause it. The cause seems to lie in a fundamental misunderstanding of three related issues: first, the intimate linkages between the various sectors and the extent to which rural people have one foot firmly planted in the cash economy; second, the need to take account of labour supply and demand; and third, the time required for a radical transformation of agriculture.

There are extensive links between state, co-op and family agriculture. Everyone in rural areas has a family plot, even full-time salaried farm workers. The daily agricultural wage of 62.50 MT per day is not enough to support a family, and thus food from the family plot is necessary. Nor is this unreasonable. It is impractical in Mozambique today to expect one adult to support a family; everyone must produce (although one might question the tradition that it is the man who has the paid job and the woman who works on the family plot). Similarly, it is sales of peasant surplus that feed workers on the plantations and state farms.

The land surplus ensures that people usually have the option of farming their own land, and thus can choose how to divide their time between state farm, co-op and family plot. On cash income alone, state farms are best at 62.50 MT per day. Well organized co-ops, which have some use of a tractor, can generate profits of up to 40 MT per worker for a shorter day. Family hoe farming is likely to earn only 25 MT per day from cash crops. But if there is nothing to buy with the money, time is more productively spent growing food on the family farm, or on a co-op like Chinhamancungo which provides non-cash benefits.

Peasants also choose according to how hard they have to work, not surprisingly considering that a major form of colonial exploitation involved intensification of labour. A 'workday' is often defined as a set of tasks, such as weeding a certain number of rows or transplanting a given number of seedlings. Often state farms set fewer tasks in a 'workday' than their colonial predecessors, and co-ops usually set even less. People often prefer less money for less work. One co-op head said simply that he preferred the co-op because working on the neighbouring state farm 'is like forced labour'.

Also important is competition for labour at peak seasons. Most peasant crops have three labour peaks: preparing the land before the rains, weeding during the rains, and the harvest. Maize, peanuts, rice, some beans and cotton all have the same schedule. (Sunflower, cashew nuts, sweet potatoes and cassava have significantly different labour peaks, and can be used to ensure a more balanced demand for labour throughout the year.) Peasants find it more profitable to harvest their own cotton and rice, so it is not surprising that state farms have trouble getting labour now that the state can no longer force peasants to work on plantations. The peak labour demand on the Zambézia tea estates also conflicts with the peak weeding time on nearby peasant farms, causing competition for labour.

This competition for labour is not new, and the most important function of the colonial state was to resolve that conflict in favour of the capitalist enterprises by organizing forced labour and forced cropping. Indeed, Bridget O'Laughlin notes that one reason why the state cannot make the ex-capitalist farms profitable is precisely because the victory of Frelimo ended the highly exploitative system of labour recruitment on which their profitability rested. She says that, 'The major political task in socialist transformation must be a fundamental shift in the relationship between the state and the peasantry, which is necessarily also a major shift in the relationship between the state and the formerly capitalist enterprises which make up the greater part of the newly nationalized state sector of the economy.'

This requires concerted planning of all three sectors together to make labour demands more compatible. Perhaps a co-op might grow primarily sunflower and its members grow cotton as the main cash crop on their family plots, or vice versa. Much lip-service is already being paid to the need to stabilize state farm workforces; that is, to make them full time instead of seasonal. In particular, this means a more varied cropping pattern in which there is work to be done all the year round, with some of the slack time from cash cropping used to grow food crops like cassava and sweet potato to feed workers.

But the pressure from central Government was always to produce a few key crops such as cotton and rice, and this pushed aside good intentions. Co-ops are frequently forced to grow cotton by the Government and cannot plan a balance with members' family plots. State farms were forced to expand their main crop rapidly, which increased rather than decreased monocropping.

In stressing highly mechanized, monocropping state farms, Frelimo failed to recognize the full dimensions of this issue. Despite mechanization, their crops still require seasonal labour, particularly for the harvest. The continued expansion of monocropping of rice, cotton and maize assumes a reserve labour army willing to work at peak seasons even when no longer forced to do so. As we have seen, this clearly does not exist. Rapid mechanization was often justified precisely by the shortage of labour, but that shortage was quickly forgotten when acreage was expanded still further.

More fundamentally, however, Frelimo ignored the dominant form of labour recruitment in the south: mine labour. When South Africa cut back mine recruiting, it left tens of thousands of men unemployed. They thought of themselves as workers, not peasants, and would not be easily reabsorbed on family farms. Hardest hit were the young men, who had not yet been to the mines and who needed mine wages to start a family and farm. At the same time, the collapse of the marketing network sent many people who had formerly raised cash crops on to the job market. Thus there was a double crisis: massive rural unemployment with tens of thousands of people looking for full-time work at the same time as a lack of seasonal labour for the plantations.

Agricultural mechanization is usually a device to push farm workers off the land and into urban factories. Yet in the south of Mozambique, the need was the opposite. 'The problem is one of stabilizing and reabsorbing the worker-peasant on the land, which calls for a labour absorbing strategy through the spreading of investible resources so as to maximize the output for given investment,' argued the CEA's Marc Wuyts in 1978. A return to hoe farming would be no solution. The abandoned colonial farms had used some machinery and their productivity depended on it. Rather, the need was for more and smaller machinery, and possibly even the partial use of oxen instead of tractors, to create more jobs and give a higher return on investment. Wuyts noted that it might not generate the biggest marketed surplus, but it reduces the pressure on that surplus by stabilizing people on the land. It also avoids one of the crucial problems of seasonal and migrant labour, which is that it is unskilled and is automatically sent home as soon as it learns its task. This was acceptable for the colonial state, which could unload all the costs of reproducing the family on to the family farm, but it is unacceptable now. Productivity gains must be made through increased worker skills: a permanent labour force will learn to use and maintain machinery and irrigation systems, recognize plant diseases, and take an active part in running the enterprise.

The collapse of marketing also led to an ancillary crisis and a suggestion. The crisis was in the supply of traditional foods such as maize, beans and peanuts to the cities. The colonists had grown rice, potatoes, vegetables and other expensive, high-quality, middle-class foods. The operation of the new state farms at a time of marketing collapse forced workers in Maputo to switch from traditional to middle-class foods, yet these are much more expensive to produce because they require more inputs. The suggestion, then, was that one way to maximize output for smaller investment was for the state farms to grow the crops like sweet potatoes and beans that people actually wanted and which were cheaper anyway. Yet another CEA study called for the setting up of small rural workshops which would use the mechanical skills of returned miners and provide tools and consumer goods for local people.

The CEA's work was largely ignored at the time. The push continued for highly mechanized state farms producing crops for middle-class consumption and for only large factories making tools and consumer goods. Only with the Fourth Congress did this begin to change. In 1977, the CEA's study *The Mozambican Miner* warned that if nothing was done, the countryside would be unable to absorb the extra labour. Nothing was done, and there was a massive migration to Maputo. In 1981 O'Laughlin cautiously asked: 'Are the young men of Gaza and Inhambane flooding into Maputo because they do not want to work, or because they need a wage before they can set up a household and begin family farming?'

But in 1983, the urban unemployed were dubbed 'marginals' and 'lazy' and expelled from the cities. It seemed that little had been done to provide conditions to stabilize them on the land. And the Government was using the expulsion to forcibly recruit plantation harvest labour. One group of 700 was sent to Lioma in northern Zambézia, which is not even based on an old colonial farm; it is entirely new, but it follows the same pattern of highly mechanized monocropping (in this case maize) and suffers the same problems of shortages of harvest labour.

O'Laughlin also pointed out that because the colonial economy was so closely tied to primitive peasant family farming, the transformation of capitalist agriculture to more productive state farms requires a parallel transformation of family farms into more productive forms. Thus support for state farms and peasant farms cannot be separated. And she concluded that cooperativization is 'a historical necessity' in Mozambique now.

Cooperativization is possible because peasants are already embedded in the market economy (and the crisis in family farming comes largely from the collapse of official marketing and the supply of consumer goods). Peasants are anxious to produce for the market and are willing to take up newer, more productive technologies. The nature of cooperatives may vary according to region. In the south, for example, co-ops experimented with a controversial system of daily 'advances' on future co-op profits, to provide something like a wage to worker-peasants who expect wage labour.

Cooperativization is necessary because it provides the only practical way to modernize peasant agriculture with Mozambique's limited financial resources. Investment in a co-op can serve more people and thus be more profitable than investment in individual family farms. But 'to make cooperative production immediately more productive than family agriculture generally requires at least some limited form of investment', notes O'Laughlin, because 'there is no gain to be reaped in Mozambique by simple cooperativization of land because there are no landless peasants'.

Thus investment must be balanced in such a way as to satisfy the dual needs of producing urban food and export crops, while at the same time stabilizing worker-peasants on the land and increasing their productivity. The bias towards highly mechanized state farms clearly does not maintain this balance. One can only wonder if, instead of giving the Limpopo valley over to the giant, expensive, mechanized state farms, it would not have produced more food, at lower cost, and with more jobs, if the area had been divided up into irrigated, partially mechanized co-ops with more diversified crops.

It is a question that will never be answered. While overseeing the breakup of Cail (Limpopo Agro-Industrial Complex), the new Agriculture Minister João Ferreira decided that land should be distributed to peasants and private farmers, but that no new co-ops should be created on the grounds that they would take too long to produce results.

Ferreira has clearly taken seriously the Fourth Congress orientation that: 'Private farmers who demonstrate a capacity for work, management, and initiative must be properly organized and supported. They must be able to obtain the resources they need to carry out their work successfully. . . . At the same time, fiscal and pricing policy must be adapted so that the producer will take an interest in developing his work and in investing his profits in small and medium-scale undertakings.'

One of Ferreira's first meetings after his appointment was an all-day outdoor session with private farmers from Maputo Province. He listened to their complaints and ordered substantially more help for them, in the form of inputs and machinery.

The Central Committee told the Fourth Congress that support for private and family farmers would provide a 'short-term solution to the current food supply problems'. Thus the irrigated Limpopo valley land was distributed to those peasants and private farmers who showed they could make immediate good use of it; in other words, that they already had agricultural equipment. This restricted the distribution of good irrigated land to existing private farmers and to those peasants who were already the richest and best established, leading to increased class differentiation. Co-ops had been seen as a way of avoiding such class differentiation.

Despite the chopping and changing, Mozambique's agriculture policy has actually been consistent. It has consistently ignored the two essential tasks of socialist transformation – changing the relationship between the state and peasant, and modernizing peasant agriculture – and has instead consistently tried to obtain quick results.

The Third Congress saw state farms as the 'quickest way'. That view carried with it the assumption that machinery, expensive, imported hybrid seed and fertilizer 'must' produce more.

The Fourth Congress looked to family and private farmers as the 'short-term' solution. So the same machinery, seeds and fertilizer are given to private instead of state farms.

There is no quick road to the socialization of the countryside. It is a long slog to improve peasant and state farm agricultural techniques and technology to the point where expensive, imported hybrid seed and other modern inputs will produce more than cheaper local seed. The organization of cooperatives and stabilization of state farm workforces are not just political goals; they are the only means of raising the skills of the bulk of the rural population and thus making that necessary technical leap.

People are hungry. Mozambique is desperately short of foreign exchange. Drought, South African aggression, and the world economic crisis have made all these problems more severe and given Frelimo much less room to manoeuvre. Yet Frelimo's own policies have exacerbated the effect of these outside forces. By concentrating on 'accelerated development', Mozambique is probably less developed now than it would have been if Frelimo had stuck to its political goals. And there is a real danger that Frelimo has squandered its political capital: that after eight years of sacrifice, peasants and workers are less willing to make the further sacrifices necessary to bring about real socialization of the countryside.

13. Communal Villages: The Backbone of Rural Development

When we arrived, there was a crowd around the cooperative shop. A few bicycles were being sold, and the new owners were wheeling them away from the shop, proudly showing them off to neighbours. More than 400 grass-roofed adobe houses stretched out in neat rows behind the shop. Most had small gardens with cassava, papaw trees, and a few vegetables. Some houses had flowers in front. This was Josina Machel Communal Village in Nampula Province.

The village president, José Sumana, proudly showed me the school, which now has 250 pupils in the first four primary classes. There are three teachers, two with six years of primary school and one with just four. Sixteen local children are in the fifth or sixth class of primary school in nearby Iapala. The primary school teachers are the most educated people in the village, and they also help with adult literacy classes. Sumana, who has four years of school and can therefore read and write, had just come back from a training course for village presidents and was bubbling over with new ideas for Josina Machel.

The village is already reasonably organized. There is a village health worker, a People's Tribunal (court), a council, and a Party cell with 22 members. There is a well with a hand pump for drinking water, although the village was intentionally sited next to a stream and many people prefer that water. There is a cooperative farm, based on an abandoned settler farm. It has 75 members and grows tobacco and sunflower. There are also carpentry and brickmaking co-ops; the latter supplied bricks for a new health post now under construction. Some people work on a nearby state farm.

Everyone has a family farm. The soil is good and the crops are varied. Everyone grows maize (some of which is usually sold), sorghum, cassava, beans and sweet potato, and keeps a few pigs or chickens. Many also grow pumpkin, peanuts, garlic, onions, tobacco, sunflower, cotton, cashew nuts and bananas. Mango trees are so common that they have no owners and anyone can pick the fruit.

Most people in this part of Nampula Province still live on their individual plots. Encouraged by Frelimo, some people moved together in 1977 to form Josina Machel, and they seem happy there. Indeed, more people are drifting in to the village, and several houses were under construction when I visited. The school, co-op shop and health post seem the main attractions. 'Before, many more of our children died,' Sumana said. He also pointed to the better social life and the cultural activities like dancing. Women often have most to gain from moving to a village. They can participate in community life for the first time, and learn to read; the proximity of neighbours means their husbands beat them less.

Josina Machel is typical of many other communal villages that I have visited during my stay in Mozambique. Some are better, some worse. It is easy to see why Frelimo calls communal villages 'the backbone of rural development'. They provide a new and better life, and they are frequently popular with the residents.

Villagization is hardly a new idea. Many countries with dispersed populations have realized that there is simply no other way to provide a minimum of services such as health, education and clean water to the people. Mozambique talks of communal villages as 'urbanization of the countryside' and sees them as providing a better and more interesting life that will reverse the flow to the cities. Villages must become centres of modernization where people learn new ways of living, better agricultural techniques and so on. Most important, Frelimo communal villages have an essential political purpose: only when people come together can they learn to take political control over their own lives, and participate actively in the political and economic development of Mozambique.

Communal villages are modelled on the way people came together in the liberated zones for protection by the guerrillas. There they received some medical care and education, and did some collective production to support the struggle.

The economic base of the communal village is expected to be collective production: agricultural and artisanal cooperatives and state farms. Eventually it is intended that family farms will be reduced to vegetable gardens of less than two acres to provide food but not a cash income.

Since independence, 1,350 communal villages have been created. They have 1.8 million inhabitants, 14% of the total population and 18% of the rural population. They are in various stages of development; for example only 515 have Party cells, 460 have village councils, and fewer than 300 have village health workers. Probably more than 200 have been burned by anti-Government MNR rebels, some several times; not all have been rebuilt (see Chapter 21).

The problem of collective production was discussed in the previous chapter: there are only 375 co-op farms in the entire country; fewer than 4% of the adult residents of communal villages are members of agricultural cooperatives.

All things considered, then, there must be fewer than 200 villages that have reached the stage of development of Josina Machel. Even that must be seen as significant and dramatic progress; real evidence that a socialist transformation of the countryside is possible in Mozambique. But it pales into insignificance beside the need. Socialization of the entire countryside requires 10,000 villages. To achieve this in a decade as promised in the ten-year plan would require 1,000 villages a year, whereas Mozambique has only built 1,300 villages – and fewer than 200 real communal villages – in eight years. Thus the central question is not the principle of communal villages, which seems the only choice both in practical and political terms, but rather why the process has been so slow.

A basic contradiction of villagization is that it is necessary as a means of development because of the lack of resources, yet that lack impedes the process itself. One estimate is that simply bringing clean water to 10,000 communal villages will cost £150 million. And there are no technicians to plan the villages. The people who pick the sites are usually young and inexperienced, with only primary schooling themselves, and too often they select locations where good farmland or water nearby are insufficient.

Inevitably, a great deal depends on a few individuals – local administrators, village presidents and so on – and their ability to organize and motivate people. I visited Mozambique Unity Communal Village the day before I visited Josina Machel. In both, the province was building new two-room schools, and in both the walls were finished but the roof had not yet been built for lack of beams and roofing sheets. The rains were starting, and in Mozambique Unity, the president, Nicolão Macoro, had organized a group to go out and cut bamboo poles and gather grass to put a temporary roof on the school. Thus they could use the building this rainy season and let the Government finish it when materials became available. In Josina Machel I asked president Sumana why he wasn't doing anything to put a temporary roof on his school. He shrugged and replied, 'It's not our fault. "They" promised to finish in time.' Initiative and imagination count for a lot, and it has moved Mozambique Unity into the forefront. Macoro is a hustler, repeatedly going into Nampula city to push for building materials and other goods for the village, and constantly bending visitors' ears about what he needs. And he is an organizer. Because the village is so good, it has become a model that official delegations come and visit. So Macoro had the villagers build a restaurant to sell meals to the visitors. A cinema and creche were under construction when I visited.

Ernesto Napote is a full-time worker from the provincial villages commission assigned to Mozambique Unity. He is a former president of a nearby village, Namecona, which has not been a success. Ernesto said the big difference was the creativity and initiative of the officials, and how well they involve the villagers. 'Here they plan well and discuss with the people, triggering the ideas of the villagers. In Namecona the Party just gives orders; it doesn't mobilize and draw on people's own ideas. We never got a village council going. We cut down the trees to build a house for the tribunal, but never built it. Someone built a house in the Namecona village square; no one stopped him and he still lives there.'

But resources are also important. Ernesto noted that Mozambique Unity has very good land. It has both a lorry and a tractor while many villages do not even have one vehicle; Josina Machel, for example, has no transport. It is much easier for Macoro to organize a work party to cut roofing poles for the school when they can be brought back on a tractor; a similar job in Josina Machel would require the villagers to carry the poles on their heads for at least 15 miles.

And the rule too often is: to him who hath shall be given. In its warehouse, Mozambique Unity has more than 100 sacks of cement, surely more than has been given to any other village in the province. The first small maize mill to be given to a village in Nampula Province went to Mozambique Unity, too. Unquestionably, good use will be made of it there, but it would have had more political impact and been a more important focus of mobilization if it had been given to Josina Machel or to Napala, the struggling but successful village mentioned in the last chapter. Similarly, Mozambique Unity is the only one of the 250 villages in the province that has a full-time worker assigned by the provincial villages commission.

Mozambique Unity is unlikely to collapse under too much help, the way Necheche has, in part because people *are* so well organized and motivated to do things themselves. Undoubtedly, better use is made of resources there than in other villages, and it is important to demonstrate to Mozambicans themselves just how much is possible. But more capital has been put into that one village than will be available to most other villages until the end of the century, so it will remain a show-piece for foreign visitors and an island of development in a sea of poverty.

Villages face a host of small problems which will take time to resolve. There are the inevitable feuds between clans and neighbours. Party and village officials sometimes create problems with silly rules. For example, once I was going to help a village build a school on a Sunday afternoon, when I passed many of the men walking down the road in the other direction. It is customary to brew maize beer and have a party after the work session, but this village banned brewing, so the men were going to the next village where they could get beer. And no work was done on the school. (By contrast, a nearby village made the more sensible choice of banning brewing out in the bush, but allowing it in the village where it could be more easily monitored and controlled.)

One of the continuing divisions in many villages is between those who work on the cooperative farm and those who do not. One reason is that as cooperative production was intended to be the economic base for each village, the village health worker and others who provide services such as

Joseph Hanlon

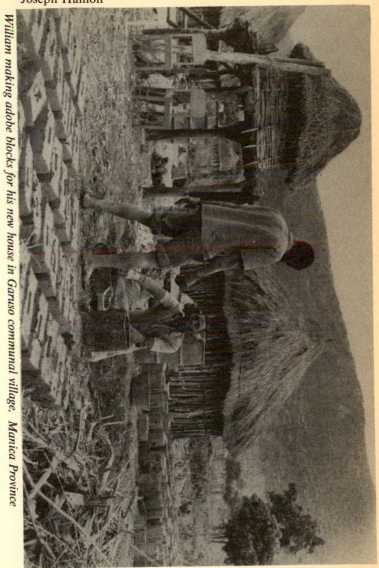

William making adobe blocks for his new house in Garuso communal village, Manica Province

creche workers and officials (while on village business) are meant to be treated as cooperative members and receive an equal share of the profits. Sometimes more than a third of recorded workdays are not directly productive for the co-op, and co-op members complain that they are supporting the village and that non-members are benefiting. The same is true if farm co-op money is used to start the co-op shop. Sometimes, as in Josina Machel, it is the opposite. The co-op shop there is independent of the co-op farm and members of the latter complained that non-members had more time to queue and thus got more from the shop.

In better villages, such problems are resolved locally, either in meetings or by the village council. In Josina Machel it was agreed that the co-op shop would open in the afternoon instead of the morning, as people work on the co-op farm in the morning only. (It is being argued there and elsewhere that giving priority to farm co-op members for scarce consumer goods would also encourage people to join the co-op farm.) Many villages have taken to paying the health worker directly instead of from the co-op. An annual whip-round, for example, can usually raise as much in cash and kind as the health worker would earn if he worked on the co-op farm. At least one village allowed the health worker to make an (illegal) token charge of 5 MT (8p).

But many village health workers have abandoned their jobs because they receive no support and could no longer afford to spend time in the health post instead of growing food to support their family. (It remains an anomaly that the Government pays village schoolteachers but not village health workers.)

Socialization of the countryside and the building of communal villages were envisaged as the 'decisive factor for the victory of socialism in our country', according to President Machel. But socialization of the countryside as it affects the majority of peasants has never been a priority in practice, and this is the real root of the problems of lack of resources, people, and organization which face so many villages. The bias towards state farms rather than co-ops has already been discussed. There is also a bias towards urban areas and big projects, which leads to incidents like one in which a drilling rig intended to bring water to villages in drought-stricken Inhambane was diverted to Maputo to provide water for fruit trees to beautify the airport.

The issue is symbolized by the National Commission for Communal Villages, created in 1978 to oversee and assist villagization. Like the co-ops commission, it was never given adequate staff or resources. In 1980, President Machel announced that he would shortly appoint a Secretary of State for Communal Villages, to give the villages commission much more political clout. He never did, which was a clear sign that those at the top had lost interest. People rightly assumed that communal villages were less important than, say, cotton or cashew nuts, both of

Annual rethatching at Mavili Communal village, Nampula Province

Joseph Hanlon

A public meeting; communal village, Nampula Province

Joseph Hanlon

which had secretaries of state. Reduced to an impotent shell, the Commission was finally closed down in 1983 and responsibility for villagization given to the new Minister of Agriculture.

A central problem is that relatively few villages really conform to the Frelimo model, typified by Josina Machel, of peasants voluntarily coming together to form a village, based on a mix of political motivation and their own desire to improve their lot. Some villages were formed in that way, especially in the former liberated zones. But most villages result from war and natural disaster and involve a high degree of compulsion:

*More than 100 villages in the Limpopo and Zambezi River valleys were created after the disastrous floods in 1977 and 1978, which killed more than 100 people. To prevent similar disasters in the future, Frelimo ruled that people could not return to the flood plain but should live in communal villages on high ground. This policy definitely saved lives in floods on the same rivers in 1981.

*Some communal villages were created to house workers on state farms and other large development projects.

*Many villages in the north house refugees who returned from Tanzania and Malawi after independence.

*Many villages in the north are simply converted *aldeamentos*, the 'fortified villages' created by the Portuguese to keep peasants away from the influence of Frelimo.

*More than 200 villages in Manica, Sofala, Inhambane, Tete, and Zambézia were created by the military to keep the peasants away from the influence of the MNR.

In all these cases, it is housing that comes first, followed only later by any form of communality. All too often, large numbers of people are moved into a small village which had been formed voluntarily, swamping the original inhabitants and their political motivation and organization. When government officials talk of creating new communal villages they always stress services, such as health, education and water. Farming, which must be the economic base of most villages, is often forgotten.

Planning can be quite bad, and sometimes there is not enough good farmland nearby, so that peasants have to walk many hours to their fields. Even in Josina Machel, a well-organized village, some fields are five miles away and people keep a hut there and stay in their fields during the peak labour seasons. In Josina Machel, people like the village and come back after a period of heavy work, but in unpopular villages people really live on the family plot and maintain only a token presence in the village.

An important issue rarely raised publicly is forced villagization. Since 1978 the army has moved people into what are called communal villages, but which bear little relation to the Frelimo political goals. When I first spoke to officials, they denied this was happening, as they did to other journalists.

But faced with first-hand reports, they became more open. Job Chambal, then National Director of Communal Villages, said: 'When it is said that we are forcing people into communal villages, it is true. Because if we don't, then the enemy will use these people to destroy their own future. These people are being liberated.' He admitted that often they cannot leave the villages: 'Why would they want to? To support the enemy.' But he stressed that they are different from the Portuguese aldeamentos. 'The objective of the aldeamentos was to impede our liberation struggle. In our villages people will have their own political bodies and cooperative farms and shops for their own benefit.' In practice these are often not created, and people see little difference. There are reports of people burning their own villages and blaming the MNR. I visited the village of Buapua, in Manica Province, shortly after it had been burned. The village secretary said he was convinced that a resident had told the MNR when the best time was to attack; almost surely it was one of the women forced to move into the village by the army.

How much physical force is used is never clear; peasants frequently talk of houses being burned and of people moved at gunpoint, but I could never get a first-hand report. Often people are threatened by being told that 'just over the mountain' people had their houses burned, and they will too if they don't move. What is clear is that, in practice, people have no choice.

Like the Portuguese before them, Frelimo will have to make its own decisions about the military merits of forcing people into villages. But I think forced villages are an important source of recruits for the MNR, and are building up antagonism to Frelimo that will take years to remove.

Nor is the military the only agency forcing people into villages. Considerable administrative pressure is also used. In Manica, Governor Manuel António set a personal goal of total villagization of the province not by the end of the decade, but by the end of 1982. I saw the effect in mid-1981 in Garuzo, a new village near the provincial capital of Chimoio. Villagers told me that in May they were simply given two weeks to move from their dispersed houses to a new village site. Two weeks later, unarmed local militiamen visited all those who failed to move and told them to move immediately. They had to sleep out in the cold winter rain until they built temporary shelters. António's haste may have had some military reason, as the MNR was already active in the south of the province, although not at that time near Garuzo. Some months later the MNR did pass through, burning the new village. I wonder if their passage was made any easier by those forced into the village, who wanted an excuse to return to their old farms.

António's crash programme had neither the political nor the technical cadres to carry it out. Explaining to people the advantages of villagization is a long, slow process; people do not easily give up their old homes and ways which have served them well for generations. Official policy is that inevitably some people will hold out and that they should be allowed to do so and only move when they see that life in the village really is better. And the governor and provincial director of communal villages mention the Partly line that villagization is voluntary. But they put most stress on the governor's order that 'no one can remain outside villages'. The caveats fall away, and inexperienced and harassed administrators simply tell people to move. Sometimes they use false promises of blankets, houses and wells, that cannot be kept.

Similarly, Manica had too few staff to plan villages. Some lacked both water and good farmland, and had to be moved. In some, people abandoned their new villages, only to be found by militiamen and told they must move back.

Inhambane started down the same road at about the same time. There had been a serious drought in 1979–80. Inhambane is one of Mozambique's driest zones in most times, so it was decided to move people to areas with sufficient land and water to prevent disasters in future droughts. And there was popular enthusiasm for this, largely because of a groundswell of support for Frelimo resulting from the highly successful drought relief programme the year before. People told visitors: 'We know Frelimo cares about us. If it hadn't been for Frelimo, many people would have died.'

But under Politburo pressure, Inhambane set the target of moving everyone in one year. It had the same shortage of skilled and experienced people as Manica, and officials accepted that it would be impossible to motivate people and that the move would require force. There was even insufficient staff to plan the villages, so most sites were randomly picked from maps, independent of the capacity of the land, which is quite fragile in that zone. (In one area, an excellent local administrator called on the oldest, most experienced farmers and asked them to go out and select the best sites for villages. They chose well, but the experience was not repeated elsewhere as it took too long.) There was also insufficient time and resources to provide water; resettling everyone in the drought zone would have required 450 wells in one year, double the number dug in the entire country the previous year. Finally, some of the best land was unoccupied for good, practical reasons; it has rich, heavy soil that cannot be farmed with hoes and requires oxen and ploughs. Thus some time was needed to provide equipment and teach villagers new techniques, although it would have been an excellent development scheme.

In the end, Inhambane's villagization target was quietly scaled down, but only after considerable protest and lobbying by technicians who warned that it was not only impossible, but also dangerous: not only would the villages fail but the land would be turned into a desert. But they had to overcome fierce resistance from officials who argued that they had been given targets 'from the highest level' and that their duty was to fulfil them, come what may.

In part, this reflects an underlying problem with Mozambique's whole central planning process. Civil servants see their job as implementing the central plan, and so long as plans mean numerical targets they will do their best to fulfil those targets. This will continue until plans say more about how targets are to be fulfilled, and method is given the same importance as results.

Mozambican journalists have never been allowed to write about forced villagization in their own country. But in August 1981 there was enough worry for the Mozambican weekly magazine *Tempo* to carry an article mentioning Tanzania's 'forced collectivization of the countryside'. It pointedly noted that Tanzania's plans had been overambitious, that many errors were made in locating villages, and that 'in some cases peasants were moved to Ujamaa sites without any political mobilization'.

Clearly there are disturbing parallels. Ujamaa villages were to be based on cooperative production and voluntary mobilization. In 1968 President Nyerere stressed that, 'No one can be forced into a Ujamaa village.' But Tanzania, too, lacked the skilled political and agricultural cadres to plan, organize, and motivate rapidly. Instead, the process increasingly became one of simply creating villages to fulfil quotas. Even the political goals changed. Ujamaa was replaced by 'development villages' which did not have collective production. By 1973, President Nyerere declared simply that 'to live in a village is an order'.

Caught in the middle, in Mozambique as they were in Tanzania, are the inexperienced and overworked lower-level government officials. Will they continue to be given unrealistic targets without the resources to implement them? Frelimo's leaders were in Tanzania at the time of Ujamaa, and with the majority of Mozambique's villages still to be created, there is time to learn from that experience.

Part V
Party and People

14. People's Power

'Our tradition is to go to the people to discuss the people's problems, seeking strength and inspiration from the people. The people's participation in the discussion of problems and in decision-making guarantees not only that the decisions are correct, but also that the people are consciously committed to their implementation,' explained the Central Committee at the Fourth Congress. This system, Frelimo argues, is 'popular and democratic' and forms the basis of all organs of People's Power.

At independence, Frelimo could not simply take over embryonic democratic institutions already established by the colonial state. The entire administrative system was profoundly racist and fascist, and had to be rebuilt from the ground up. During the Transitional Government and for more than a year after independence, Frelimo relied entirely on the Dynamizing Groups (GDs), which were composed of eight to ten people, and existed in every workplace, urban neighbourhood and village. Great stress was also placed on mass meetings, held as frequently as once a week, to raise problems and look for solutions, as well as to keep the GDs in check.

The GDs and mass meetings were highly successful, not simply in keeping the country going, but in convincing people that they had the ability to transform Mozambique. As the Central Committee told the Fourth Congress, the GDs 'played a fundamental historical role in mobilizing the people, in denouncing the vestiges of colonial behaviour, and in consolidating our independence. They . . . were an important school where the people learned to exercise power and practise democracy.'

The GDs had been flexible, serving a host of functions as the remains of the colonial administrative structure collapsed. They were the representatives of Frelimo and organized and motivated people, they served as local councils and managed factories, and they were the courts and social workers.

By late 1976 and early 1977, these functions were divided up and given to a series of new bodies. The Third Congress established Frelimo as a 'Marxist-Leninist Vanguard Party' made up of the 'best revolutionary working people'. Its central role was to ensure that politics remained in command. For the bulk of the people there were established 'mass democratic organizations' for women and youth, plus 'production councils' which formalized the various kinds of workers' committees that had been set up and which were seen as a first step to trade unions. These mass organizations were envisaged as 'the connecting links between the Party and the people'. Finally, there were established a series of elected People's Assemblies, ranging from local councils to a national parliament.

In addition, as administrative structures developed they were able to take on much of the work previously done voluntarily by the GDs. The Ministry of Health developed a social work section. People's Tribunals were created, with a few professional judges and a majority of lay magistrates. Managers were appointed to run factories and businesses. The police and council workforces were reorganized and strengthened.

The GDs still remain in cities, where they serve as neighbourhood councils, as well as in some villages and other places that still do not have Party cells.

These organizations are still extremely young and are only finding their way. Because of fascism, people had no experience of democratic organizations before independence, and they are still learning. The lack of trained or even literate people plagues all of the new bodies (8% of the delegates to the Fourth Congress were illiterate, and many others did not speak good Portuguese). Combined with extremely poor communications systems, this means poor linkages between national offices and local groups. And the roles of the various bodies remain unclear. Factories have a manager, a Party cell and a production council; towns have an elected council, a Party committee and an appointed administrator. What exactly are the roles and responsibilities of each of the three?

Because Mozambique has not had time to establish a complete new administrative and legal apparatus, the Party retains an administrative role. For example, where Portuguese law is still in force or where new laws are unclearly drawn, Party directives have the force of law. Thus, before parts of the new Family Law were introduced liberalizing divorce, the Party had already issued a directive to Tribunals which bypassed the Portuguese code still theoretically in force. In any case, Tribunals are supposed to act on common sense and revolutionary principles as well as law, and the local Party officials are the guide for that.

Frelimo works through 'democratic centralism', the essence of which 'lies above all in the existence of a single centre, which enjoys the confidence of all militants and of the masses in general, to lead the Party organizations in their entirety. Our Party represents the interests of the labouring classes as a whole, and not the private interests of individuals or isolated groups. Therefore the Party has to carry out the gigantic task of bringing together all the forces existing within the masses, and orienting them in the direction of a single objective, thus lending unity to disparate actions. The Party can only realize these tasks if the leadership is centralized,' explained the Central Committee to the Third Congress. But the goal is that the Party will also be democratic and thus there is 'a centre expressing the will of all'.

The Central Committee made clear that it realized the need to steer a course between excessive and bureaucratic centralization, on the one hand, and anarchy, lack of discipline and lack of forethought, on the other. But this has remained a problem, especially for the mass organizations, which are regularly enjoined to carry out Party orientations and which have not been given the freedom to raise issues of concern to their members.

The rise of the independent trade union Solidarity in Poland led to considerable debate inside Frelimo. It was concluded that such a challenge to the Communist Party was not permissible, but at the same time that the Polish Communist Party had created the problem by losing touch with the base. The debate reinforced the fears of Frelimo leaders that they, too, might be losing contact with the grass roots, and thus creating conditions for a similar event in Mozambique. The creation of trade unions was postponed for several years while the matter was rethought.

Frelimo's answer was a mixture. On the one hand, it made strong efforts to rebuild the Party at the base, and the build-up to the Fourth Congress was especially intended to do this. On the other hand, it reasserted the primacy of the Party. In April 1983, when it was announced that trade unions would be created, Political Economy Secretary Marcelino dos Santos declared: 'The head is the Party, and thus there cannot be contradictions between the Party cell and the union.' Democracy comes through 'study and profound, systematic discussion', and is not considered to consist simply of elections. Frelimo's leaders choose the issues to be debated in the Party, the mass organizations and the press. This system leads to a more thorough discussion and usually to some kind of consensus, and it allows Frelimo to concentrate its attention on a few key problems rather than spread itself too thinly. In particular, it avoids the wasted energy and acrimonious debates and slanging matches that often paralyse apparently more 'open' societies. However, it does depend very strongly on the leadership's being in close touch with the people, and responding correctly to their demands. So far, the Party and the top leaders have a good record. An example is police brutality, which could not be dealt with in the press but by 1981 had become a matter of concern for many people; the Party was listening, and suddenly there was a Presidential speech and a crackdown on the police. On the other hand, the leadership missed the importance of empty shops in the rural areas, which would have been made clear in a more 'open' system.

Elections of all sorts are tightly controlled by the Party as well. No matter what the election – officials of a Party cell, villagers electing a council, Party members selecting delegates to a Congress, etc. – it is Party officials who nominate a list of candidates. They are then publicly discussed by the electors and only those who 'enjoy the confidence' of the electors are finally selected. At the first national elections in 1978, about 10% of candidates were rejected. I attended several election meetings in 1980 and was impressed by the openness of the discussion and by the extent to which the candidates did seem genuinely popular.

The system is similar to those in the United States and Britain in that candidates are picked by a small elite; in Mozambique there is no choice between candidates, but I think the people elected are in practice more acceptable to the bulk of the voters than are those in the UK and US. And both systems can be used to exclude those who rock the boat or try to raise issues the Party does not find opportune.

One of the strongest justifications for this system is that Frelimo is not simply trying to build socialism; it is also trying to forge a nation where a national consciousness never existed before. Open elections would surely be divisive, and would be fought on tribal and racial grounds. Instead, Frelimo pushes for unity by choosing candidates in such a way as to blur those distinctions.

In the end, the success of People's Power and democratic centralism will depend on how they evolve over the coming years, as they become more established and as the electorate becomes more educated and experienced with democratic structures.

The Party

The original Front for the Liberation of Mozambique (Frelimo) was a mass movement open to all opposed to Portuguese colonialism and fascism. At the Third Congress it was agreed to turn it from a mass movement into a 'vanguard party'. Although it was to be a Marxist-Leninist Party, theoretical knowledge or even basic literacy were not criteria for membership. Instead the Party was for the workers, peasants and intellectuals who, in the words of President Machel, 'are the most aware, most advanced, and most dedicated to serving the people'.

It was the people themselves who were to choose. During the 1978 membership drive, anyone could put him or herself forward or be put forward by others. Existing Party militants (those in Frelimo during the armed struggle, who were automatically members of the new Party) did preliminary investigations at candidates' homes and workplaces to reject those obviously unacceptable. But the main filter was a mass meeting of co-workers where the candidates' attitude and conduct towards fellow workers, wives and husbands, and neighbours were discussed at length. Many people were rejected.

Not only did the system have the important political advantage of directly involving the people in selecting Party members, it also had a vital practical advantage. In the majority of the country not affected by the liberation war, the old Frelimo militants had no prior contact with the workers and peasants, and thus could not have picked out the best people

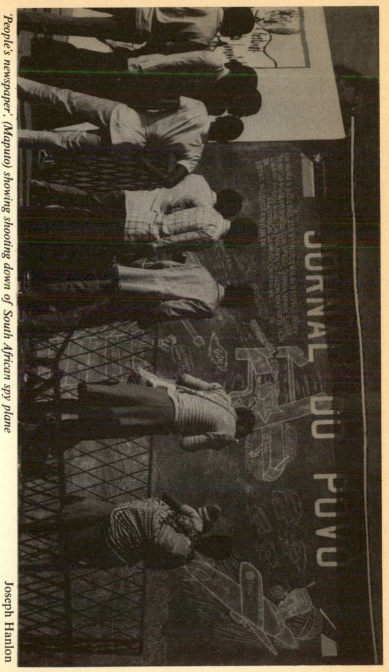

'People's newspaper', (Maputo) showing shooting down of South African spy plane

Joseph Hanlon

on their own – or screened out the worst: some candidates were recognized as secret police agents by people in meetings.

As was admitted later, the new Party apparatus was inevitably weak and fell into a host of traps. It became too bureaucratized and communication between top and bottom became formal and irregular. Provincial and district Party officials did not help or guide individual cells, which were unsure what to do. Many cells restricted themselves to holding periodic meetings and chanting slogans. Others simply became social clubs.

At the same time, the division between Party and state was unclear. The Party is meant to set the strategy and tactics and then monitor their implementation by the state apparatus. At the lowest levels, the Party cells often just continued to work like the old GDs, as a parallel authority which inevitably came into conflict with state and company administrators. At national level, all the top Party leaders were also ministers and there was no clear distinction of function. Furthermore, more than half the Central Committee elected by the Third Congress came to hold government posts as ministers, governors, ambassadors and provincial military commanders. Thus the Central Committee was not an effective check on the Government.

To reverse this, sharper lines were drawn between Party and state. In 1980, two Party secretaries, Jorge Rebelo and Marcelino dos Santos, were relieved of ministerial posts to concentrate full time on revitalizing the Party and making it less bureaucratic. They also tried to rebuild contact with the base, and ensure that Party cell members took an active part in the life of their workplace or village. In many places Party cells again started meeting regularly to discuss and try to resolve local problems, and holding frequent meetings with workers and villagers.

The build-up to the Fourth Congress was used to shake up the Party cells and other structures. Cells were purged of inactive or inappropriate members, and many new members were admitted. For the first time members elected the cell secretariats by secret ballot instead of simply approving a list handed down from above.

At the Congress itself, the Central Committee was expanded from 54 to 128. Only nine members of the old Central Committee were not re-elected, but the vast majority of the new members are outside the central state apparatus, which means the Central Committee for the first time can serve as an independent check on the state.

The run-up to the Congress also gave a quantitative jump to the Party, whch now includes about 2% of Mozambican adults. Membership was announced at the Congress as 110,000, of whom 54% are peasants and 19% workers.

Delegates to FRELIMO 4th Party Congress, April 1983

Anders Nilsson/AIM

Mass Organizations

For the bulk of the population not in the Party, there are 'mass organizations' of youth, women and workers. The women's organization was established during the liberation war and is discussed in the next chapter.

The youth movement (OJM) was set up in 1977 and is expected to involve youth in the main tasks of development, as well as to organize recreational, sporting and cultural activities 'to stimulate the useful, joyous, wholesome collective organization of young people's spare time.'

The Third Congress said that the mass organization must 'enable Frelimo to feel and to know at every movement the problems, needs, opinions, criticisms, and suggestions of the various sections of the population'. At the same time, the mass organizations are given guidelines and directives by the Party. In general, the Party has dominated. The youth and women's movements have not provided a forum to air and deal with the special problems of their constituencies, and neither group has attracted many members.

Production councils were set up in late 1976 as mass organizations of workers. In 1984 they are to be converted into trade unions. Their role has only been clarified over time, and they now have four tasks:

*ensuring active and effective participation of the workers in the planning and control of production and in solving problems;

*maintaining discipline, although actual disciplinary actions are the responsibility of management;

*improving working and social conditions; and

*combating the black market by ensuring that their products go to the proper destination.

The three bodies in the workplace – management, Party and union – are expected to work together 'with the single objective of increasing production and productivity'. In practice, as a national meeting of production councils admitted in early 1983, 'It has not all been a sea of roses.' There have been conflicts among the three groups as they tried to work out their roles. Especially in factories where GDs had virtually taken over management in the early years of independence, the workers lost considerable power when directors were appointed. Autocratic decision-making by the new directors did not help. In any case, workers had little experience of trade union organizing, so there was a long learning process.

In the early years the production councils received little respect from the workers as they seemed purely an arm of management, and indeed were sometimes chosen by it. They only disciplined workers and harangued them to work harder. When I visited Texlom in Maputo in 1981, the head of the production council solemnly told me that in colonial times it had been possible to provide face masks and other safety devices, but Frelimo could not be expected to do as well as the colonial managers until the employees worked harder and increased production to pay for protective equipment.

Increasingly, production councils are taking a more positive role. They run national 'socialist emulation' campaigns in which prizes such as bicycles, radios and holidays are given to the best workers. And stress is being put on workers to use their initiative and experience to solve production problems, particularly making spares that were previously imported. The production councils are also taking a greater role in social issues, for example helping to organize creches, canteens and social centres. It is not uncommon for the employer to donate the material for a creche and for workers to build it outside normal working hours or during slack periods.

The production councils at their 1983 meeting also stressed that 'security at work is indispensable and must be a priority'. They have signed a national agreement with the Ministry of Health under which workers' health and safety representatives are being trained. They monitor the health of workers, encourage pregnant workers to attend antenatal clinics, and ensure that workers with tuberculosis continue their treatment. They are also expected to improve safety standards and press managers to provide safety equipment.

In addition, every state company board of directors has a workers' director and a Party director. Company director-generals still have final decision-making power, but they must consult the production councils and need good reasons to override their views.

The production councils have had assistance from trade unions in socialist countries which, for example, have trained 315 future Mozambican union leaders. But Mozambique will encounter the central contradiction of trade unions in socialist countries: they are expected to represent the workers' interests but not be in conflict with management which also represents the workers who, through the state, own the factory.

This represents a central dilemma. As I will show in the following part of this book, there is an intense class struggle under way and managers often do not represent the interests of the working class. Workers gain consciousness through their participation in the class struggle, and trade unions are the traditional vehicle. Yet, with thoughts of Solidarity and Poland very much in mind, Frelimo has made clear that organized workers cannot participate in the class struggle in that way – they must work through the vanguard Party.

Even in those areas within the ambit of the new unions, there are potential areas of conflict with management. The Government puts great stress on fulfilling production targets and on the role of production councils in assisting this. Managers are reluctant to divert scarce resources to build creches and buy safety equipment when these will not increase production. It remains unclear how much power the new unions will have to push safety and other social improvements on recalcitrant managers.

People's Assemblies

Of all the various groups, the role of People's Assemblies is least clear. The Party sets policy. Mozambique has continued the tradition of an all-powerful administrative structure inherited from the Portuguese. In effect, then, the elected assemblies have neither policy-making nor legislative functions.

In part, assembly deputies are supposed to be leaders, taking a central role in implementing national campaigns from literacy to planting sweet potatoes. But most deputies are also in the Party and mass organizations, where they have a similar role.

The National People's Assembly is supposed to be a parliament which must approve all laws. After the first elections in 1978 there were discussions in parliament and laws were even amended. More recently it has not even met the statutory twice a year, and some of its sessions have been token meetings lasting just a day or two. Laws are promulgated by the Permanent Commission of the People's Assembly, composed of six Politburo members and nine high government officials, and are only retrospectively approved by parliament.

Disregard for the National People's Assembly could not have been illustrated more clearly than in early 1983 when two harsh new laws were introduced, extending the death penalty to economic crimes and reintroducing flogging. Both were controversial and might have provoked debate. The National People's Assembly met from 21 to 23 March. The death penalty was introduced on 16 March and flogging on 31 March, one week before and one week after the session. There was nothing the parliament could do about the former. The latter was not even discussed, although a retrospective reading of the speech to the assembly by Justice Minister Teodato Hunguana makes it obvious that the Government had already decided to reintroduce flogging.

At local and provincial levels the results have been more mixed. The Central Committee admitted to the Fourth Congress that the assemblies have made little impact and sometimes just met to fulfil the legal requirement. But some do serve as a forum for serious discussion of local issues. This could improve, because as part of the decentralization ordered by the Fourth Congress, local assemblies are to be given 'precise powers over sectors that are important to the people, such as planning and distribution of the means of production necessary for the family sector, control over supplies, and, in urban areas, control over management of state housing.' If carried out, this would shift power from administrators to the People's Assemblies, and give them a clear role.

Power

The problems with the mass organizations and People's Assemblies really relate to power, and to the tension between democracy and centralism built in to 'democratic centralism'. There is a similar tension between the strong authoritarianism inherent in the leadership and the use of public meetings.

The President, ministers, governors, and even district administrators have immense personal power. They can order that a person be arrested, sent to re-education, flogged, transferred, dismissed, and so on. And they are expected to use this power; during meetings or visits to villages or factories, they are expected to issue orders and immediately resolve problems. Similarly, ministers frequently summon national directors to appear before them immediately, no matter what else they are doing. If the President is to visit a provincial capital, the general public are told to be at the airport several hours before his scheduled arrival, and even provincial directors have to be there an hour or so before. This is intended to show respect for high officials and to demonstrate their prestige and authority.

This seems to arise from the confluence of three different traditions: Marxist democratic centralism, Portuguese authoritarianism, and Mozambique's own feudal traditions. Machel and some others in the leadership are descended from noble families linked to Gungunhana, the last Mozambican feudal ruler in the south. Speaking in Chibuto where Gungunhana was defeated by the Portuguese in 1895, the President spoke favourably of how Gungunhana personally and publicly executed criminals, and how he ordered prostitutes to be impaled on stakes. Frelimo's leaders attribute many of Mozambique's problems to their own failure to exercise power. Machel reminded the People's Assembly that 'the *régulos* [chiefs] had their laws and severely punished criminals in their zones. Thus they did not have anarchy.'

Undoubtedly centralized power does work. Just one of many examples was the simple story of the student hostel in Chimoio. After Governor Manuel António had heard repeated stories about bad conditions which never improved, he summoned provincial directors to the hostel. He established what was necessary for the repairs, and ordered the appropriate directors to provide the materials and workers. It was a graphic demonstration that despite all the excuses and denials, the problem could be solved with available resources.

Governor António did resolve the problem of one hostel. But did he improve the linkages between the provincial directorates of education, agriculture (which supplies wood) and public works, so that his intervention would not be required next time? Probably not.

These problems often arise because people are afraid to take the initiative, and wait for orders from above – not surprising considering the inexperience and colonial upbringing of most officials. But there are few rewards for successfully taking risks or showing initiative, while the price of a mistake is very high. Officials are afraid of being hauled up before a minister and punished for doing something wrong. And there is little chance for people to explain themselves. The pressure to take snap decisions means that the subtleties are lost; wrong decisions are made, and it is extremely hard to get them reversed.

And the whole style of summoning people can be immensely time-wasting. For example, a group of provincial directors arrived in Maputo for a meeting to find that the national director who called the meeting had himself been told the day before that he must leave immediately to accompany the minister. So the provincial directors cooled their heels in a Maputo hotel for a week until the national director returned and the meeting proceeded. All too often systems which are supposed to show respect for higher officials simply take the form of disrespect for those below. And it is contagious. If the President can keep people waiting four hours, and a minister two hours, then a lower-level functionary must show his status by keeping people waiting, too.

Undoubtedly the countervailing force to this authoritarianism is the importance still placed on public meetings, where people are manifestly free to speak their minds. Leaders always hold such meetings when they visit a factory or village. More important are the special purpose meetings to resolve problems. The meeting of workers of the national airline with Marcelino dos Santos went on for ten hours as complaints poured out, including evidence of mismanagement, corruption and incompetence. At a meeting in Nampula Hospital, the Health Minister simply said: 'You tell me why this hospital has such a bad reputation.' And for four hours they did, with tales ranging from staff bringing in witch doctors to male nurses raping female staff.

The presence of a high official gives people confidence and allows them to criticize their superiors to a degree that would be uncommon even in Europe. This is an important reversal of the authoritarian, hierarchic systems normally in force which often make people afraid to voice complaints. But at the same time it reinforces part of that tradition. It is the high official coming in from outside who provides the protection and makes it all possible. But it does work, and it is a mark of how much confidence Mozambicans still have in their leaders.

More than anything else, it was by holding thousands of meetings throughout the country in the build-up to the Fourth Congress that the leaders realized the anger and resentment that had been growing because of the economic problems in rural areas. All of Frelimo's top officials spent several weeks going to these meetings. In one, Marcelino dos Santos and several other officials were sitting at a table at the front of the meeting. A peasant stood up and said to dos Santos: 'Do you want to know where the problem is? It's under the table.' Dos Santos and the others looked, but saw nothing. 'Look again,' the peasant said. Still nothing. Finally he said: 'There are shoes under that table. You are wearing good new shoes. We produce the wealth of this country, but we are barefoot.'

15. 'Women Must Demand Their Emancipation'

'Women's lives have changed a lot since independence. There is no more oppression and exploitation of women by men. We women can do the same work as men and earn the same salary. Women participate in making decisions. None of this could have happened before,' explained Cecilia. She speaks from experience. In 1982 she became president of the Mozambique Cooperative Farm on Josina Machel Island in Maputo Province. A woman in her forties with six children, she is also a magistrate and a local councillor.

It was not always that way. 'When the cooperative started in 1977, only men went to the meetings, even if it was their wives who worked on the co-op and they didn't. But Frelimo said the people at the co-op meeting must be those working the land. For us it was a new thing to be on an equal footing with men. We never went to meetings before; women had no say, not even in the family, much less in public.'

Equally dramatic is the change in Cecilia's home life. Her husband works at the nearby sugar plantation, and his attitudes have changed along with his wife's. 'Before, a woman couldn't eat the food she cooked for her husband. Each day I cooked in two different pots, one for my husband and the other for myself and the kids. The meat was for the man; we ate vegetables. Now all of us eat the same food, and the whole family eats together.'

'I go to literacy classes and can read a little now. Before, women almost never did that; my parents said any woman who could read and write was a prostitute. Things are better at home since independence, too. Men don't order their wives around so much; now we sometimes discuss problems,' explained Edalina, a stall holder in Maputo's suburban June 25th Market.

But for the market woman, it was not as easy as for Cecilia. 'I started working because my husband didn't give me enough money to feed the children. He drank it all, and beat me when he was drunk. At first he didn't like me working. But now he does, and he stopped beating me,'

Edalina said. But some of the market women separated from husbands who never accepted their working.

And problems continue. 'Men say women are lazy now. But it's not true. Women have a lot to do. They cook and carry water in addition to going to work and attending literacy classes and political meetings. My husband says "Why didn't you wash my shirt?" But there isn't time, and he never thinks of helping. Women are slaves to men because of bride price. He says "I paid for you, so keep this house clean." But Frelimo says we have to go to meetings too.'

'During the armed struggle women were very active, bearing arms and carrying materials and growing food for the soldiers. Our husbands never said anything. If men forbade their wives, action was taken against them. During the armed struggle women were respected; men and women were equal. They did the same tasks, one week the man, the other the woman. And when the wife was away, her husband did the housework and took care of the children. We struggled to end the traditional divisions between men and women,' remembered Habiba in the Mueda Communal Village in Cabo Delgado.

'Frelimo told us, "We are struggling for the emancipation of women." But it seems they were just organizing to beat the Portuguese, because they don't do this now. There is no more discussion of the problems of women. It's all collapsed and the woman is at the bottom again. Here in this village women want to take jobs but their husbands prohibit it. Men leave their wives because they are old and they want a younger one. At independence, we never thought women would be pushed down like this. Now a woman is nothing.'

Two high officials were dismissed for marital misconduct in August 1982. Aurelio Sumbana, district administrator of Marracuene, near Maputo, was sacked for his 'constant physical aggressions against his wife which sometimes forced her to be hospitalized'. The case was considered all the more serious because 'sometimes these actions were carried out in the presence of family and subordinates'.

The other official was the foreign affairs secretary of the Mozambican Women's Organization (OMM), Helena Zefanias. She was sacked because of 'adultery' which showed 'bourgeois attitudes . . . which conflict with the principles which guide our struggle for the emancipation of women'. Unlike the case of Sumbana, details of Zefanias' offence were not published. But it is understood that four months earlier she had separated, by mutual consent, from her husband. He is a high Party official and both were highly respected and dedicated workers. She was sacked on the instructions of the Party, which apparently said it had evidence that she had gone out with other men after the separation. She was given no opportunity to defend herself, and no action was taken against any of the men with whom she was said to have committed 'adultery'.

Emancipation of women has been a central tenet of Frelimo policy since early in the liberation war. Now it is trying to find a route to that emancipation in a country which has inherited strong attitudes about the inferiority of women from feudalism, missionaries and the colonial bourgeoisie. What women themselves see as 'emancipation' varies widely both geographically and in time. It can be simply eating with their husbands. Or it can be the right to take jobs and hold responsible posts. Often it relates to equality in social issues like divorce.

Equally, progress towards the 'emancipation' of women varies considerably, as the quotes at the beginning of this chapter show. For Cecilia, the co-op president, and for many women like her, Frelimo's victory has transformed their lives. Yet there are many others like Habiba in Mueda who feel cheated by the promises of emancipation. Probably the vast majority are in the middle – they have made some gains, but these gains fall short of what was possible. This chapter is an effort to analyse why this has happened, and what the prospects are for women's emancipation.

This is a sensitive issue, both in Mozambique and in Europe. When I wrote an article in the (London) *Guardian* comparing the cases of Aurelio Sumbana and Helena Zefanias, one government minister reportedly said it showed I did not understand Mozambican women. There is a very real danger of that, and I feel that it is normally bad for men to write about women's emancipation. Nevertheless, it is an important issue in Mozambique, and gains for women are one of the victories of this revolution. To try to bridge the gap, this chapter has been written in close collaboration with several women, both Mozambican and foreign. What emerges I hope reflects their perceptions as well as my own.

Women as Chattels

Women throughout the world are exploited and oppressed, 'but it is in countries like ours, where the traditional conceptions about the submission of women combine with colonial conceptions that the oppression reaches its most extreme degree,' said the OMM at its first conference in 1973.

The vast majority of Mozambican women who were not White or *assimilado* faced all the effects of colonial repression. It was they who grew the forced cotton and who had to feed the family while their husbands were away for months doing forced labour at starvation wages. And they faced special abuse, particularly rape, from colonial soldiers and *cipaios* ('native' policemen).

149

This oppression came on top of their traditional position of being effectively owned by their husbands. In much of the country a man pays *lobolo* (bride price) to the woman's family. Once it is paid, he owns her labour and that of the children she produces. In a society where farming is almost entirely done with hand tools and where there are no landless labourers to hire, a wife represents *the* major capital investment. Greater production is gained by investing more capital to buy more wives.

This pattern is true in rural areas throughout the country, although there are wide regional variations. Lobolo is most common in the south where men traditionally use a large part of their wages from their first mine contract to buy a wife. Lobolo there reaches 50,000 MT (£800). In the north it is usually a token 500 or 1,000 MT, often given directly to the wife.

Half the country (the south and far north) is patrilocal, which means the wife goes to live with her husband in his family's area. Zambézia, Nampula and parts of Cabo Delgado and Tete are matrilocal, meaning the husband moves to the wife's area. This gives the woman more freedom, but she always remains under the authority of a man, usually her father or her mother's brother. Polygamy is widespread; in some areas it is the norm, involving most married women, while in others it is only a few well-off men who take another wife.

A whole series of other customs have grown up around the position of the wife as chattel, producer and reproducer. (These are strongest in the south and not all apply in matrilocal areas.) If the husband dies his wives are inherited, along with his other property, usually by a brother. If she dies or fails to produce children, the man can demand his money back or demand another wife from her family. Thus women may become wives without their consent. If the marriage does break down, especially if the man throws the wife out of his house, he still owns the children. Where lobolo is high and it takes time to earn the money, women are usually married to men much older than themselves. As older men become wealthier, they often buy younger wives, so it is not uncommon for a man to be three times the age of his wife.

In all parts of the country, girls traditionally undergo initiation rites as soon as they begin to menstruate. Apparently clitoridectomy and other mutilation are rare in Mozambique. The rites are a mix of sex education, teaching about housekeeping and the role in the home, instilling respect for elders (which is not required of smaller children), and especially teaching the girls to be submissive to their men. 'These initiation rites, veiled in an aura of mystery and religious solemnity, have a very strong psychological impact which causes the girls to blindly accept the teaching and traumatizes them for the rest of their lives,' the OMM said at its first conference.

Usually the girls marry soon after initiation, in the north to boys their own age, and in the south to older men. Often the marriage contract was made years before.

Water hole Mueda plateau, serving village for drinking, washing and laundering

Joseph Hanlon

For some years before independence, urbanization and forced and migrant labour had been causing changes in these patterns, particularly by making relationships less stable. Men were away from home for months or years. In the polygamous tradition, they would take other wives or have extended relationships with girlfriends in the city. Some abandoned wives are forced to enter other relationships as a means of support. Thus sequential relationships, whether informal or officialized in a traditional ceremony, are common.

On the other hand, the cities provided women with a chance to break out of unacceptable marriages. Many came to the city to take jobs, particularly in cashew-nut factories. Some became prostitutes, serving tourists, returning miners, and the growing colonial army. It was a harsh life, but it was the only way they could earn enough money to repay the lobolo and thus buy their freedom from an oppressive or brutal marriage. For many women whose husbands abandoned them, were killed in the mines, or were arrested by the secret police, prostitution was the only way to support themselves and their children. In either case, men still retained overall control, either as bosses in the factories or the buyers of prostitutes' bodies. But for the first time there was a large group of women with an independent income who were no longer completely owned by men.

Setting an Example

At independence, Frelimo moved quickly to introduce rules promoting the equality of women, in particular by forcing women into decision-making positions. Dynamizing Groups, tribunals, and local councils were forced to have women members.

In the 1977 elections, the percentage of women elected ranged from 28% on local councils to 12% in the National People's Assembly. Journalist Stephanie Urdang notes that this was the highest percentage of any African country reporting to the UN conference on women in 1980; the median for Africa was 12% and 6%.

Communal villages also help. The very existence of an OMM group can encourage women to speak at meetings and take an active part in political life. Social and political pressure in the village can also reduce wife beating and maltreatment of women.

Frelimo has tried to set an example itself. Party and government officials were not allowed to contract new polygamous marriages after the Third Congress. Those who do are required to leave their posts. This is in sharp contrast to neighbouring countries where the 'return to our traditional heritage' has often involved leaders taking additional wives. Similarly, the case of the Marracuene district administrator, although extreme, is unusual for Africa. Elsewhere it might be a case for the courts but would not lead to a much publicized dismissal.

Frelimo has also taken a strong line against sexual harassment. There

Anders Nilsson/AIM

Matama state farm. Women expelled from Maputo to Niassa help with harvest

have been a number of cases reported in the press of men, for example head nurses, being disciplined for using their position to force women working in their departments to have sexual relations with them.

Together this creates a different climate. I saw this at an election meeting in Manhiça in Maputo Province in May 1980. Candidates are selected by the Party and presented to a public meeting, where the crowd says whether or not those candidates have public confidence. When one man was presented, a woman in the audience asked about his wife. He said she left to live with another man. Another person said 'he is lying'. In further discussion it turned out that he had thrown his wife out, and he was unanimously rejected.

Another candidate was a woman who had left her husband and was living with another man (who himself had another wife). The crowd asked why. She told a soap-opera story of how her husband had gone to the mines and not given her any money, but said she could not take a job. She wrote to him and said she had to work. He wrote back to say 'my wife must stay at home. If you want to work, don't be there when I come home.' She wasn't. She was elected.

The most important aspect was that there were women candidates and that women in the audience spoke up and expressed their views. Before independence, neither would have been possible.

Frelimo has also introduced a series of laws to protect women, including a two-month maternity leave and the right to time off work to breastfeed young babies.

Part of a new Family Law has been introduced giving women protection in areas of divorce, desertion and child custody. Previously there was little a woman could do if her husband left her, for example if a man left his country wife whom he had married in a traditional ceremony in order to take a city wife whom he then marries in a civil ceremony. Sometimes men refuse to support their younger children, although they may later exercise their traditional right to take the children back from their mothers when they reach the age of six or eight.

A central legal problem in dealing with this is that few marriages are registered; most couples are married in traditional ceremonies or simply live together. Frelimo also faced the problem that it was impractical to legislate against polygamy, lobolo and other customs still accepted by the vast majority of the population. So it has tried to give women legal protection without giving legal sanction to these older customs.

Thus the new law defines 'de facto marriages' as monogamous relationships where the community accepts the couple to be married. Either party can register a de facto marriage, and a woman can use this to force her husband to provide some support for her and their children, to claim her husband's death benefits, and so on. Similarly, de facto marriages and polygamous unions are considered an impediment to a new

Pounding grain in village, Cabo Delgado Province. Women prepare all food

Joseph Hanlon

civil marriage, so the country wife can intervene to prevent her husband taking a new city wife.

The Family Law also radically changes the rules on divorce and child custody from those of Portuguese law and tribal custom. Divorce is much easier, and is possible by mutual consent. The courts are expected to divide common property, and to decide child custody on the basis of the interests of the children rather than traditional ownership rights. The law also permits a woman to petition a court to dissolve a polygamous union in such a way that her husband can still be required to assist her and her children.

Despite these real gains, however, progress on the social front remains limited. Initiation rites continue, although more covertly. According to the OMM, lobolo is actually spreading to places where it was not common before. Polygamy is on the increase; in some places officials are taking additional wives despite Frelimo's prohibition. And even some Party and state officials stop their wives from taking jobs and participating in OMM and Party activities.

Frelimo and the OMM are only now discovering that these issues are more complex than they thought, and it is not sufficient to chant simply 'down with lobolo'. For example, initiation rites have positive aspects in that they teach sexual hygiene and respect for elders. In a survey in Cabo Delgado, women stressed that the initiation rites 'are our only celebration'. They involve a grand party with only women, in which they turn the world upside down; they drop the modest pose they are expected to maintain in front of men and instead sing, dance, tell sexual jokes, and insult men.

Lobolo is not simply buying a bride. It is an agreement between two families which can give increased stability to the marriage.

Polygamy can actually reduce the workload of a woman. In areas where water is several hours' walk away, shared water collecting can mean that the polygamous wife works an hour a day less than her monogamous sister. And in areas with a large emigration of young men, at least some women face the choice of a polygamous relationship or none at all.

Thus the problem is not so much to abolish these customs as to change them or provide alternatives to suit modern times and Frelimo policies. Until recently, however, Frelimo has tended to downplay these continuing problems as being less important than the overall struggle to build socialism.

The Principal Task

'It makes no sense to end the foreign exploitation of women and leave the exploitation of women by Mozambican men,' commented the Central

Committee when it decided in 1972 to set up the OMM.

But to Frelimo, ending exploitation by Mozambican men does not mean fighting against men. Thus the OMM accepts as a fundamental principle that 'the antagonistic contradition is not between women and the men at whose side they fought colonialism. Rather the antagonistic contradiction is between women and the system of exploitation of man by man.'

The OMM First Conference in 1973 'called the attention of the delegates to the danger of being diverted from the real target, as exemplified by the position of the so-called "women's liberation movements" that proliferate today in capitalist countries. These movements direct their combat against men, blaming them for the oppressed state in which they find themselves.'

In his speech to that conference, President Machel warned that

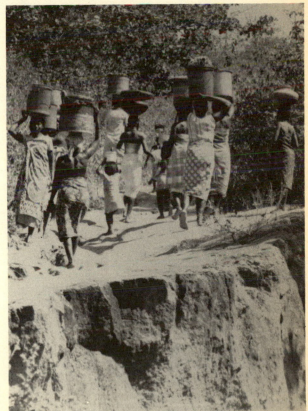

Joseph Hanlon

These women must walk 5 or more hours to get water;
there is none on the Mueda plateau

capitalist societies intentionally try to direct the actions of women against men in order to impede the struggle against the exploitative society. The 'primary contradiction' is between women and the social order; conflicts between men and women, although often very serious, are still secondary. On the other hand, Machel stressed that 'the idea that we can wait until later to emancipate women is wrong, because it means leaving reactionary ideas to grow so that they are harder to fight later.'

According to Frelimo, women's inferior position is built into the division of labour. This is what must be changed if women are to be emancipated. For example, the OMM notes that 'men discuss and decide, while the role of women is to carry out those decisions – to serve.' And Samora Machel told the OMM Second Conference that 'in the social division of labour it is always the man who has the task of transformation while the woman is always restricted to secondary tasks, essentially of maintenance, to . . . support the person who carries out the principal task.'

Thus Frelimo argues that women will be emancipated only when they participate fully in the 'principal tasks', namely in the transformation of society.

During the liberation war the 'principal task' was fighting, and the essential advance for women was bearing arms. From the first, women participated in vital supporting roles: transporting material, intelligence, political organization (especially in areas not yet liberated), sabotage, health and education. But it was only with the creation in 1967 of the Women's Detachment that women received military training and actually began to fight, and it was only then that they began to play a more active role in Frelimo. The very presence of the Women's Detachment, and of armed women marching into remote villages, helped to change the attitudes of men both inside and outside Frelimo.

After independence, the 'principal task' necessarily changed. Speaking to the opening session of the OMM Third Conference in March 1980, Mariano Matsinhe stressed that 'the problems of Mozambican women are, more than anything, problems of underdevelopment.' Thus women must be involved in development and building socialism. So the new 'principal task' must be participation in socialized production, particularly in wage labour and cooperatives. But Matsinhe stressed that, 'It is not sufficient for women to physically participate in the work of the factories, cooperative farms, state farms, and public service. . . . It is necessary that, side by side with men, women contribute to the organizing and planning of the work, and refute the ideology inculcated by feudal and capitalist societies.'

Participation in the principal task really has changed the lives of many women. For Habiba in Mueda, it was participation in the armed struggle. For Cecilia, the co-op president, and Edalina, the market woman, it was organized production. Yet these women are still a minority and some women like Habiba have lost ground. The line has not proved as effective as Frelimo expected. What went wrong?

First, it is necessary to ask why participation in the principal task has been successful for some women, and then to look at why it has not been more widely effective. The common and liberating factor of participating in armed struggle and organized production is that both take women outside the home. For part of the time they are no longer under the direct authority of a husband or male relative, and it gives them an identity independent of the family. And as the women cited at the beginning of this chapter show, there is a direct relation between the woman's life inside and outside the family. By working outside, the woman's image of herself changes as does men's image of her. This, in turn, changes her role inside the family. But it is a long process. In 1972 the Central Committee pointed to the need to further change women's attitudes and roles so that they could remain outside the home: 'Sometimes women who participate in the Women's Detachment do not consider this a normal and permanent attitude, but rather an exceptional moment in their lives. After two or three years, militants of the Women's Detachment abandon the ranks of the army to return to their families to marry, raise children, and stay in the house because this is the social function that is considered their destiny.'

The difference between the present and the liberation war is that there

Joseph Hanlon

May Day 1981 in Maputo. Women of the OMM (Mozambican Women's Organisation)

is now no urgent need to get women out of the home. Victory once depended on having as many women as possible on the supply trails and battlefields. That urgency is gone, so it is not surprising that the Central Committee no longer talks about getting women out of the home as it did during the war.

Frelimo always tries to analyse its experiences in the armed struggle and apply them to the present. In the case of women it developed the concept of 'principal task'. When this analysis was made in the first years after independence, talk was of rapid development. The President and others were worried about shortages of workers. There would be a need to take women out of the home and into jobs. Had this actually happened, millions of women would have taken paid jobs and joined co-ops. This would have involved as high a proportion of women as the armed struggle did in the liberated zones, and would have meant a similar change in women's lives.

In the event, this did not happen. For a variety of reasons discussed elsewhere in this book, Mozambique failed to create new jobs and instead faced massive unemployment; worse, the collapse of the co-op movement eliminated the possibility of socialized production for most women. In many ways, Mozambique is now little different from other countries after a war and facing high male unemployment: women are pushed back into the home.

The problem comes not from the initial conception of the principal task, nor from choosing socialized production as the principal task after independence. Rather, the problem comes from the choices that were made once it became clear that the new principal task was not feasible.

'Production' was subtly introduced to take the place of 'socialized production outside the home' as the principal task. New stress was put on the primary role of the woman as wife and mother, flying in the face of the 1972 Central Committee statement. Both of these are inside the home and family, and thus do not contain the liberating elements of the armed struggle and organized production. Indeed, they contain basic elements that work against women's emancipation. This is a return to the colonial position where women were responsible for both production and reproduction, supporting their husbands who are in wage labour. And to urge women simply into 'production' is to ignore the fact that women already do most of the country's production, namely family farm labour.

Peasant women in particular have a hard life. They are responsible for most of the farm work as well as maintaining the house, caring for children, collecting firewood and water (often from a great distance), washing clothes and cooking. They do all the day-to-day drudgery. Men only do special tasks, such as clearing new farmland, collecting and putting up the main poles for a new house, and sometimes helping with the harvest. And they traditionally do wage labour.

This maldistribution of labour is encouraged by the renewed stress on the family as the 'basic cell of society' and on the woman as wife and mother. Yet this is an immensely complex problem, because the family is a mix of security and oppression. In Mozambique, social life is centred predominantly on the extended family; despite the mobility created by a century of forced and migrant labour, people still relate most closely to home and family. Thus, the women who work in the cashew factories in Maputo, who have an independent home and income and seem freer, still feel that they are unlucky; they would not return to the oppression they fled, but they would much prefer a happy marriage and family. There is not the great demand to leave home that we often find in Western cultures.

Furthermore, the overwhelming majority of Mozambicans do not question that it is the woman who has the primary responsibility for the home and family. Cecilia may be president of her co-op, and she may cook from one pot instead of two, but she still cooks. (The issue of housework may not receive much emphasis because in the cities most women who are Party militants or government workers have house servants.)

Whatever women think of the family, being a wife and mother is not easy. Most Mozambican women give birth ten times or more during their lives, although typically only four or five children survive. Mozambican women, even in cities, see their role as mothers as extremely important; all the doctors I talked to say they get many more requests for treatment for infertility than for contraceptives.

The result is that women have no free time while men do. So it is the men who largely become the village officials, who in many parts of the country dominate the cooperatives, and who have time for special courses and training that are important in development. It is only when women are taken out of this home environment, as they were during the armed struggle, that they can begin to think about their own emancipation.

Thus the real central task is to change relations inside the family, to free women from the burdens of production and reproduction at home so that they can take part in the principal task outside the home. Frelimo underestimated the continuing struggle at home, and the links between this and paid work, which are shown in the examples at the beginning of this chapter.

It will take a long time to reduce the unequal burden on women, because, whatever the rhetoric, Frelimo still sees wives as inferior to their husbands. For example, Mozambique's constitution states that 'the emancipation of women is one of the state's essential tasks. In the People's Republic of Mozambique, women are equal to men.' Yet Frelimo approved a nationality law at the same time as the constitution under which women lose their Mozambican nationality if they marry foreigners, while men do not.

And Samora Machel, in his speech to the OMM First Conference in

1973, warned that emancipation of women should not be seen as the 'mechanical equality' which, he said, was demanded in capitalist countries: 'If I wash the dishes today, then you wash them tomorrow, whether or not you have time.' And he warned particularly that emancipation of women does not mean drinking, smoking, wearing mini-skirts, sexual promiscuity, refusing to have children or 'accumulating diplomas'.

The implication of this is that the paid labour of the men is more important than the unpaid labour of their wives. In his impromptu 1983 May Day speech, Machel even stressed the importance of women making their homes more comfortable for their men so as to help them win 'socialist emulation' awards at work.

Single Women and Morality

Not all women accept this line, however. Many women in production, in the Party, and in state jobs have a higher consciousness than their husbands. When men force them to choose between political work and their husband, sometimes they choose the former. And many women now have the courage to leave polygamous or brutal relationships. Thus an inevitable result of Frelimo's support for women's emancipation is many more divorced and separated women. The upheavals of independence and modernization have also left many abandoned women. Finally, Frelimo's commitment to education for all means that many girls remain single and continue their schooling instead of marrying at puberty. Thus there has been a major demographic change since independence: there are many more single women.

The response of many Mozambicans, and of Frelimo itself, has been intensely puritanical, and has resulted in the application of a very traditional double standard. Perhaps this is because of the petty bourgeois and Protestant mission-school background of many in the top leadership. The result is a continuing campaign against prostitutes, women with lovers, and women who commit adultery (but the men are rarely mentioned).

Prostitution has become an extremely emotive issue. President Machel frequently inveighs against it. On 5 March 1982 in Xai-Xai, he abandoned his prepared speech to launch into an hour-long attack on immorality, and especially prostitution. 'We are preoccupied because we hear prostitution is gaining ground here. A prostitute is a foul smelling, putrid person. When you pass by, you have to hold your nose.' And he warned women in the audience: 'Beware, a prostitute can take your husband. They are hunting men.'

Prostitution was widespread in the cities during colonial times, and at independence thousands of prostitutes were sent to re-education camps. Undoubtedly there are still traditional prostitutes in the cities – women who have sexual relations with a large number of men for immediate cash payment. Some were prostitutes before independence, who were sent to re-education and then returned with no other way to earn a living.

But the problem is that many Mozambicans regard any single woman, and particularly a single mother, as a prostitute. The OMM Second Conference in 1976 noted that 'as a general rule the single mother is marginalized. Society does not accept that a single mother can be an honest woman, simply because she lives alone.' This pushes single women into any possible relationship with a man, including polygamous and temporary ones.

Men are rarely willing to go through a 'proper' marriage to a woman who already has children (who traditionally are the property of the father and thus not the responsibility of the current husband or lover). So many women have little choice, especially if they are poorly paid, as in the cashew and biscuit factories in Maputo, and are receiving no support money from the father of their children. Such a woman may enter into a regular relationship with a man who, typically, is already married, but who gives her housekeeping money just as he does his official wife. Indeed, both men and women see this arrangement as in keeping with the polygamous traditions, but it is in a grey area verging on what some call prostitution.

There are also an increasing number of women who do not want another official marriage. Often they came to Maputo and worked hard to pay back the lobolo and buy themselves out of an oppressive marriage, and do not want to be owned by any man. They have freed themselves only to be labelled as prostitutes.

This opens up a whole range of abuses, as became clear when the unemployed were forcibly expelled from the cities in 1983. It was up to male-dominated neighbourhood councils to decide if women were in stable relationships and should be counted as housewives, or if they were prostitutes. A few single mothers with permanent jobs were labelled prostitutes and sent to Niassa, sometimes because they refused to sleep with neighbourhood council officials.

One ironic aspect of these moral judgements is that they marginalize a group which should be in the vanguard: women workers. They have long experience of struggle and are working class, so they should be leaders of both Party and OMM. Yet they are not, because of moral censure of single mothers.

The double standard of Frelimo's harsh morality shows particularly clearly when applied to single women undergoing the training which is essential to bring them into the principal task of organized production. Many girls still drop out of school after the initiation rites, and women are still a tiny minority in training programmes. But an increasing number stay at school, join the army, or go on for further training in Mozambique and abroad.

This puts the girls in a social situation for which they are not prepared.

Customarily, girls begin sexual relations soon after initiation rites, or even before. So it is hardly surprising that many single women in their late teens and early twenties do so. The result is a very high pregnancy rate among women in many training courses.

Frelimo takes a strict moral line on this; single women who become pregnant must leave school. And when teachers on a nursing course began distributing contraceptives because they were alarmed at how many students were having to drop out, they were stopped by the Health Minister who said it was 'illegal' to give them to single women. 'Nevertheless, the men who cause the situation of single mothers are tolerated and never censured,' comments the OMM.

This is a clear case in which moral judgements are stopping women from participating in the 'principal task'. And this was not done during the liberation war. Then it was argued that women were too valuable to lose, so they had their babies and continued in the Women's Detachment.

The same dual standard applies to adultery. At its Second Conference in 1976, the OMM complained that, 'When a woman commits adultery, she is marginalized, but with a man it is considered normal and creates no scandal.'

This is particularly true of the Frelimo leadership, as is shown by the case of Helena Zefanias, one of the women who organized the Second Conference. By contrast, at least one married male minister who had regular affairs was never publicly chastized or penalized. The moral conduct of top male officials seems to be taken into account only when they are doing their jobs badly, as happened with the first Minister of Agriculture, or João Pelembe, the Governor of Gaza dismissed in 1982.

In part this also reflects another aspect of Frelimo morality. The top leaders feel they must be seen to be paragons. Top leaders cannot divorce by consent – the lower-ranking partner must be at fault. Thus Salomé Moiane, OMM General Secretary, is separated from her lower-status husband, but Helena Zefanias could not leave her higher-ranking spouse. This was shown most dramatically by the case of Politburo member Mariano Matsinhe. On 10 November 1980 the Politburo granted him a divorce and broadcast an official statement, a device normally used only for the most important announcements. The statement was a ten-minute-long vitriolic denunciation of Matsinhe's wife, Margarida Mandlate. At the end of the statement, Matsinhe's colleagues expressed their 'sympathy and consideration' and 'encourage[d] him to overcome this difficult moment in his life'. His former wife was sent to re-education.

Can Men Liberate Women?

Frelimo may have strict rules about women being represented on local bodies, but it does not apply them to itself. The top leadership of the

Party and state is male. There is only one woman minister, Graça Machel, and no women governors, secretaries of state, or high-level military commanders. The entire Politburo is male. At the Third Party Congress only 14% of the delegates were women. By the Fourth Party Congress, 26% of Party members were women, but only 15% of Congress delegates were women.

Protocol requires that all major speeches be given by top Party leaders. So it is always men who give the major speeches on Women's Day and at OMM conferences, and thus all major policy statements on women have been made by men. Mariano Matsinhe gave the opening speech to the OMM Third Conference just a few months before his spectacular divorce.

And it is men who decide what the emancipation of women is. This is shown most starkly by the new Family Law, which establishes the essential conditions to enable women to participate in the principal task of production ouside the home. The draft law was ready in 1980 and it has been blocked ever since by the Party and the Council of Ministers. Finally, virtually in secret, the courts were allowed in 1982 to introduce the sections on divorce and recognition of de facto unions mentioned earlier in this chapter. But no publicity was permitted, which means few women know they have gained these rights. These parts of the law have not been published, and even lawyers have difficulty in obtaining copies. So it remains hard for women to extricate themselves from oppressive marriages and win child support.

And the bulk of the law remains blocked. Its content is similar to progressive family laws introduced in other countries, including the Soviet Union. But it is clearly too strong for some at the top. Included in the parts of the law still not introduced is the establishment of equality in marriage: it is emphasized that both husband and wife must 'contribute to household duties' and that both 'husband and wife are free to engage in all political and social activities and have the right to freely choose their profession.'

'The fundamental role of the OMM is to be an arm of the Party, one of the links between Party and people,' Party secretary Jorge Rebelo reminded the OMM in 1981. Like the youth movement, the OMM has no right of independent action. And the Party has steered the OMM away from dealing with specifically women's issues and towards those which affect everyone in the country. Economic development became dominant; for the Third Conference in 1980 the Party told the OMM it could only talk about women in production, and not the social issues which were keeping women out of socialized production and which were uppermost in the minds of women. After protests, the Party agreed that a Special Conference could be convened on social issues. But it was unenthusiastic and the Special Conference was repeatedly postponed. In

1981 Rebelo told the OMM that their 'central activity for this year is to support the fulfilling of the state plan for 1981'. The concept of the principal task as production has become so diffuse as to have lost all meaning; women could be relegated to their traditional 'support' tasks and there was no sense of which actions had an emancipatory effect and which did not.

Working as an arm of a largely male Party may explain some of the weaknesses of the OMM. Others clearly come from the inexperience of the women themselves. The OMM was set up in 1973 to incorporate the vast majority of women who were not in the Women's Detachment. It had considerable success in Cabo Delgado, where it became involved in health, education and social issues. After independence, there was spontaneous support for the OMM and groups were set up all over the country. But at national level it faced serious problems. The best cadres of the Women's Detachment and OMM were given government and Party jobs. Other militants dropped out because they were embarrassed by their lack of Portuguese and by their peasant ways. So the OMM just drifted, unable to give guidance or co-ordination to the newly formed local groups.

In late 1976 the Party intervened and appointed a whole new set of women to organize the Second Conference. They called in women from throughout the country and the conference was a major success. It was outspoken both on social issues and on the 'principal task'. It stressed the need to change the old ideas of both men and women. For example, it chastized women for their 'passivity in the face of their husbands' adultery'. On production, the conference noted that 'in the countryside, in reality it is the women who have always planned, organized, and carried out production, but we now find women relegated to merely carrying out instructions in our communal villages and cooperatives.' It stressed that women must take on traditional men's jobs, that work groups must be mixed, and that women should be proportionately included in decision-making bodies.

But the conference did nothing to see that its strong resolutions were carried out. Only later did the Party appoint new OMM officers, and they were inexperienced and unsure what they should do and how much power they had. The OMM proposed programmes to the Party and months passed without a response. The Party bypassed the OMM on a key issue, the establishment of People's Tribunals (magistrates' courts). These took over the main role in family disputes which had previously been a key OMM area and was one of the reasons why women had supported it, especially in urban areas. An attempt to study the problem of battered wives was blocked by male doctors and not supported by the Party.

The OMM never saw itself in conflict with the Party and genuinely looked to the Party for guidance and support. After all, it was Frelimo which had made women's emancipation an issue in the first place, and which had organized the Second Conference. Thus there was never any attempt to bypass the Party. Faced with a lack of support from the Party and its lack of interest in the issues defined as most important by the Second Conference, the OMM leadership became demoralized and confused. In the end, it restricted itself to simply passing vague Party directives down to local groups.

At the local level, the results were highly varied. As with communal villages (see Chapter 13), it really requires one or two dynamic people to get the local OMM moving. In some areas local OMM secretaries took the Second Conference directives seriously, and insisted that women occupy a fair share of decision-making positions and move into formerly male jobs. A few women became stevedors, tractor drivers, engineers, judges, mayors and co-op presidents. Many women began attending literacy classes and special OMM courses. OMM sewing and farming co-ops were established.

But all too often, without national support, local OMM groups just drifted. In most villages, the OMM consists of just officers and a few others. Many local OMM officials themselves continue in polygamous relationships and approve of lobolo and early marriages for their daughters. Husbands would not allow OMM officials to go on courses, saying they had to stay and take care of the farms and children; and the OMM did nothing. Both local OMMs and local tribunals discourage divorce as a way of settling marital problems, and encourage women to stay in polygamous relationships even if their husbands take another wife, in order to keep the home together.

Even in areas like the Mueda plateau, where women had a militant tradition and took an active part in the liberation war, the local OMM was not strong enough to resist the onslaught of men trying to recoup the privileges they had lost during the armed struggle.

Thus local OMMs tended to drift into dealing with only traditional women's tasks, ignoring social issues and thus unable to promote the 'principal task' of production. In a 1981 survey of 38 OMM village secretaries in northern Manica Province, 26 said the OMM's main job was to clean the village. The next most commonly mentioned items were gathering water and firewood for guests in the village, and assisting women with births. Only a few mentioned production or the fight against social ills.

This is in keeping with the OMM at national level. Its 'action plans' for the three years 1981–83 are very similar. They stress women in production and defence and implementation of the state plan. But production only involves consolidating the few existing OMM co-ops and starting a few new ones. Literacy is also given importance. But the main campaign in all three years was 'maintenance of houses' – women keeping their homes and villages clean and in good repair. It is exactly relegating women to the secondary task of maintenance which Samora Machel noted was their traditional role.

Party Secretary Marcelino dos Santos admitted to the Fourth Congress that the house maintenance campaign 'did not spread to the masses to the extent that had been expected'. This might be interpreted as a silent protest against the OMM and Party. The conflict came out into the open when a Maputo provincial OMM official went to the Vigilance Cooperative Farm to encourage the house maintenance campaign. The co-op comprises mostly women and is highly successful. It has a tractor and irrigation pump; the women work on the co-op four days a week compared to only two on the family farm. Far from lauding their productive work and involvement in the 'principal task', the OMM official was harshly critical of their not keeping the village clean enough. She became angry at their responses that they were too busy with production to worry about special maintenance campaigns.

This highlights two central problems for the OMM and Frelimo about the emancipation of women. First, there seems to be no distinction between those tasks which can advance the liberation of women, like work outside the home, and those like house maintenance which reinforce the subordinate role of women. And second, the stress so far has always been on women taking on *additional tasks* in production, health, cleaning, etc. There is a limit as to how far this can be carried, when women already do most of the work in the country. Without a fundamental change in social relations in the home, and especially without men taking on a significant part of the housework and subsistence farming, women will never be able to play an equal role.

Finally, in 1983 Frelimo recognized that it was failing to incorporate women into the new principal task. This has again forced it to confront the social issues that are blocking the advance of women. The Fourth Congress mandated that the much postponed OMM Special Conference on social issues should be held in April 1984.

On the model of the preparations for the Fourth Congress, there are to be meetings at all levels before the Special Conference. Great emphasis is being put on the freedom of women to speak out, and on the decision that the meetings are to collect information and not to give orientations. This will open the floodgates to the anger expressed by people like Habiba in Mueda. It could, for the first time, give vitality and direction to the OMM and again promote the emancipation of Mozambican women.

The Party secretariat issued an unusually strong statement on the Conference. It noted that women cannot participate in development if they are still 'oppressed by social problems'. And it listed some: 'At home, it is still frequent for a woman to be oppressed, exploited, and the victim of maltreatment by her husband. At work, the woman is often passed over for promotion and her access to positions of responsibility is blocked. In general social relations, innumerable forms of discrimination against women continue.'

These are strong words not heard since 1976. Furthermore, there was an important shift away from the tacit assumption that Frelimo would emancipate women. 'The liberation of women is, in the first place, a task of women themselves. No one can liberate women. They must take over totally the combat for their emancipation.' And using the word 'demand', which is rarely heard in Mozambique, the Party secretariat says that women themselves must 'demand their emancipation'.

But as Graça Machel told the preparatory meeting for the Special Conference: 'The Party thinks that because it created the OMM it can direct it. So the OMM will have problems when it begins to threaten the privileges of men.'

16. The Compromised

Every day as they go to the railway workshops in Inhaminga, workers pass a small concrete bunker. In 1974 it was a Pide (secret police) torture chamber. Hundreds of people passed through it before being killed in a vain effort to stop Frelimo's advance.

Pide did not work alone. It was assisted by the much feared Voluntary Police Organization (OPV), composed largely of black Mozambicans. At independence, some OPVs fled. But most stayed. Some used old friend-ships and intimidation to gain power over workers still traumatized and frightened by the massacre. Varsy Khan, a worker in the Inhaminga wagon repair section, told me how Luis Paul was appointed head of his section in 1976. 'We objected, because we knew Paul had been an OPV and had pointed out workers here who were arrested and then killed.' But the workshop director, who had held his job since before independence, confirmed Paul as head of the section. Ex-OPVs became heads of other sections, gained control of the social club, and even determined housing allocation. Frelimo militants were given dirty jobs, were refused time off for Party work, and were arbitrarily fined. 'All the workers were afraid. Even Party members were afraid. We remembered the colonial times and the power of those men then. We saw their power now. We thought Frelimo had forgotten us.'

Eventually the oppressive power of the ex-OPVs brought chaos to the railway. They never directly sabotaged operations. Rather they pre-vented the introduction of the collective work methods Frelimo hoped would compensate for the flight of skilled Portuguese technicians, and they discouraged workers from showing any initiative. As workers be-came discouraged, production and work quality fell. Accidents rose and finally Surface Transport Minister Alcantara Santos visited this remote workshop 120 miles north of Beira. He discovered the fear and demoral-ization. A dozen ex-OPVs were arrested and a new workshop director was appointed.

More than 100,000 Mozambicans of all colours participated voluntarily in organizations supporting the colonial-fascist state. These ranged from a group of women called the Matrons of War who wrote letters to soldiers at the front, to members of the fascist ANP, to those who joined the most brutal anti-Frelimo units. These last included Pide and its private army, the *flechas* (arrows); commandos and special paratroops (GEPs) who did the dirty work of the Portuguese army; and the OPV and Special Groups (GEs) which were anti-Frelimo militias.

The GEs and OPVs were organized particularly in areas like Inhaminga which were the focus of Frelimo infiltration. A similar zone was Meluco district in Cabo Delgado. Defence Minister Alberto Chipande visited there in 1983 and noted that in colonial times 'a majority of men in this district were linked, in one form or other, to colonial puppet organizations. Here the war was very difficult. Whenever you saw a Frelimo guerrilla, you beat your drums to warn the Portuguese.'

Members of all these groups were known as 'the compromised' because they compromised themselves by voluntarily supporting the repressive colonial apparatus. Frelimo distinguished between those who voluntarily took part in the repression and those who did not. Ordinary colonial civil servants, the tens of thousands of men forced to serve in the colonial army, and even regular colonial policemen were *not* considered 'compromised'.

Instead, the compromised were the large number that collaborated willingly, like the drafted soldiers who chose to take extra training as commandos. It was the commandos, the GEPs, the flechas, and others who were responsible for the atrocities that made Mozambique's liberation struggle particularly brutal and nasty. In many other revolutions, those people would have gone before a firing squad, or been torn limb from limb by guerrillas whose comrades had been killed and tortured.

But not in Mozambique. None was executed. A few who had committed the more horrendous crimes were sent to re-education centres. Most were free to walk the streets and allowed to keep their jobs and homes; the only restrictions were loss of civil and political rights. They could not vote or hold public office and could not join the Party.

It was an extraordinary act of clemency, as well as a gamble that most of those people would change their attitudes. Not all did. The Portuguese had destroyed most of their lists of collaborators, so many were not known, especially if they moved to a new job and home. Some infiltrated the Dynamizing Groups. Others were only spotted at the public meetings to vet prospective Party members. Even that screening was insufficient. In 1978 Frelimo found that the year before it had elected a former Pide agent and a former ANP member to the Central Committee; both were expelled.

Finally in November 1978 President Machel announced that the names and photographs of the compromised were to be posted in their workplaces. Partly it was an effort to end the secrecy, both so as to prevent blackmail and take the load off their consciences. And partly it was so that workmates could keep an eye on the compromised and help them with what Frelimo calls 'mental decolonization'.

In some places, even that was not enough. Luis Paul and the other OPVs at Inhaminga had their photos posted, but it made no difference. Most of the compromised did come to terms with Frelimo, however.

The process of reintegration came to an emotional close at a series of meetings in 1982 between President Machel and more than 1,000 of the compromised in Maputo.

With former political prisoners jailed by Pide looking down from the balcony and most of the Politburo participating, the meetings lasted seven days. It was like theatre or psychodrama. The President talked to individuals, sometimes for an hour each, and drew out stories of villainy and tragedy that gave some hint of the climate of fear that pervaded colonial Mozambique.

Alberto Elias told how he was standing in a queue when a white woman walked to the front. Just a cheeky teenager then, he muttered, 'Some day you won't be able to do that.' He was reported to Pide and jailed for five months while he was questioned about possible Frelimo connections. After he was released, Pide called him in and said: 'You are our client now.' They suggested it would go easier for him if he joined the fascist party, ANP. He did, becoming one of the compromised.

António Pope told how, while he was still at mission school, he and three other boys were called in by the priest who directed the school. The boys had been found 'good jobs' without having to finish school. The 'jobs' were as Pide agents. 'We accepted, as always, what the priests told us,' Pope commented.

Others were more sinister. Jaime Maté told how Pide paid his way through school in the early 1960s. In exchange, he infiltrated the African Students Movement. 'I denounced many people. Too many to remember,' he admitted. 'How many people were arrested because of you?' the President asked. 'I don't know. They never told us what happened to our reports,' Maté replied. Machel pressed him: 'You must have seen people disappear. How many?' Finally, in a low voice, Maté admitted: 'Many.'

A man who worked in the public telex office where I sent my articles turned out to have been in Pide. He mixed with passengers on trains going towards the border, to try to pick out those fleeing to join Frelimo. Any he caught were put back on the train to Lourenço Marques, and were often dead on arrival.

A group of Pide drivers initially said they had only been chauffeurs of top officials. But Machel did not accept that. And slowly the men began to tell stories of ferrying people from prison to Pide headquarters and later taking the bodies to the morgue or to be dumped at sea. Others told of carrying agents to isolated places to execute people.

Sometimes it was horror piled on horror. Two commandos told how they were present at the Wiriamu massacre, when Pide agents threw hand grenades into a crowd of suspected Frelimo supporters. More than 100 were killed. 'It took us three days to bury the bodies,' one of the commandos told the hushed audience.

Samora Machel drew out stories of how fascist education and especially church schools had moulded people. And it came out clearly how the Portuguese had promoted a few Blacks to control the rest. A journalist who was the only Black on his newspaper wrote glowing articles about the commandos, and he joined the ANP. He and others were compromised by climbing in colonial society at the expense of their brothers and they adopted a colonial mentality to justify themselves; they thought of themselves as Portuguese and better than other Blacks.

The first black pharmacist clearly felt like that. He even joined the ANP and became a district head. Yet under intense probing by Machel, he had to admit that he had been repeatedly passed over for promotion by the colonial health service because he was black. It seemed as if he had never admitted this to himself and always rationalized his failure to advance.

Machel stressed that people must understand how they came to be compromised. 'No one is born perfect'; everyone makes mistakes, Samora said. But they must 'look into the mirror', confront their past, and talk openly about it if they are to 'throw off the burden' of past mistakes.

This was shown dramatically by João Jorge, who told how his daughter had seen him in a newsreel filmed at the opening session and shown in the cinema before the meetings finished. For the first time he was forced to admit to his children that he had been a Pide agent. 'It lifted a burden off my mind. It liberated me.'

It was also an emotional series of meetings for Machel and the Frelimo leaders who attended. Some met again the Pide agents who had denounced them and caused them to be jailed or have to flee. Machel reminded the collaborators and their victims that the Portuguese had not returned one Frelimo prisoner of war. All had been tortured and killed. Frelimo fought to end that kind of repression and would not replace it with another. But it seemed that even Frelimo's leaders could not forgive those people without first confronting and understanding them. Both sides needed the catharsis.

Not everyone was prepared to admit the past. A worker at a Maputo hospital denied all involvement with Pide and said he had been falsely accused by his co-workers. The President summoned the accusers. In an emotion-charged scene in a later session, they came on to the auditorium floor and confronted him as the man who had revealed the existence of their Frelimo cell, and caused them to be jailed. He broke down and admitted his guilt.

Some former Pide agents bragged about what they knew was public and lied about the rest. José Fumane told how he infiltrated Frelimo in Dar es Salaam, but said he left the secret police when he returned to

Mozambique. He had to shamefacedly admit his continued work as the President presented him with details of his later spying. Others held out. A known Pide agent who infiltrated the Negroes Association flatly denied his role.

A journalist who served as clerk of the fascist legislative assembly and wrote many of its reports told the President that others wrote the reports and 'I only changed a few commas.' ANP members said they never attended meetings; even officials claimed they did nothing and headed moribund branches. Machel commented: 'To listen to you, the ANP only existed in the imagination of Salazar and Caetano.'

Throughout the meeting, Machel stressed that this was the final rehabilitation of the collaborators. Whether they confessed their guilt or not, they were no longer 'compromised'. Their photos came down off the office notice boards. They regained full civil rights and would be permitted to join the Party, if they otherwise qualified.

During the seven days of meetings, the tone changed dramatically as the compromised slowly became convinced of their acceptance by Frelimo. On the final day, most joined enthusiastically as the former political prisoners in the balcony led the singing of Frelimo songs. Reconciliation had been achieved. Only a few former members of the ANP, implacably arrogant to the end, refused to sing.

Part VI
The Class Struggle Continues

17. The Worker-Peasant Alliance

Mozambique's constitution says that 'power belongs to the workers and peasants, united and led by Frelimo'. In turn, 'the Frelimo Party relies essentially on the alliance between the working class and the peasantry', according to the Party Programme, which goes on to explain: 'The working class is the leading force of the Mozambican revolution. It is the leading class of history. It alone is capable of embracing the whole process of transformation of nature and society and of promoting and guiding this process. . . . The peasantry, which is the most numerous stratum of our population, is the principal force of the revolution in our country. It constitutes, in alliance with the working class, the political basis of people's democratic power.'

This is a goal rather than a reality. The peasants are dispersed and disorganized. And as the Central Committee reminded the Fourth Congress, 'Our working class was historically recent, numerically weak, and with a low level of class consciousness.

'To suggest that our working class has already assumed its directive role is to forget our history,' explained President Machel. 'Fundamentally, who unleashed and developed the national liberation struggle? It was the organized peasants. Here, in our country, it was the peasants in the liberated zones who gave the example of organization to the workers.'

And he went on to explain that through the correct mobilization, organization and education, 'the peasant masses gained a high level of consciousness that permitted them not only to defeat Portuguese colonialism, but also to beat the new exploiters'.

Thus the essential task to guarantee the success of the revolution is to organize the workers and peasants to take power. This must be done through production, which in turn requires a total reversal of the relationship between state and people. As I noted in Chapters 3 and 11, the main role of the colonial state was to organize labour – migrant labour for the mines, forced labour for the plantations, and forced peasant crops – in a way that ensured maximum exploitation and minimum worker power. Frelimo must now develop and structure industry and the large agricultural enterprises so as to build a strong working class. This means permanent instead of casual workforces, skilled instead of unskilled labour, and strong worker organizations. Peasants must be brought into co-operatives so that they can work together instead of separately. Finally, the role of the new Frelimo 'vanguard' Party must be to ensure that there are militants everywhere pushing this transformation forward.

Changing Production Relations

Nationalization is not the same as socialism, commented Sergio Vieira. Capitalist countries also nationalize, he said, pointing to British coal mines and railways and French cars, factories and banks. Then he said: 'Fundamental is the introduction of new social relations of production, and these were introduced with the state enterprises. They liquidate the antagonism between the proprietors and labour, because they link the labouring classes not only to production but to the management of the actual production process.'

This must be the goal. But it had not been achieved in 1977 when Vieira gave his speech, nor has it been achieved since. There have been some gains. Production councils and other forms of worker organizations have been introduced; the Party has some influence in the running of industry; some social choices are now being made about the products to be produced. Nevertheless, Mozambique has yet to pass very far beyond the first stage of nationalization. 'The best factory we have in Maputo', according to Samora Machel, is the Mabor tyre factory. Majority-owned by the Government, it is managed by a US multinational, General Tire, and is like a well-run capitalist factory anywhere in the world.

Neither do Frelimo's campaigns of 'socialist emulation' and 'voluntary labour' change the relations of production. They are usually about increasing production rather than productivity. All too often awards go to people who work harder rather than those who organize better to improve productivity permanently. Extra days of 'voluntary work' are known increasingly as 'compulsory voluntary labour'. It seems as if Frelimo has reverted to the Portuguese tradition of increasing exploitation to increase production.

More important, Frelimo has failed to change the most basic element of colonial capitalism: migrant and casual labour. The colonial 'working class' (that is, permanent skilled and semi-skilled workers) were largely white Portuguese who went 'home' at independence. Black Mozambicans usually did manual labour on a daily basis, for example on construction sites and in the ports, or else did migrant labour. Thus to build a working class it is necessary first to create a permanent workforce.

Sometimes this has proved more difficult than Frelimo expected. In Maputo port Frelimo did turn the casual workforce into a permanent one. Yet the complex historical relationships between different groups of workers, as well as Frelimo's own inexperience both with the working class and in running ports, has created unexpected problems in actually giving the workers a greater role in running the port. The exercise has required considerable study and the full-time involvement of a Central Committee member.

Frelimo justified the development of the state farm sector precisely on the grounds of 'creating an agricultural working class'. But working conditions and relations to the 'bosses' seem to have changed little since independence. Indeed, the new state farms seem to be modelled on the old plantations. There is talk of growing a wider variety of crops in order to balance peaks and ensure employment during the entire year, and thus build a permanent workforce. Yet the agricultural priority has been to expand monocropping: this has increased the demand for seasonal labour. In 1983 tens of thousands of urban unemployed were forcibly shipped to plantations to help with the harvest, little different from the forced labour of colonial times. Some were sent to state farms like Lioma in Zambézia and N'Guri in Cabo Delgado which are entirely new and did not inherit the labour practices of abandoned settler farms or plantations, but introduced these same labour practices from scratch.

Even where the workforce could have been made permanent under present conditions this has not been done. On the tea estates, for example, the demand for labour at the 'slack' time in September is half the labour demand of the January to April peak. So half the labour force could be permanent even if nothing was done to change cropping patterns. Yet all workers are casual and seasonal, just as in colonial times. Indeed, some state farms have permanent workers but do not know it; they pay by the week and keep no records of workers, so they assume all are casual when in fact many have worked there consistently for years.

This means, in turn, that most agricultural enterprises do not have effective production councils or much worker input into the planning and running of the farms. This has been a key element in their disastrous results. Some of the workers are much more experienced than the new, young state farm managers, and could have told them they were making foolish decisions – if anyone had asked, or if they had been organized to tell. Furthermore, effective farming requires a host of small daily decisions in response to actual conditions – to delay planting in one spot because the ground is too wet, or to spray early because a pest is appearing. Small farms are more effective because the owner-manager is working the land and can take these decisions; large farms can only be efficient if the workers are motivated and involved – and are listened to.

Frelimo's policy towards the working class is literally the carrot and stick. It has given preferential treatment to the working class, for example by the 50% increase in the minimum wage in 1980, the massive £20-million annual subsidy to consumer prices, the Maputo ration system which guarantees at least a bare minimum of staple foods without queuing, social benefits such as canteens and creches, and certain preferential treatment in health and education.

On the other hand, the working class has borne the brunt of harsh new laws. Workers from the traditionally most militant sectors, the ports and railways, were in 1983 the first to be executed for economic crimes and the first to be flogged. Executed in public beside a wealthy trader and prawn smuggler was a train driver convicted of stopping his train and selling off some of the sugar he was carrying. The first public floggings were not of black-market kings, but of two stevedores who stole food and clothing from the port of Quelimane. A central problem in the black market is the participation of distribution workers. Clearly, as Frelimo says, the working class has a low consciousness. And the new harsh penalties seem popular. But it is wrong to argue, as some in Frelimo do, that the new laws are 'class' justice directed against the bourgeoisie.

Peasants

In most parts of the Third World, development benefits only the better off in rural areas, widening class divisions in the peasantry. Frelimo saw socialization of the countryside as the way to prevent this. In carrying out this policy, however, it made two mistakes. First, it overestimated the existing class differentiation, and concentrated on the division between poor and middle peasants; this may be an important issue elsewhere, but not in Mozambique. Second, it failed to support poor peasants.

Surprisingly little is known about Mozambican peasants, and the regional variations are very lage. Frelimo's experience in the liberated zones of the north is not immediately applicable to the rest of the country. Some studies have been carried out since independence, especially by the Centre of African Studies (CEA) of Eduardo Mondlane University. They suggest that differentiation between groups of peasants is much smaller than in other African countries, and that the relationship between middle and poor peasants is usually non-exploitative.

It seems that the particular form of Portuguese colonization prevented any large differentiation. Peasants simply could not accumulate capital. They could not compete with the colonial state for labour and thus could not exploit other peasants. And they could not gain control of large tracts of land because the colonial state wanted to prevent landlessness to ensure that migrant workers always had land to return to.

As this table shows, even by 1970 there was not much differentiation in the peasantry:

	Families		
	Number	%	% of land
Poor 0–5 acres	1,258,000	76.4	47.3
Middle 5–14 acres	344,000	20.8	39.3
14–25 acres	38,000	2.3	9.8
Rich 25–50 acres	7,000	0.4	3.6

Poor peasants are usually simply hoe farmers. Middle peasants generally lease or own improved means of production, such as oxen and ploughs, or even tractors.

The better-off (rich and upper middle) peasants came from four small groups. First were the *régulos* (traditional chiefs appointed by the Portuguese) and their entourages, who were exempt from forced crops and labour because they were part of the colonial apparatus, and who themselves could control both land and labour. Second were peasants along the highland border areas who were able to break commercial monopolies by smuggling. Third, with the growth of the liberation war, the Portuguese not only curbed the abuses of forced crops and labour, but also tried to create a class of richer peasant farmer, called *autonomos*, who would support the colonial regime. The Cotton Institute and Cereals Institute gave technical advice, credit and inputs, and leased tractors to richer Blacks as well as to Whites. A few were even able to buy tractors. There is some overlap between the first and third groups, as it was the régulos and traditional healers who were most able to take advantage of these facilities. And the numbers were always very small; in 1970 the Cotton Institute lent money to only 1,724 autonomos. Fourth, some miners in the south were able to invest in tractors and other equipment, and it is here that differentiation was probably largest. Even so, a study of miners by the CEA showed that all peasants in the south were dependent on mine labour for survival. The only difference was that middle peasants had been able to take the money from two or three contracts and acquire oxen and ploughs, whereas poor peasants remained permanently dependent on the mine wage to feed their families.

Middle peasants and artisans often hire wage labour, but the CEA studies on both the south and the north found that this was usually casual labour for a few days at a time. Indeed, since there is surplus land in most of the country, it is usually more profitable to go off and open a new plot than work under exploited conditions for someone else.

Equally important, the CEA found that 'middle' and 'poor' were not fixed groups; peasants regularly moved from one to the other. Sickness or a bad harvest can force a middle peasant to sell productive implements or return to the mines, and as middle peasants grow older, they often become poorer.

Nevertheless, Frelimo maintained a hostile policy to the middle peasants. For example, the Central Committee said in 1976 that communal villages were to be only for 'poor peasants, workers, and exploited labourers'. Middle peasants could join only if they contributed their means of production to the village, and each family was to be limited to two acres for private production.

This policy was never carried out, which was probably just as well. But villagization is still harder for middle peasants, who are more likely to have fixed assets like fruit trees, permanent houses and water tanks which they must leave behind if they move to a new village. Reluctance to abandon these possessions causes resistance to villagization, and in some areas Frelimo cadres seem to have forced middle peasants into villages precisely because of the levelling effect. In its 1977 study on miners, the CEA warned that middle peasants were being made apprehensive about joining communal villages, and that this was dangerous because they 'are the backbone of agricultural production in the peasant economy. Many of them are excellent agriculturalists, and they work extremely hard on the land.'

Other policies, too, hit the better-off peasants. For example, the cereals and cotton institutes were closed at independence. This caused a drop in production, but it instantly cut the levels of those peasants whom the institutes had helped.

Pushing the middle peasants down to the level of poor peasants would have been reasonable if matched with programmes to raise the level of both poor and middle peasants. Cooperativization was the obvious way. And unlike rich peasants, middle peasants accept cooperatives as an alternative to personal accumulation. The failure to back co-ops and family farms hit both poor and middle peasants hard; they had no route to economic development, and have probably become poorer.

Nor has this policy had its intended effect. If anything, differentiation has increased. While most peasants were getting poorer, the better-off peasants were finding ways to develop. For example, with the growth of planning and the bureaucratic desire to include as much as possible in the plan, some rich peasants were able to get themselves included in the district agricultural plan, and thus obtain resources not available to co-ops and family farms outside the planned sector.

The black market benefits rich peasants who produce more and thus can profit from it, while it only squeezes the poor peasant by making his terms of trade worse. Peasants with non-farm incomes particularly benefit. Mine wages are used to buy cars and vans so that the owner can go into the very lucrative transport business. When I visited Chibuto, in Gaza, it seemed that most vehicles had South African registration numbers and thus had been brought back by miners.

Also, in at least a few cases in Gaza and Manica, rich and middle peasants have been able to use co-ops as a way to accumulate, for example by leasing oxen and ploughs to the co-op at high prices, by joining the co-op because it can get a tractor and then using the tractor to plough members' individual plots, or by using the co-op to take over good land and then giving some to members for individual use.

Access to good land is probably the most important catalyst to differentiation. Land nationalization was used to prevent individual peasants from grabbing abandoned settler land. For example, it was said in Maputo just after independence that when Samora Machel's father tried to take back the land which had been taken from him in the 1950s, and was now being abandoned by the settlers, the President personally went to his father's house to nationalize the land.

It did not always work like this. There were instances of even early land redistributions benefiting better-off peasants. This increased as the criterion for land distribution became the farmers' ability to use the land. Thus in 1982 in Marracuene district in Maputo Province, the criteria for redistribution of high-quality land were: ordinary peasants received two acres; those with oxen and ploughs (in other words, middle peasants) received 10 acres; and those with more than one set of oxen or a tractor or money to hire a tractor (in other words, rich peasants or 'private' farmers) received 25 to 40 acres. This was a clear case of giving most to those who have most. It dramatically increased the differentiation which Frelimo said it was fighting.

The other group to receive land in the 1982–83 redistribution were the so-called 'private' farmers. This term has never been defined. Originally it was a euphemism for white farmers, but it has now come to cover two groups: larger farmers, say with more than 50 acres, and people with non-agricultural income that can be invested in farming. Typically the latter group is composed of the local shopkeeper or restaurant owner, returned miners, professionals like nurses, and higher paid skilled workers on state farms.

Both private farmers and better-off peasants have also been given priority for credit, inputs and equipment. This kind of support was further increased after the Fourth Congress. Except for a massive import of hoes, there has been little support for poor peasants.

The argument for this is that food shortages are becoming serious, so it is necessary to support those farmers who have the know-how, experience and some equipment, and can respond quickly. This may be true, but it would have been unnecessary if co-ops and family farmers had been supported in the first place. And it is having the effect of dividing the middle peasants, pushing the weakest further down while promoting the strongest into a new group of rich peasants.

Misunderstanding?

Frelimo has largely failed to build peasant and worker power. What went wrong?

One factor must be the misguided worry about the middle peasants, which led Frelimo to support rich peasants while failing to realize that 'middle' is a relative term and that in Mozambique middle peasants are extremely poor and closely linked to poor peasants.

A second factor must be the widely-held misconception that peasants and the unemployed could simply return to subsistence farming. Coupled to this is the failure to appreciate the almost total overlap between workers and peasants: nearly all Mozambican men have done wage labour, particularly in the mines or on plantations, while most workers remain dependent on family plots for some or all of their basic food. They are 'worker-peasants'.

There is a real demand for wage labour and thus a serious unemployment problem. Many ex-miners think of themselves as workers, not peasants. And even young men who expect to be farmers need wage labour to earn enough capital to start farming.

Over several generations, the peasant subsistence economy was destroyed; there can be no 'return to subsistence'. After cash crops and forced labour, peasants grew barely enough food to survive. They became dependent on cash earnings from crop sales and wages to buy the basic means of production such as farm tools, as well as items such as soap and seeds that in a less oppressively controlled system they might have had time to produce themselves. Furthermore, their surplus fed the workers on the plantations and in the cities. Mozambican worker-peasants are permanently integrated into the cash economy, which is why the empty shelves in rural shops, the lack of support for peasant agriculture, and the decline in mine and city jobs produced a peasant crisis.

The third and overriding factor is the class position taken by the people carrying out Frelimo's policies, the managers and bureaucrats. Many have simply taken on the mantle of the former capitalist proprietors, and have actively opposed peasants' and workers' power. Yet they use Marxist rhetoric to justify their actions. They talk of preventing peasant differentiation as an argument for supporting the rich peasants instead of the middle peasants. They justify the rapid expansion of state farms by the need to build a working class, but keep the old relations of production on those farms.

Frelimo calls this group the 'aspirants to the bourgeoisie'. In the following two chapters I will try to identify this group and trace its continuing realignments, as well as to show how Frelimo first promoted and then fought it.

The peasants and workers see the failure to change social relations of production. Workers can do little about it because strikes are illegal. Yet they have taken action. Go-slows by women at the Cajuca cashew factory won the dismissal of the director. Sisal cutters in Zambézia ran a year-long go-slow in a successful bid for a wage rise.

But it has been the failure to resist the advance of the South African-backed Mozambique National Resistance (MNR) which has highlighted the class conflict most clearly. Parts of the military pushed a pro-peasant line at the Fourth Congress because they could see that Frelimo was losing the support of the peasants. Perhaps the most dramatic example was at Muaquiua in Zambézia, at the headquarters of a 2,500-acre state farm based on an abandoned Portuguese farm. When an MNR band swept into the village in October 1982, they held a meeting and said: 'Who gets all the food and cloth? The bosses.' The workers agreed, and joined the rebels in burning down the houses once occupied by the Portuguese owners and now occupied by the state farm managers.

18. Aspirants to the Bourgeoisie (1975–80)

Frelimo 'took revolutionary measures to eliminate the economic power of the colonial bourgeoisie and to prevent that power from falling into the hands of the local bourgeoisie', the Party told the Fourth Congress. The state now owns the most important industries. Land, health, education, housing and legal services are all nationalized. There is no significant group of local industrial capitalists, nor does foreign capital dominate the country. Mozambique *is* a sharp contrast to what Marcelino dos Santos called 'the sad reality of many African countries where power is in the hands of a minority of exploiters intimately linked to and dependent on imperialism'.

But if Frelimo did not simply change the colour of the bosses, neither has it given power to the workers and peasants, as the previous chapter shows. There is an intense class struggle under way, and as the *Report on the Preparations for the Fourth Congress* admitted: 'The internal bourgeoisie now has more economic power than it held soon after independence. It has infiltrated the trade circuits and the state apparatus.'

The eight years since independence are much too short for well-defined classes to have formed. Class positions and aspirations have changed radically since independence and are still changing. Inevitably, this makes analysis difficult, and, some might argue, premature. But as Frelimo often stresses, this issue pervades all others. Something, however tentative, must be said.

Frelimo itself is clearly struggling with the problem. There are no textbooks or handy East European Marxist formulas that can simply be applied to Mozambique's particular history. Frelimo continuously analyses the issue and its views have necessarily shifted. Machel often inveighs against the 'bourgeoisie' and 'petty bourgeoisie'. Information Minister José Cabaço talks of a 'national bureaucratic bourgeoisie'. The report on the preparations for the Fourth Congress mentions an 'internal bourgeoisie'. Increasingly, though, Frelimo has taken the sensible course of arguing that there is no properly formed bourgeois class. So it tends to use phrases like 'social stratum' (instead of 'class') and 'aspirants to the bourgeoisie'. According to the President, 'they are still "aspirants to the bourgeoisie" because they do not yet have economic power'.

Frelimo remains extremely reluctant to discuss publicly its still incomplete class analysis, which means that official statements are normally mere slogans. Indeed, the only recent analysis of this aspirant stratum was one page of the 174-page Central Committee report to the Fourth Congress, and thus it is worth reproducing it in its entirety:

> Our country has a social stratum that enjoys levels of consumption unavailable to the overwhelming majority of the people.
>
> From the social point of view, it consists chiefly of citizens originating from social strata that were already privileged in the colonial period.
>
> Politically, this social stratum is opportunist, elitist, unscientific, and hopeful of transforming itself into an authentic bourgeoisie.
>
> All it admires in the bourgeoisie is its corrupt consumerist nature.
>
> From the cultural standpoint, aspirants to the bourgeoisie are alienated and estranged. They are unaware, or pretend to be unaware, of the value of Mozambican culture and they spurn the people's wisdom and knowledge. These individuals are slaves to everything that comes from Europe, and particularly from the West.
>
> For this reason, they try to distort the class character of our revolution by transforming it into a technocratic process through which they can control power.
>
> This social stratum actively opposes any measures that aim at simplifying organization and methods, democratizing leadership, or increasing the workers' share in planning and controlling production.
>
> Because of their book-learning, aspirants to the bourgeoisie despise solutions from the people. They are unable to learn from the people.
>
> So they reject the experience of the liberated areas. They reject the small-scale projects that require the intelligence, sensitivity, and understanding of the people and prefer the projects that come ready-made from abroad.
>
> The characteristics of aspirants to the bourgeoisie make this social stratum extremely vulnerable to the insidious action of the enemy. Strict class vigilance must be exercised over these individuals. They must be detected. The recalcitrants must be isolated and the waverers won over.

For a Marxist party, this class analysis is remarkable sociological, looking entirely at consumption patterns and recent history. The core issue of controlling production is only mentioned once. Does Frelimo really believe that its 'aspirants to the bourgeoisie' act against the people because of 'book-learning' rather than vested class interests? And does Frelimo honestly think that its technocrats look particularly to the West and not equally to their East European counterparts?

Nevertheless, this analysis is a good starting-point. Clearly it is the desire for continued and improved group consumption that brings the aspirants together. They do largely come from strata that were privileged in colonial times. And part of the group is trying to control power through technocratic means.

In the rest of this chapter I will try to look more closely at just who are the 'aspirants to the bourgeoisie' and how they became so powerful. In the following chapter I will look at Frelimo's later moves against them.

In broad terms, I see two different kinds of aspirants, the *commercial group* and the *state group*. The first is based on private commercial capital and is accumulating largely through the black market. The second is promoting a form of 'state capitalism' in which the bureaucracy does not 'own' the means of production but can still control it in order to divert a significant part of the surplus for its own benefit.

Frelimo explicitly rejects the concepts of state capitalism and state class, but I think this second group is related to what Cabaço called the 'national bureaucratic bourgeoisie' and what others see as an emerging technocratic elite.

The commercial and state groups are not well defined and remain fluid. They are not highly organized or coherent; individuals and subgroups change their positions; alliances form and shift as individuals and subgroups change. Sometimes bureaucrats and traders seem allied; at other times, the bureaucrats seem to ally with the workers and peasants against the traders. Sometimes the conflicts are expressed as between Party and state, sometimes as within Party or state, and sometimes as between state and private.

This should not be seen as an active 'conspiracy'. Individuals make a variety of conscious and unconscious choices, particularly in terms of maintaining and improving living standards, and they do not always see the full implications. Political guidance plays a vital role. People do respond to dynamic leadership from Frelimo militants; where that is lacking, quite committed individuals can drift into choices that support group interests.

Upward Mobility

To understand the unusual fluidity in class positions now, it is necessary to look back. Mozambique was mainly a service economy, earning money from ports, railways, and miners in South Africa. The plantations were owned by non-settler (and largely non-Portuguese) capital. Locally owned trading companies did grow up based on the exploitation of peasant production, but none was very large. With the attempts to encourage local capitalists in the 1960s, there was some increase in settler investment in industry. But there never was a settler capitalist class such as grew up in Rhodesia, for example, where it controlled a significant and reasonably integrated part of the economy. The weakness of Mozambique's settler capitalists and their relatively small amount of capital are demonstrated by the ease with which they abandoned their investments at independence.

The Mozambican elite, then, was not one of capitalists but of managers, professionals like engineers and doctors, government functionaries, and traders and shopkeepers. It was, literally, 'shopkeeper colonialism'.

The flight of 90% of the Portuguese meant the disappearance of virtually the entire colonial bourgeoisie and much of the petty bourgeoisie. Their jobs were taken by those few Mozambicans with at least a basic education. Overnight, clerks became managers and orderlies took charge of health centres. During the next few years, night school and recycling courses led to upward mobility for many others. Tens of thousands of Mozambicans were promoted and moved quickly into new social strata.

Those who moved up so rapidly came from groups which had been relatively privileged in colonial times: the remaining Whites, Asians, Coloureds (mixed race), and a few Blacks, often either the families of régulos or *assimilados*. Until the mid-1950s, assimilado was the official status of Blacks considered 'civilized' enough to be honorary Whites; they had to prove they acted and thought like Portuguese, spoke Portuguese at home, ate with a knife and fork, listened to Portuguese music, and so on. The régulos were traditional chiefs who had been steadily transformed into the lowest state administrators. Régulos who opposed the Portuguese were simply deposed and replaced by someone more compliant, usually a brother or cousin so that the prestige of the traditional noble family could be maintained. They retained some local respect and sometimes became quite wealthy.

Although discriminated against in comparison with most Whites, these non-white groups were exempt from forced labour, were allowed to run businesses, and had some access to the colonial education system. And it was at this level that Portuguese colonial society was more class than race based. An educated and well-dressed assimilado was better treated in Lourenço Marques than a white peasant just in from the countryside.

In response to the liberation wars, Portugal increased opportunities for non-Whites in all of its colonies. Assimilado status and forced labour were abolished, and there was easier access to education. By independence, there were a significant number of non-white nurses, primary school teachers, clerks etc.

Special note must be taken of two racial groups, Whites and Asians. For both, it was easy to think of going to Portugal, and most did; they required stronger reasons to stay behind than middle-class Blacks who had extended family ties in Mozambique. Some Whites and Asians stayed on because they were committed to Frelimo and the anti-fascist struggle, others because they had been born in Mozambique and thought of themselves as Mozambicans even if they would have preferred a bourgeois government. An important and overlapping reason was that those who stayed did much better in Mozambique than they ever could have done in Portugal. With so few educated people remaining, a university degree or even secondary school training ensured a high post. Class played a part, too; many poorer Whites and Asians had not been able to pay for secondary school or university for their children, and those children definitely gained better jobs in independent Mozambique than they would have in Portugal.

As a result, agriculture, education, information and some other areas have a disproportionate number of Whites in decision-making positions, for example as national directors. Many are militant backers of Frelimo policy; some are not.

As elsewhere on the east coast of Africa, the Asian community held an important commercial role in the colonial era. Many Asians went to Portugal at independence. But others stayed and moved into bureaucratic and professional jobs at independence. Finally many took the opportunity to replace white businessmen in the cities, often moving from small rural shops. Leaders of the Asian community estimate that it now controls more than three-quarters of the wholesale and retail trade that is in private hands.

Most non-Whites who were privileged in colonial times saw themselves, culturally at least, as Portuguese. Indeed, Portugal was more successful at 'mental colonization', as President Machel calls it, than at economic colonization – perhaps because of its really tight control of education. When black children arrived for their first day of mission school, they had to take a 'Christian' name instead of their own (African) name. Textbooks were only about Portugal. To become an assimilado, it was required to forget African culture and learn about Portugal. 'Cultured' Mozambicans knew more about Portuguese *fado* singers than about their own songs and dances.

President Machel comes from just this background. His grandfather had been in the court of Gungunhana and his father was a wealthy régulo until he was dispossessed to make way for the Limpopo valley *colonato* settlement scheme. Samora Machel became a nurse, one of the highest positions a Black in colonial Mozambique could reach. At a dinner in Nampula in 1977, he reminisced about his past. 'I was an assimilado. I was Portuguese, not because of my identity card, but because of the way I acted. I was a functionary for 11 years' and accepted the same values as everyone else. 'I had great admiration for the bourgeoisie.' Before he finally fled Mozambique in 1963, he worried about losing his salary and status. Eventually, 'I liberated myself and fled. I threw away the salary, but I also threw away the colonial mentality.' It was the liberation war itself that changed him. 'If Salazar had granted independence in 1964, our capital today would still be Lisbon. Without a revolution, we would be Portuguese and enjoy neocolonialism.'

At its first meeting in Maputo, less than a year after independence, the Central Committee concluded that there was a 'middle and small national bourgeoisie' which applauded the victory of Frelimo only because it hoped to take over the role of the colonial bourgeoisie. It was *needed*, and the Central Committee concluded that it could be prevented from copying the colonial bourgeoisie and could be 'reintegrated' into the new Mozambique.

Although the rate of social mobility has now slowed considerably, the reverberations of the rapid early moves are still being felt. The dynamic of the early years of independence was moulded in part by the interaction of this group with the victorious guerrillas, both new to their jobs and only feeling their way, and both responding to highly contradictory influences. On the one hand, the effects of 'mental colonization' were very strong. Furthermore, many of those who moved into higher positions expected the salaries, life styles, and other trappings of the Portuguese they replaced. On the other hand, independence did mean something new, and the revolutionary rhetoric and example of Frelimo were equally strong influences. People did radically change their ways of thinking.

Managing the Economy

After the initial bitter struggle against the retreating colonial bourgeoisie, a focus both of the transformation of attitudes and of the class struggle was the fraught problem of managing the economy and social services Frelimo had taken over.

The Dynamizing Groups played an early vital role, often actually running neighbourhoods and abandoned firms when there was no one else. At their best, they were an embryonic form of people's power and there was some hope that they might become a permanent form of workers' and residents' control.

But they were trapped by the heritage of the colonial education system, which meant that few Dynamizing Group members had management or other technical skills. Some problems proved too technical to be resolved by good will and pooled knowledge. Sometimes the education gap meant that Dynamizing Groups were dominated by people who had an education, and who were exactly the aspirants to the bourgeoisie against whom the Dynamizing Groups should have been struggling.

Frelimo itself faced the same problem. It had mobilized people to fight a highly successful guerrilla war, but its leaders had little technical or managerial experience. It had to depend increasingly on the aspirants and on East European experts.

By 1978 there was a feeling of confidence. The worst was over. The infiltrators and the bad administrators had largely been found and Frelimo felt it could really take control. Production had stopped falling. But it was not increasing. The foreign exchange squeeze was beginning, which meant that for the first time critical choices had to be made about resource allocation.

Frelimo's new advisers argued that the problems were largely technical. A National Planning Commission was set up with East European help at the end of 1977. In individual enterprises and institutes, the view was increasingly expressed that people's power had served its purpose; it had been a vital check on the worst abuses, but the people now in management positions had proved themselves trustworthy. Management must have more power and more freedom to deal with basically technical issues.

Frelimo was listening. In August 1979 the President stressed the need to 'concentrate the power of directors'. And he added: 'Power cannot be disputed.' Nevertheless, there was still a balancing role for people's power. He used the analogy of the hammer. The director concentrates the force like the head of the hammer, but 'the handle is the democratization of work methods and collective direction'. A director should take decisions only after ample discussion with the workers, to ensure their confidence.

But this caveat disappeared from speeches to health workers in December 1979 and at a rally in Maputo in March 1980. 'Power is exercised by the manager; it is the manager who decides,' Machel said. The individual responsibility of the director comes first; collective responsibility only comes through reporting back afterwards. 'During the war, we admired the impeccable organization of nature, that water does not run up the mountain.' And people's power? 'We must establish the authority and prestige of the director as the representative of people's power.'

A parallel change took place within the military. Mozambique's army did not introduce formal ranks immediately after independence. But on Army Day, 25 September 1979, after watching a parade of heavy artillery and other equipment, the President said that the transformation of a guerrilla army into 'a modern, strong, and well-equipped regular army has reached a phase which requires defining levels of responsibility with more rigour and clarity, which implies the establishment of clear hierarchies with officers, NCOs, and soldiers.' And he stressed that the new 'sophisticated arms' required new technical skills. A year later, the military was given ranks, shoulder stripes and medals.

This new line of manager's power was not introduced without a struggle, particularly at first. British engineer Peter Sketchley tells the story of the Cifel steel mill where he worked. In 1977 the Industry Ministry appointed a new administrator. He had been a member of the Lourenço Marques city council and still owned two small factories, but he stayed on after most others of his class had fled. Because of his technical and managerial skills, he was able to unblock bank credit and increase production. But he totally ignored the workers' council, and set up a rigid administration based on six Portuguese technicians. And he was backed by the head of the Dynamizing Group, an assimilado lab technician, who even went to the factories owned by the administrator to lecture the workers on discipline and sacrifice. But when a Party team arrived as part of the 1978 national campaign to establish the vanguard Party, it discovered the problems; the Dynamizing Group was replaced and the administrator dismissed.

But the newly powerful directors continued to marginalize workers' committees, and increasingly they gained Party support. The June 1980 edition of the Party newsletter, *Boletim da Célula*, took note of continued complaints about this and admitted there was a problem of 'authoritarianism'. But by then the ideology of strong directors had become dominant. The article laid the greatest stress on misunderstandings by workers' groups about their role in the firm. It strongly criticized them for defending workers in disciplinary actions and for suggesting they should have another chance. The director 'has the authority to punish those who are undisciplined, regularly absent, or negligent'. The 'fundamental role' of the Party, Dynamizing Group, and production council is to 'motivate workers for greater engagement in production'.

Party officials stressed that directors were appointed by ministers and thus had the confidence of the Party; it was not the role of workers' bodies to interfere.

New in this period was the stress on the 'prestige' of directors. Machel emphasized that society itself had hierarchies. In the health speech he said that, 'The people like to see their officials well treated.' They would not expect to find a director behind them in the bread queue. And he went on to ask: 'Is it right for a director to be in the same hospital ward as his subordinate, for the wife of a minister to be in the same ward as the wife of a cook, or for a doctor to be in the same ward as the servant who takes care of her children?' And he answered his own question by ordering the larger hospitals to set up private rooms for officials.

In addition to private hospital rooms, higher rank brings an increasing series of perks. They mean a life style that, while hardly luxurious, can be considerably better than that of other Mozambicans. At lower levels, they mean access to a concrete house instead of a wattle-and-daub one; at higher levels they mean a better house. In a country with few private cars, higher rank includes use of a state car. And officials often have access to special shops; these do not provide many special goods, but do give priority access to meat and similar items which are in short supply to the general public. Another perk is foreign travel and the ability to buy foreign consumer goods.

Some of this is necessary. Many Mozambican officials work incredibly hard and have little free time for social life, even without shopping or waiting for buses. Furthermore, they are expected to be available at short notice for late meetings and urgent trips, which makes domestic organization difficult. Shopping, health service visits, and travel all require queuing and a high degree of organization which simply is not possible for many high officials because of the demands placed on them. On the other hand, all officials are assumed to have servants to shop and take care of their children. It is not the official who goes to the special shop, but the servant. The line between keeping officials healthy and efficient and giving them privileges is very fine, and perks are a growing source of grumbles from below.

Having won power over state resources and official sanction for its privileges, the state group set about manipulating state investment to benefit itself and strengthen the dominant position of its members and their families. This was not done through an overt or organized process, but rather in a form of mutual back-scratching which ensured that decisions were taken which kept power in the hands of the state group, invested capital to benefit that group, and diverted surplus for group consumption.

The state group has strengthened its own position by building and supporting large state institutions: favouring state farms over co-ops, heavy industry over appropriate technology, improved hospital care instead of rural health posts, etc. This has been done by convincing the political leadership that this is the correct path. Leaders without a technical background are encouraged to believe that Mozambique should have the most modern technology and not be fobbed off with less sophisticated 'second-class' techniques.

Up-to-date equipment usually means fewer jobs and thus a smaller working class, while it increases the power of managers and technocrats. In Mozambique this tendency was strengthened by the development of a highly centralized, compartmentalized and secretive planning system. All important decisions were taken by the National Planning Commission, which also made all the links. Each sector of industry knew only its own annual plan; companies were not allowed to talk to suppliers. This led to the ludicrous position in which the Beira water company was told it was to get water pipe from the Lusalite factory in Beira, when officials of the two companies had talked informally (thus violating the rules) and knew no pipe was available.

This system was not accidental, and it gave the technocrats enormous economic power. They added a special twist by convincing the leadership that Mozambique was special and could have growth rates never before achieved in Africa. This encouraged a system in which totally unrealistic targets were set during the early 'political' phase of the planning process. As each year moved on, and it became clear that resources were not available, the technocrats made the choices as to where the resources went. As the Council of Ministers pointed out about agricultural co-operativization, these are class choices benefiting big state projects. It was the peasant hoes that were left out, not the tractors. Similarly the Third Congress orientation to grow white potatoes on state farms (for urban middle-class consumption) was carried out with vigour, while the other Congress directive to distribute and promote improved varieties of sweet potato and cassava for peasant cultivation was completely ignored.

At provincial, district and factory level, unrealistic plans mean that unplanned allocation decisions must be made, and this increases the power of district administrators and factory managers. The obsession with secrecy that surrounds planning means these directors can limit the amount of information they give the workers about such 'technical' decisions.

The state group has used its power to direct resources, for example, to investments in the cities where this elite lives. A high Party official stressed to me the importance of peasants becoming more self-reliant and not expecting help from the state, for example by making soap at home instead of expecting to buy it in shops. Then he went on to say how necessary it was that the Government is spending millions of pounds improving the Maputo city water system.

Similarly, there is the personal (and often formally authorized) use of state and company resources. Ministers build themselves bigger houses. Lower-level people use company cars to take food home from the canteen.

Finally, there is corruption. From the growing number of reports of mayors, company directors, and lower officials arrested, it is apparent that this is becoming more widespread. And there are now previously unheard-of tales, like customs officials asking for money to clear goods in the port. Will dash, or 'something for breakfast', become normal in Mozambique, too?

The attitude is illustrated by the director of a state company in one of Mozambique's larger cities. He delayed his transfer from Maputo for some weeks until a bigger house was found for him, then spent his first weeks of work arranging furniture, etc. He assigned to himself a sack of rice intended for company workmen doing emergency repairs. And he had the company pay for the repair of telephones and air conditioners in his new house. None of this is serious and would hardly raise eyebrows elsewhere in Africa, or in England for that matter. But it annoyed his workers, which is partly a sign of what is still expected in Mozambique.

It is essential to put this into context. Ministers' houses, while big by Mozambican standards, are modest by the standards of other countries; they build second houses in their home villages, as do most African leaders, but the ones I have seen are simply the normal wattle and daub, improved with cement wash and cement roofing sheets instead of thatch. And state officials in Mozambique remain remarkably honest. There is no diversion of international drought aid to feed the bourgeoisie, as there was in West Africa.

And Frelimo itself has been compulsive about applying its rules to itself with utmost severity. When officials are caught with their hands in the till or misusing their posts for personal gain, they are tried and their names prominently published in the newspaper. The most dramatic example was the case of Central Committee member Francisco Langa, who died in May 1980. The Central Committee statement praised Langa as one of the heroes of the liberation war, but it went on to say that he had committed suicide because he had been caught embezzling state funds. Instead of sweeping the story under the carpet, as many countries would have done, Frelimo used it to make a political point.

Private Capital

In parallel with the increase in prestige and power for the state group, 1979–80 also brought a boost for the commercial group. Publicly Frelimo has always said there is a place in Mozambique for private business, but gave it no encouragement or support in the early years of independence. Few firms were directly nationalized, but the Government did take over hundreds of shops, restaurants, hairdressers, workshops and so on abandoned by their Portuguese owners. Usually the workers had not been allowed to gain the slightest management experience, and considerable government time was spent sorting out tiny problems. Nevertheless, many were disasters. A chain of People's Shops had permanently empty shelves, while the workers paid themselves inflated wages and the Bank of Mozambique covered the debts.

The state was overstretched, while the remaining private sector had stabilized and was now prepared to expand. The obvious choice was to return these small businesses to private hands. At the end of the privatization, the state controlled only 40% of wholesale trade, and consumer co-ops had 20% of retail trade.

In this same period, there was new encouragement for medium-size private farmers, especially in the 'green zones' around the main cities. Also, President Machel made a personal appeal for the return 'home' of black Mozambicans who had gone abroad during colonial times to set up businesses because the Portuguese would not allow them to do so in Mozambique. Private foreign investment was also encouraged, but response was largely limited to private Portuguese firms, particularly in the textile industry, some of whom were simply rehabilitating factories in Mozambique which they already owned.

It was virtually impossible for private capitalists to accumulate wealth legally. The severe shortage of consumer goods meant there was not enough to sell. Rigid price controls meant that for some items traders were actually expected to work at a loss. Special licences needed to move goods from one district to another were frequently not granted.

This meant that the only way the newly expanding capitalists could accumulate was through illegal and speculative dealings, which they did. Products were increasingly traded on the black market, known as *candonga*. Road transport remained largely in private hands and vehicle owners charged high rates.

In some provinces, more than half of commerce was candonga. The profits were vast, and prices of smuggled vehicles and consumer goods like video cassette players were up to 20 times their value if imported legally. Traders began to invest their speculative profits in farming and fishing, both to provide a cover, and as a route to further illegal trading. Many of the new private farmers, for example, sold their produce directly on to the black market.

A few Mozambican bureaucrats did move into private trade, either by leaving their jobs and buying restaurants or other businesses, or keeping their jobs but buying transport or running farms through relatives. Largely, however, bureaucrats do not use their state positions to assist their own private accumulation. Thus they are not like the Tanzanian 'bureaucratic bourgeoisie' with its taxis, chickens and bars on the side. Rather, the technocratic and bureaucratic elite sees its basis of power and accumulation as being the state itself. This means that the state and commercial groups remain as two distinct parts of the internal or aspirant bourgeoisie.

The relationship between the two groups is extremely complex, varying over time, geography and bureaucratic rank. At first, the two groups had a community of interest. Whatever their later divisions, they continued the colonial tradition of an upper stratum composed largely of bureaucrats, managers, professionals and commercial capitalists. Both state and commercial groups were obviously opposed to worker and peasant power. And tighter state control of the economy brought the two closer together; capitalists could only accumulate with the tacit approval of the state apparatus, while shortages of goods meant that the perks for the bureaucrats often had to come through the private sector. In some provincial capitals, private businessmen ran the special officials' shops, or officials were able to buy before the general public from private shops. Luxury restaurants in Maputo were privately run, but with special allocations from state warehouses and a blind eye turned to black-market purchases.

Often, the two groups developed a semi-legal symbiotic relationship. The demands of the middle-class life style in a rural area, and especially the demands of entertaining visiting delegations in the style which is expected, mean that a district administrator must have certain items like soap and cooking oil which are not available on the open market. He obtains these from the district wholesaler. Superficially it is above board;

the wholesaler says that they are part of a small amount kept back for government use, but in fact that has long been exhausted and both know the oil and soap come from candonga. Similarly, the district wholesaler needs a licence from the district administrator, to take maize out of the district for example. The administrator will give a licence for a few sacks, ostensibly for the legal purpose of feeding workers at a shop outside the district owned by the wholesaler. In fact, both know the licence will be used again and again, and the goods sold on candonga.

Sometimes the administrator and the wholesaler are already friends; perhaps they knew each other before independence, went to school together, or have family ties. But the worsening shortage of food and consumer goods means that these links are increasingly forged through necessity. A doctor may have to treat the local wholesaler as a private patient in order to get enough food for the hospital. Schools, the army and state farms all depend on candonga to get enough food. Obtaining building materials or scarce spare parts for vehicles often requires a back-door arrangement. And a manager is much more likely to get into trouble for not fulfilling his plan than he is for resorting to under-the-table dealings to do it.

The way in which state-owned small businesses were sold also showed the close relationship between the state and commercial groups. There was no attempt at continued social ownership, no control of new owners, and little protection for the workers. There was no attempt to distinguish unsuccessful businesses from successful ones that could profitably have been kept in state ownership; Maputo's best restaurant was sold off along with some of the worst. Equally curious was the failure to encourage cooperatives, which would have been an alternative form of social ownership preferable to privatization. A strong network of consumer co-ops already existed, and some shops were given to these co-ops. But there was little support for neighbourhoods to take over shops to form new co-ops where none existed. And there was no encouragement for the workers in businesses to form cooperatives to take them over, even though non-agricultural co-ops had been encouraged at the 1976 co-ops seminar. Indeed, the workers were all tarred with the brush of being lazy and overpaid and received short shrift. The new private owners were allowed to take only those workers they wanted; the state would assign to new jobs, usually in agriculture, those the new owners didn't want.

Even more questionable were some other aspects of the sales. Wholesale firms, which provide a much bigger opportunity for either state control or private candonga, were also sold off. Businesses were sold to the highest bidder at prices which could not be justified by legal profits. New owners were allowed to close restaurants for 'redecoration' which sometimes lasted for two years, while they continued to pick up their allocation of food and beer and sell it on the black market.

It was the sale of government wholesale and retail stores that helped prepare the ground for the candonga explosion, and it must have been clear to both sides that illegal trading was intended. Apparently the state group saw this as a good thing, and believed it would get more through candonga than through normal channels.

This kind of relationship drifts into more blatant corruption. Private traders are able to pay massive bribes. A prawn smuggler bought the entire customs staff at the Namaacha border post, giving the customs head a car. In another case, a major Nampula wholesaler paid electricity workers to ensure that his house always had power when there was supposed to be a rota of cuts. At a lower level, candonga usually requires official connivance, in the form of a warehouseman, port worker, or policeman looking the other way.

Kickbacks are another form of corruption. For example, a state company director approved a massively inflated bill to an electrician for work done at the company (the bill, for £600, claimed that 2,000 yards of wire had been used instead of the 20 yards actually needed). In exchange, the electrician did free work on the director's house. Maputo bureaucrats protected rather than disciplined the director when the issue was raised.

Life Style

Social factors are also important for this stratum. All those with an education, in particular government and Party workers, have tried to develop a life style different from peasants and workers. This has led to a separation between mental and manual labour, which is one of the traditional divisions between bourgeois and working classes. Frelimo sought to break down this division during the war. Everyone was expected to do manual labour, and Samora Machel noted that 'our pride is in our calloused hands'. After independence, this continued. Schools, for example, were expected to grow some of their own food. Eventually the attempt died away, and little was heard of manual labour except for the odd special morning of 'voluntary' work.

Similarly life styles developed patterns in sharp contrast to Frelimo rhetoric. The rigid hierarchies of the workplace carry over into social life. Mozambican life is very formal, and directors rarely mix with their subordinates. This was encouraged by the 1979 health speech, and for a while in some hospitals, doctors could not drink their tea at the same tables as nurses, and nurses could not use the same tables as porters. A Party meeting on ideological work in July 1981 noted that 'many Party cadres isolate themselves *deliberately* from the masses, living in closed circles; they refuse invitations to participate in people's meetings as well as in parties and social events organized by the population. Imbued with the bourgeois spirit of officials, they wrongly think that their contact with the masses will cause them to lose a so-called respectability.'

There was also an effort to differentiate the city from the countryside more sharply. In the period shortly after independence, civil servants and flat dwellers filled every bit of vacant land in central Maputo with vegetable gardens, both to provide food and in response to political encouragement for manual work. This declined and was ended when the President announced in his March 1980 speech that 'in the centre of the city we don't want vegetable patches. We want flowers; we want beauty.' In the same speech he said Maputo needed luxury restaurants where a glass of beer costs double the normal price, men have to wear ties, and women cannot enter carrying babies on their back (as most women do). Three years later he backed this up with another discussion about not bringing the bad habits of the countryside into the city; he told women that breastfeeding their babies on the street or even plaiting their hair in public was as bad as pissing or spitting in the street. It seemed little different from what the Lourenço Marques bourgeoisie said about their country cousins 30 years before.

Education plays a central role, both in the 'aspirants to the bourgeoisie' gaining their position, and in ensuring that their children will follow in their footsteps. Frelimo puts great stress on education as being essential if the workers and peasants are to take power, and it gives the highest priority to training Party militants with special accelerated courses. Nevertheless, most people in higher positions were educated in colonial times and thus were children of the petty bourgeoisie, and they have seen to it that education has not changed significantly. Textbooks used in the Frelimo schools during the liberation war were not introduced after independence on the spurious grounds that they were not academically acceptable. Despite some rewriting of course material, the style remains the colonial one: highly theoretical with little practical application or relevance to the students. Learning is by rote; teachers lecture and students copy down every word with no discussion. It is fitting that the rector of Eduardo Mondlane University uses a medieval Portuguese title, *O magnífico*, the magnificent.

In 1980 I attended a seminar on mathematics teaching. At one session led by Education Minister Graça Machel, several educators spoke in flowery Portuguese about didactic methods and teaching aids. Finally, a primary school teacher from Niassa stood up. In basic but clear Portuguese he pointed out that this elevated discussion was meaningless when he did not have a blackboard or textbooks, taught classes of 60 pupils or more, and he and his fellow teachers only had four years of primary schooling themselves. The audience broke into laughter. It was a time when an astute political intervention could have reversed the meeting. The Minister could have said it was important to consider the problems of the bulk of the teachers. Instead, she joined in the laughter. The embarrassed teacher sat down, and the colonial-trained educators continued their discourse.

In such an environment, it is the children of the elite who do best at school, and who are likely to go to university. This was reinforced with a 'new system of education', written in 1980–81 and finally introduced in 1983. It is rigidly streamed, with the decision as to whether or not a child will go to university (and thus become part of the leadership) being made after seven years of primary school. It is not unlike Britain's old 11+ exam. A decision was also taken to teach only in Portuguese, which is the first language (and thus spoken at home) only of those who received an education in colonial times. Altogether, the new system will restrict the entry to university of the children of peasants and workers who do not speak Portuguese at home and will fall behind at school from the first.

Furthermore, academic requirements for jobs have been rigidly tightened. In the period after independence, people were pushed into jobs without concern for formal education; increasingly, however, paper qualifications are becoming most important.

An apparently contradictory piece of wage legislation, passed in 1980, makes more sense in the context of this education system. Universally known by its number, 4/80, the law: sharply increased the minimum wage, rigidly linked starting salaries to educational attainment, called for a job evaluation exercise which would set wages on the basis of skills and responsibilities, and barred all other salary increases. The minimum wage was set at 62.50 MT (£1) per day for farm workers and 2,100 MT (£33) per month for other workers. Starting salary for someone with nine years of schooling is 5,500 MT (£87) per month, and with a university degree 10,000 MT.

At first viewing, it was a major income redistribution. The new minimum wage raised the incomes of tens of thousands of workers. No one had their salaries cut, but school leavers suddenly found that they were to receive less than half what they expected, which was a strong blow to middle-class aspirations.

But it had a more subtle effect as well. As an immediate sop to the aspirants to the bourgeoisie, the minimum wage was declared non-applicable to house servants. And as André de Carvalho, Secretary of State for Technical Education, later pointed out, it created a rigid rule that more edcucation means more money. Thus those who go through technical courses and then to work are always disadvantaged compared to their colleagues who continued in the academic stream at school. Skilled workers and middle-level technicians are permanently inferior to those who continue in school and become office workers and bureaucrats. The early streaming affects a child's lifetime salary potential and class position, and will clearly be influenced by the class of the parents.

There were always nagging objections to the growing power both of the bureaucrats and the private sector, but in 1979–80 doubters tended to be dismissed as 'leftists'. In one particularly vitriolic speech, President Machel reviled critics of the technocrats as 'opportunists who bring with them the virus of treason and capitulation' and who must be expelled by the revolution. Small wonder that critics held their tongues.

But the mood in 1980 was also important. Independence in Zimbabwe brought peace for the first time, and there was optimism that it would last. Finally, Mozambique would be able to concentrate on development and everything seemed possible. Frelimo's leaders were prepared to do almost anything the technocrats suggested.

It remains unclear how much the growth of privilege reflected conscious concessions to the aspirants to the bourgeoisie, and how much it really was seen as the appropriate accoutrement of higher rank. But it was clear that those who were later dismissed as aspirants to the bourgeoisie had the ear not only of the President, but of Frelimo's entire leadership, and in 1980 reached the peak of their power.

19. 'Stop Making Concessions' (1981–83)

'When we arrived in Maputo in camouflage uniforms wearing pistols, the aspirants to the bourgeoisie said, "You know, Mr President, that is not elegant. A suit and tie would look much better." And we took off our pistols. We gained elegance, but they had our weapons. We lost our ability to detect the enemy,' declared Samora Machel at a rally in June 1982. He strapped on his pistol again, and said: 'We must stop making concessions to the bourgeoisie and the aspirants to the bourgeoisie.'

Was he thinking back to his own speeches of just two years before? The tone was surely different. Instead of talking of 'authority and prestige of the director as the representative of people's power', he now called for 'breaking definitively with the bourgeoisie to consolidate people's power'.

The change began in early 1981, particularly in the military. The raid on African National Congress (ANC) houses in Matola on 30 January 1981 and the March expulsion and arrest of CIA agents showed that parts of the new officer corps were corrupt and compromised. Two of the eight new lieutenant-colonels were arrested: Fernandes Baptista had been in the army general staff and was a member of the Frelimo Central Committee, which meant the CIA had penetrated one of Frelimo's most important bodies; Jossias Dhlakhama had been head of the armoured cars division in Maputo. The shock was compounded when the two escaped 16 months later, probably with inside help.

The army was also failing to curb the spread of the anti-government Mozambique National Resistance (MNR), in part because it had forgotten its guerrilla heritage and was relying on the new heavy weapons. Finally there were widespread complaints about misconduct and maltreatment of the public by the army and police. Both reflected the move away from involving the people and towards technical solutions and status.

In a speech in late 1981, Machel lamented that 'in training our new officer class, we did not place sufficient value on the criterion of class. We gave too much importance to levels of education. We did not establish a correct balance between the army's technical growth and its political growth.' And he complained that 'many commanders acquired a taste for comfort, for the easy life, and even for luxury.'

On the economic front the debacle was as bad. There, too, the aspirants to the bourgeoisie were failing to deliver the goods. Production was not rising as fast as promised and giant state farms remained stubbornly unprofitable. The ten-year plan, the culmination of technocratic dreams, was due in June 1980, but was repeatedly delayed. Initial drafts were hopelessly unrealistic, even for that optimistic time. It was only presented to the People's Assembly in late 1981, more than a year later; it was never published and was given a hasty (if secret) burial. By then there were public criticisms of Frelimo managers acting like capitalists. They were locking themselves in their offices, making elementary mistakes they would have avoided if they had talked to workers.

By 1982 the issue was being expressed explicitly in class terms. In analysing the failure of the cooperativization of agriculture the Council of Ministers in April blamed 'middle-level officials in the state apparatus and in state companies who have a social democratic mentality or a technocratic vision of the process of cooperativization. They spread wrong ideas that oppose the conception and principles of the Party.' Furthermore they delay and misdirect equipment going to co-ops 'with the intention of undermining the cooperativization process'.

The President himself admitted to the Central Committee in August 1982 that 'the acute shortage of cadres with political convictions and maturity and a high technical capacity continues. Because of this, we had to make some concessions with regard to the class character of our cadres. This meant that we have not always been able to guarantee the predominance of new values.'

The basic problem was that the technocrats of the state group were neither red nor expert. Had they possessed the technical competence they claimed, they might have been able to manage the economy in a state capitalist way with some efficiency. Many of the mistakes in the National Planning Commission and on state farms were pure incompetence. Had they been political, they could have drawn the workers in, through the production councils and other bodies, to overcome at least some of their own technical lacks. They failed because they did neither.

The knowledge that too many concessions had been made to the bourgeoisie came at the same time as a similar realization that by concentrating so much on the technocratic elite, Frelimo was losing touch with the base. It was the war against the MNR that showed most clearly that Frelimo no longer had the wholehearted support of the peasants or of many of its other traditional supporters.

The President met with former political prisoners who had been held by Pide, and with veterans of the liberation war. Both groups complained that they had been marginalized on spurious grounds, the guerrilla fighters because they lacked the proper qualifications gained by those who stayed home and did not fight, and the political prisoners because

203

they had not gone through the politicization of the armed struggle. And there were bitter complaints about Maputo bureaucrats forgetting the countryside.

Similar meetings with the 'compromised' (see Chapter 16) and with religious leaders tried to stress that these people had a place in Frelimo and that their natural home was not with the aspirants to the bourgeoisie.

Indeed, Frelimo itself seemed to have forgotten just how fluid class positions still are. Unemployed workers will become runners for black marketeers and align themselves with the private traders. Many educated people, despite their class background, were politicized by the revolution and are prepared to push for a workers' and peasants' state. And these positions are constantly changing, as some of the fears of communism and Frelimo instilled by the Portuguese prove groundless, while some expectations of independence also prove over-optimistic.

It was in the year-long build-up to the Fourth Congress that the Party leaders realized how disaffected people had become because of the overcentralization of the state and Party. They then began to organize an assault on both state and Party structures.

It was made clear that people were free to speak at the Congress preparatory meetings, and bottled-up complaints came flowing out, showing that peasants thought they had been forgotten. Most shocking was that in areas not affected by the war against the MNR, people seemed unaware that there was a war on, and there was even reluctance to join the fighting.

This freedom continued into the Congress itself, even appearing in prepared speeches. João Ferreira, who was later appointed Agriculture Minister, told of a peasant in Nampula who, when asked why he did not produce more, said: 'When the technician is always in a hurry and won't eat the food I eat and drink my water, I think he is hurrying to where they produce more maize and cotton.'

Marcelino dos Santos admitted to the Fourth Congress that 'access to education, above all at the highest levels, is not yet governed by strict class criteria.' And the Congress itself called for a 'change in the class composition' in higher education, as well as a better 'link between the syllabus content and the practical reality of our country'.

Most dramatic, however, were the speakers from the urban shanty towns and the countryside. The very form of their comments was an implicit criticism of the formality which had been imposed on the Congress by the urban aspirants to the bourgeoisie, and which many delegates refused to accept. 'Debate' was to consist of delegates reading prepared statements, but many deviated from their prepared texts or abandoned them altogether to make bitter criticisms of the leadership.

Despite the President's caustic comments about suits and ties the year before, each male delegate who did not already have one had a suit made for him on his arrival in Maputo. 'We are well dressed here, but we await the day when it is not only for the Congress,' commented Achita Zona, a peasant woman from Niassa. She went on to say that things had been better in her area, one of the liberated zones, during the war than they were now.

The veterans of the war felt they had a special licence to speak. José N'Chumali, whose intervention is cited at the beginning of this book, was awarded a medal later in the Congress for directing the Buzi sugar mill to increase production despite repeated MNR raids. 'It is difficult to put sentiments on paper,' he said before his now famous warning about enemies inside the Central Committee and Council of Ministers.

It was two days before the President responded directly. 'Our state apparatus is corrupted, José N'Chumali. It is not directly linked to the enemy, but to comfort. We are slaves to our house and furniture. Even ministers start to think: "If I go out to the countryside, I won't have my chauffeured car with its flag flying on the front." Little by little, these things corrupt.'

The Party itself has been the centre of much of the recent class struggle. By taking authority over the state, the Party hoped to impose its more political views on the aspirants to the bourgeoisie within the civil service. In fact, as N'Chumali and others pointed out, those aspirants were entrenched in the Party.

In the original Party structuring, priority was given to practice rather than Marxist-Leninist training. Members were selected on the basis of their behaviour and attitude and were vetted by neighbours and co-workers in public meetings. It may have been shocking to the doctrinaire Marxists, but it did ensure that the majority of Party members were militant peasants and workers.

Nevertheless, higher officials are expected to be Party members, and the Party is seen as the route to advancement. So the aspirants join the Party. As was shown by the doctor in Maputo Central Hospital, it was very difficult to keep them out. Once in the Party, they tend to dominate the cell. Indeed, provincial governors and district administrators are the Party secretaries in their areas. Directors often cloak their bureaucratic position with Party credibility. So the state group is inside the Party.

Frelimo tried to move against this. A Central Committee statement issued in 1982 spoke of the state company, provincial, and district directors who, 'notwithstanding being members of the Party', transfer active Party members, try to control or sabotage the work of the Party cell, and try to prevent workers from discussing the annual plan. This 'reflects the sharpening class struggle' and also shows 'the persistence of autocratic, authoritarian, bureaucratic, and anti-popular sentiments'. Henceforth, in all companies – both state and private – the Party cell must be given whatever information it asks for, particularly with respect to raw material supplies, and must be 'consulted' in advance 'over all measures directly affecting workers' such as dismissals, punishments, awards and promotions. This was a total reversal of the 1980 instructions that the director had total power to discipline workers.

The switch to secret elections of the Party cell secretariats was also an attack on the aspirants to the bourgeoisie. Previously cell elections followed the same pattern as all others in Mozambique: the next higher body (in this case the district committee) nominated candidates who were then approved or (occasionally) rejected by the cell members. Often those named were the most articulate, who were frequently members of this upper stratum. In the 1982–83 elections, there was no nomination list at all; members wrote their preferred candidates on pieces of paper and those with the most votes became the secretariat. Often these were different from the people previously proposed by higher Party bodies.

The most dramatic change came at the Fourth Congress. The previous Central Committee of 54 people had a majority composed of ministers, governors and provincial military commanders – hardly a group that would lead to the Party taking independent control of the state. The Congress elected a 128-member Central Committee. A majority are workers and peasants not directly linked to the central state apparatus, with a significant number of guerrilla veterans and ex-political prisoners. The most outspoken delegates, including N'Chumali, were elected. Few of the state group were newly elected.

Once the campaign against the aspirants to the bourgeoisie built up steam, it was repeatedly noted that the capital had attracted all the best trained and upwardly mobile technicians. They refused to leave the city, and concentrated on making lovely plans. But no one followed the plans, because the farms and factories were run by people with less training and experience. Despite the rhetoric, however, Frelimo had been unable to dislodge them.

With the force of the Congress behind them, it was different. A month after the Congress, the President's office announced that 27 of the top technocrats – agronomists, economists, and other technicians – were to be sent out to run farms and factories. The head of the university economics faculty was sent to run a sugar plantation, while the head of planning in the Ministry of Agriculture was to run one of the large state farms.

It was just a beginning. It seems that the Congress was not the culmination of the class struggle, but only the start of a new phase. The balance of forces within the Party and state remained fragile, and no group was strong enough to evict the other. Instead, the Party took the line of least resistance, and expanded its key bodies. None of the ten-man Politburo was dropped, and one man was added. Only nine of the 54 members of the old Central Committee were dropped, and none of them was well known; rather the remaining members were swamped by the election of new militants. Economic policy remains the heart of the class struggle, and the Congress approved economic guidelines only for three years instead of five, all they could agree on. It took a month to get an agreed government reshuffle after the Congress.

But by returning to its roots, Frelimo has set in motion a continuing class struggle. N'Chumali and his new colleagues seem less likely to be blinded by the jargon of technology and central planning than their leaders have been until now. They may not accept the continued dominance of the state group, and seem likely to make the Central Committee a forum for that struggle which it has not been before.

But the aspirants to the bourgeoisie were not sitting idle. There has been considerable shifting of alliances. The commercial group moved to take control of the economy, so that the state group was under assault both from the commercial capitalists and from the workers and peasants. The result seems to have been a break between the two groups of aspirants, with parts of the state group temporarily linking up with the workers against speculative capital.

There had been a series of skirmishes before, including private traders' strikes in 1977 and 1979. The first public battles were the grapefruit and tomato wars of 1981. Maputo market stallholders and private wholesalers tended to keep retail prices high even in peak seasons, and use the glut of fruit and vegetables to push down producer prices and thus increase their mark-up; overall profits from selling a smaller quantity of fruit and vegetables at a high price were bigger than from selling more at the lower price. When the Government set new, lower fixed prices, the traders simply refused to sell the products. Using the back-up of large state farm production, the government wholesaler sold sacks of cheap grapefruit on Maputo street corners and then opened its own market stalls to sell low-price tomatoes. There was extensive press coverage, and the traders finally broke and accepted the new prices.

In 1982 the balance of power shifted. The world economic crisis, the intensifying war, and especially the worst drought in decades were pushing down both industrial and agricultural production, creating serious shortages. The black market grew explosively. Private traders used the shops and wholesalers newly bought from the state to take goods out of the official commercial circuit. This time, there were no state farm tomatoes to fight back with.

Both Frelimo and the state group had naïvely thought that the state had retained enough power over the economy to control the private sector. Instead, in many areas candonga had become the dominant market. In meeting after meeting before the Fourth Congress, candonga was raised as much more important than the MNR. The Frelimo leadership began to worry that if it was not seen to control the MNR and candonga, its own power might be threatened.

This also led to the first real battle between the two groups of aspirants. Candonga was strong enough to sabotage measures introduced by the state, and thus directly threatened state control over the economy. Furthermore, the urban middle class was now being hurt by the black market, instead of benefiting from it as expected. Bureaucrats were having trouble getting food. They saw that the traders and their families, through a tight network, were still living very well.

Elements of racism began to emerge, too, as the state group resented the continued consumption of the largely Asian commercial group and of white foreign technicians. Conflicts emerged within the state group, too. In areas like information and security, there was resentment by Blacks about Whites in key positions. In part, this was simply a demand for Africanization, to displace Whites from coveted posts they were seen to hold only because their privileged positions as colonizers had allowed them more education. But the resentment was exacerbated because some of those Whites held left-wing views antipathetic to the interests of the aspirants to the bourgeoisie.

The bureaucratic strata joined with the Party leadership to launch an assault on what were called the 'armed and unarmed bandits': the MNR and the black marketeers. In early 1983 there were summary public executions of captured MNR men and the death penalty was introduced for major economic crimes. Public flogging was begun for a whole range of economic crimes, including black marketeering. Goolam Nabi, the trader who bought the Namaacha customs staff and smuggled hundreds of tons of prawns, was convicted by a military tribunal. In April he was shot in public, to the horror of the Asian business community.

Despite this, the Fourth Congress gave an unexpected boost to the private sector. It accepted the role of the private sector more explicitly than the Third Congress had, and it revised the Party Programme to give more space to it. In part this reflects Frelimo's acceptance that Mozambique does need the resources and experience of the private sector, and in part it reflects the hope of the state group that it can discipline and redirect private capital to work as its ally rather than its opponent.

The Fourth Congress made several explicit concessions to the commercial group. Private trade was authorized in former liberated zones and in communal villages, where it had been largely banned before. Increased support was announced for private and family farmers, as well as support for local industry, regardless of whether it is private or cooperative.

At the same time, the state has tried to tighten controls. Private farmers are supposed to receive inputs from the state only if they contract to sell a percentage of their production to the state. The Congress decided that, 'We must ensure that by 1985 the state controls wholesale trade at national and provincial level and guarantees effective control of the circulation of goods.' Increased power is to be given to districts to control distribution and small industry. Shortly after the Congress, the Government set up a new State Secretariat for Road Transport to try to impose some control on private lorry owners.

Soon after the Congress, the new Agriculture Minister, João Ferreira, met with private farmers in Maputo and authorized substantially increased support, with no word about controls. Land from the Limpopo state farms, particularly Cail, was given to private farmers and better-off peasants; Ferreira specifically said he was not interested in new co-ops. This accelerated a trend which was already becoming noticeable: the creation and promotion of a new group of rich peasants. (Giving additional power to the districts could easily have a similar effect, if the district administrators, local shopkeepers, private farmers and rich peasants work together.)

What seems to have happened is that the state group has:

*accepted as necessary a three-year pause in state-dominated economic development while hoping to consolidate its position during that period and move forward later;

*joined with the workers and peasants against speculative capital because its own economic control was threatened; but

*tried to move commercial capital into production while it supported and tried to create rich peasants as new potential allies, then working with both these groups to block support for poor peasants.

The state group seems divided on all these points. For example, it has moved to reduce its dependence on the commercial group by improving and taking tighter control over the shops that serve officials. Yet some high Maputo officials are suggesting a return to private medicine and private rented housing.

Despite its internal splits, the state group will be crucial in the class struggle for the next few years, both because of its intermediate position between the commercial group and the worker-peasant dominated Central Committee, and because of its command of the state apparatus.

Part VII
Destabilization

20. Towards Regional Economic Liberation

Southern Africa is dependent on the Republic of South Africa as a focus of transport and communications, an exporter of goods and services, and as an importer of goods and cheap labour. This dependence is not a natural phenomenon nor is it simply the result of a free market economy. The nine states and one occupied territory of Southern Africa (Angola, Botswana, Lesotho, Malawi, Mozambique, Namibia, Swaziland, Tanzania, Zambia, and Zimbabwe) were, in varying degrees, deliberately incorporated – by metropolitan powers, colonial rulers, and large corporations – into the colonial and sub-colonial structures centring in general on the Republic of South Africa. The development of national economies as balanced units, let alone the welfare of the people of Southern Africa, played no part in the economic integration strategy. Not surprisingly, therefore, Southern Africa is fragmented, grossly exploited, and subject to economic manipulations by outsiders . . .

It is not the quest for liberation, but the entrenched racism, exploitation, and oppression which is the cause of conflict in Southern Africa. The power behind this is in large measure economic. Economic liberation is, therefore, as vital as political freedom.

With this declaration, entitled 'Toward Economic Liberation', the nine majority-ruled states of Southern Africa in 1980 formed SADCC, the Southern African Development Coordination Conference, and declared their intent to 'liberate our economies from their dependence on the Republic of South Africa'.

SADCC only became possible with the independence of Zimbabwe and the victory of Robert Mugabe, which brought about a dramatic restructuring of both political and economic relations in the region, and sabotaged South Africa's plans for continued economic dominance.

South Africa had always been the focus of regional development. This role actually increased as the wave of decolonization swept south and the remaining White-ruled states – Angola, Mozambique, Rhodesia and South Africa – pulled together. With UDI (Unilateral Declaration of Independence) in Rhodesia and the imposition of sanctions, British capital in Rhodesia was replaced with South African capital. Previously

Rhodesia's only rail outlets had been to Mozambique and Botswana, so a new line was built directly to South Africa.

Independence of Mozambique and tighter sanctions further integrated Rhodesia into the South African economy. And, as the physical and industrial centre of the region outside South Africa, Rhodesia was the key to any alternative strategy. The Chinese-built Tazara railway linking Zambia to the port of Dar es Salaam was the first step in linking the majority-ruled states. But Zambia, trapped in the middle, was still forced to deal with Rhodesia and South Africa.

When it became clear that majority rule in Rhodesia was inevitable, South Africa put its trust in Bishop Abel Muzorewa. It proposed a 'constellation of states' including: the bantustans; Swaziland and Lesotho, two small independent countries which are entirely integrated into the South African economy through their membership in the Customs Union and Rand Zone; Muzorewa's Zimbabwe-Rhodesia; and Malawi, South Africa's only ally among the majority-ruled states.

The victory of Zanu and Robert Mugabe put paid to that idea. Zimbabwe joined the other Front-Line States (Angola, Botswana, Mozambique, Tanzania and Zambia). Even more shocking to South Africa, they were joined by Malawi, Lesotho and Swaziland in forming SADCC.

The SADCC leaders saw as the most urgent priority the reorientation of transport and communications, which were then centred on Johannesburg. The first SADCC conference, in Maputo in November 1980, asked international donors for more than £1,000 million for projects to rehabilitate and upgrade transport and communications links. About one-third of the money was raised, and a regional transport and communications commission established in Maputo. Mozambique was the key, as its ports would serve all but two of the SADCC states.

Industry and energy are the other obvious areas of SADCC cooperation, with the particular aim of reducing dependence on South Africa for oil products and manufactured goods.

A number of changes in trade patterns did take place. The oil pipeline from Beira to Zimbabwe, closed by sanctions, was rebuilt and reopened. Mozambique stopped buying foodgrains, coal and some other goods from South Africa and bought instead from Zimbabwe. Where possible, Mozambique routed air passengers through Harare (Zimbabwe) instead of Johannesburg. Mozambique negotiated a trade agreement with Tanzania under which the countries deal in local currency, not dollars, and try to keep the amount of trade balanced each year so that neither country has a deficit with the other. This has worked well. It avoids the normal blockage to intra-regional trade, namely the lack of hard currency, and SADCC is encouraging other pairs of member countries to sign similar agreements.

SADCC itself has earned a good reputation for not building up a big bureaucracy but still moving steadily and competently to implement its

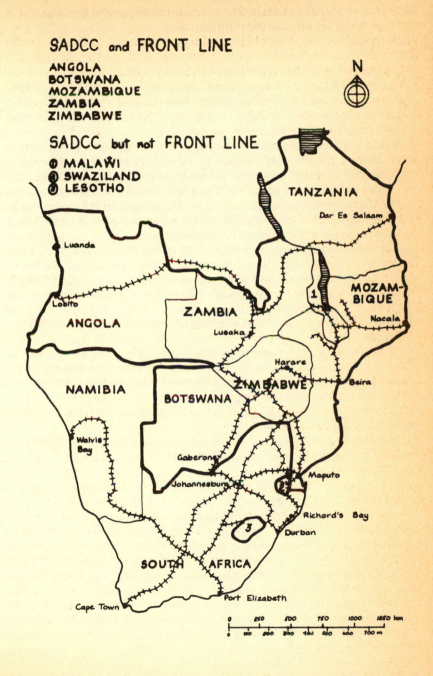

SADCC and FRONT LINE
ANGOLA
BOTSWANA
MOZAMBIQUE
ZAMBIA
ZIMBABWE

SADCC but not FRONT LINE
① MALAWI
② SWAZILAND
③ LESOTHO

N

TANZANIA
Dar Es Salaam

Luanda

Lobito

ANGOLA

ZAMBIA
Lusaka

MOZAM-
BIQUE
Nacala

Harare

NAMIBIA

BOTSWANA

ZIMBABWE

Beira

Walvis
Bay

Gaberone

Johannesburg

Maputo

Richard's Bay

Durban

SOUTH AFRICA

Cape Town

Port Elizabeth

0   250   500   750   1000 1250 km
0   100 200 300 400 500 600 700 m

projects. It works by consensus, only advancing on projects which are of mutual benefit and on which all can agree, thus avoiding conflicts and bickering.

The economic power of South Africa remains very strong in the region. Before sanctions were imposed, most Rhodesian cargo went through Mozambican ports, yet three years after Zimbabwe's independence, most of its cargoes continued to flow through South Africa. This is largely because the two main shipping agents in both Zimbabwe and Mozambique are South African: Rennies is owned by the Old Mutual insurance group; Manica Freight Services is owned 40% by Anglo-American Corporation of South Africa and 60% by Safmarine, a shipping line whose main shareholder is the South African Government. They are hardly likely to redirect traffic through Mozambique, even though it is significantly cheaper. Another important factor is containers. After Mozambican independence, the South African Government, working through Safmarine, forced the rapid containerization of most traffic, including that from Rhodesia. And Safmarine dominates the container shipping cartel which serves Southern Africa. Thus Zimbabwe's cotton and tobacco still go through the modern container port of Durban, and only non-containerized cargoes like steel and sugar were transferred back to Maputo.

South African traffic still goes through Maputo, particularly low-value bulk cargo like coal. But in 1983 South Africa began building a new railway across Swaziland to make it easier to ship cargoes to the ports of Durban and Richard's Bay from the eastern Transvaal, and thus divert more traffic away from Maputo (while giving some money to Swaziland to bribe it away from SADCC).

South Africa also backs up its economic muscle with force. It works mainly through the Mozambique National Resistance (MNR – detailed in the next chapter) to try to keep the railways from Zimbabwe to Beira and Maputo closed. Sometimes it works directly. For example, during the month before the second major SADCC conference (in Blantyre in November 1981) the bridges carrying the road, railway and oil pipeline from Beira to Zimbabwe were expertly sabotaged. The railway to Malawi remained open. But as a special slap on the wrists of President Banda for hosting the SADCC meeting, saboteurs then destroyed the marker buoys in Beira port; since the link to Zimbabwe was already cut, hitting the port could only affect Malawi. Since then, the MNR has largely kept the railway from Beira to Malawi closed, and even cut the road linking Malawi to Zimbabwe – a continuing reminder of how serious South Africa considers Banda's sin of joining SADCC instead of the constellation (despite the otherwise continued close links between Malawi and South Africa).

The third SADCC conference was in Maseru in January 1983, another insult to South Africa as Lesotho had also been expected to join the constellation. In the month before the conference, South African forces actually attacked Maseru, and the oil storage depot in Beira was sabotaged, causing more than £10 million damage to oil and facilities owned by British Petroleum. This was the base of oil supplies for the Zimbabwe oil pipeline. To fill the gap, Zimbabwe tried to import oil products from Maputo. The MNR closed the railway from Maputo to Zimbabwe, and South Africa refused to carry oil from Maputo to Zimbabwe. For several weeks there were severe fuel shortages in Zimbabwe.

In a sinister linking of sabotage and economic power, the Beira director of Manica Freight Services was convicted by a Mozambican military tribunal of links with the oil depot raid. Named Dion Hamilton, he is British but spent many years in South Africa and then in colonial Mozambique, where he had even helped train the anti-Frelimo special paratroops (GEPs).

Industry and energy cooperation have also run into difficulties, in part because of the ability of South Africa and its allies to play on regional differences and desires for self-sufficiency. For example, Zimbabwe is spending nearly £1,000 million on a series of coal-fired power stations at the Wankie colliery, which will actually reduce regional energy cooperation. It will cut purchases of Zambian hydroelectricity which had continued through the sanctions period. And the same electricity could be generated by an expansion of the Cabora Bassa power station in Mozambique that would only cost one-third as much as Wankie. The scheme has been promoted by Anglo-American, which runs Wankie. It was backed by the World Bank, which did an energy study for Zimbabwe that did not include cheaper energy souces in Mozambique because it is not a member of the Bank. (On the other hand, Mozambique presses ahead with socialist bloc sponsored planning for iron and steel production, when it would be cheaper to buy from Zimbabwe. Both sides often seem more worried about self-sufficiency than regional cooperation; no one suggests trading Mozambican electricity for Zimbabwean steel.)

It will be many years before the SADCC states can delink from South Africa (and in the cases of Lesotho and Swaziland it is probably impossible). No one is calling for unilateral sanctions. The failure of the Western powers to support sanctions against Rhodesia, which caused Mozambique and Zambia to bear the brunt, makes these countries more reluctant. Mozambique, which probably has least to lose by sanctions, stresses that its trade with South Africa is tiny compared to that of the United States or Britain. There is no point in closing the border if it simply diverts port traffic from Maputo to Durban.

Nevertheless, there are clear practical and political reasons for increased economic independence from South Africa. And, despite both internal problems and South African power, regional cooperation is increasing. The psychological impact on both South Africa and the SADCC countries is much greater than the actual shift in trade. And that is why regional cooperation has become the main target of South African destabilization.

21. Highwaymen

Half of Mozambique is like Europe in the days of highwaymen. Travelling means risking life and limb, as João Dedeus discovered. He is the student I mentioned in Chapter 2 who had his eye plucked out after the Mozambique National Resistance (MNR) ambushed the bus in which he was riding.

MNR terror and disruption are now causing economic chaos, and Frelimo actually has full control over less of Mozambique than the Portuguese did in 1974. Not bad going for an organization that is entirely the creation of foreign security services. (Unlike Unita, the MNR cannot even claim that it once was legitimate, even if it fell into bad company later.)

With independence in Zimbabwe, many Rhodesians were anxious to tell the tale of how they created the MNR. It is largely the child of Ken Flowers, former head of the Rhodesian Central Intelligence Organization, who wanted a fifth column inside Mozambique, and so drew together members of anti-Frelimo groups who had fled to Rhodesia in 1974. Some, like those who took the radio station on 7 September, felt that Portugal had sold them out and they wanted to continue the fight. But many were members of Pide (secret police), commandos, special paratroops (GEPs) and other groups described in Chapter 16, who were justifiably frightened that Mozambicans might exact retribution for past massacres and brutality. On arrival in Rhodesia, they found the only way to earn their keep was to continue the fight against Frelimo.

Ron Reid Daly, who founded the Selous Scouts, was also in on the birth of the MNR. He had modelled his Scouts on the *flechas*, Pide's private and very nasty army. And Daly tells how, in 1974, the flecha commander, Oscar Cardoso, 'with some of his men forced their way across the Mozambique border at gun-point and made their way into Rhodesia. For a time he served under my command with the rank of captain with some 40 of his men, both Black and White.' And right-wing South African-Italian journalist Giancarlo Cocca tells how he saw commando groups setting off for Rhodesia with all their vehicles and equipment in April 1974.

A central role in pulling together this mercenary force went to Orlando Cristina. One of the first Pide agents to infiltrate Frelimo in Dar es Salaam in 1964, Cristina later became right-hand man to Jorge Jardim in Beira. Jardim was godson to the Portuguese dictator António Salazar, and became an *éminence grise* in colonial Mozambique. In addition to having immense economic power, he also set up the GEPs as his own anti-Frelimo force. (Evo Fernandes, who eventually became MNR spokesman in Lisbon, also had Pide links and served as aide to Jardim in Beira.) Jardim was not acceptable in Rhodesia because he was accused of cheating on sanctions busting, but Cristina was.

Zeca Caliate later told the Portuguese newspaper *Expresso* how he was personally recruited by Cristina into the MNR in 1977. Once a Frelimo commander, Caliate went over to the Portuguese in 1973 and became part of their anti-Frelimo propaganda operation. After the 25 April 1974 coup he put together a group of 150 men and took up freelance banditry in Manica. Then he went to Portugal where he was found by Cristina.

The Central Intelligence Organization provided a training camp at 'Retreat Farm' near Bindura, north of Salisbury (now Harare). When Mozambique imposed sanctions on Rhodesia on 3 March 1976, it gave Flowers the excuse he needed. The first MNR bands moved into Manica and Tete Provinces and attacked shops and health posts near the border. (In addition to the Mozambican exiles, some ex-commandos from Angola later claimed to have been part of this first group.) In June 1976 the Rhodesians opened an anti-Frelimo radio station.

The South African, Rhodesian and Portuguese security services had always kept very close contact, and it is clear that Boss was fully informed about, and approved of, Flowers' project. Gordon Winter in his book *Inside Boss* is wrong when he says Boss 'set up' the MNR and that its first actions were carried out by South African commandos. But Winter does not exaggerate when he says, 'I was its number one propagandist right from the start.' In 1976 articles by Winter about the MNR began to appear in the South African press, and Winter admits that in 1977 he faked a picture supposedly of MNR men training 'inside Mozambique'.

The MNR did not take on a life of its own until 1977 and the arrival of André Matzangaíssa. André joined Frelimo in 1972 and became a platoon commander in the Gorongosa area. At the end of fighting in 1974 he was put in charge of Dondo, near Beira. In 1974–75 many Frelimo guerrillas felt they deserved compensation for the many years of fighting in the bush, and that they had a right to take what they wanted. The Frelimo leadership cracked down hard, and many ex-guerrillas were sent to re-education centres. André, accused of stealing a Mercedes car, was sent with other ex-guerrillas to a camp at Sacuze, near Gorongosa. He escaped in October 1976 and made his way to Rhodesia. By April 1977 the Rhodesians had made him head of the MNR. One of his first acts was to attack his old re-education camp and free other ex-guerrillas who formed the core of his army.

By 1979 the Rhodesian Special Branch had set up an operations headquarters for the MNR in Umtali (now Mutare) and established new camps at Inyanga and Chisumbanje, both close to the frontier. Supplies were flown by helicopter and aircraft to the MNR inside Mozambique. By mid-1979 the MNR was strong in Manica and northern Sofala Provinces, and was able to attack and hold a few administrative posts. It frequently attacked the railway linking Malawi to Beira.

Then things turned bad for the MNR. On 11 September 1979 the Lancaster House talks opened in London. In October the Mozambican army began an assault on the main MNR base on the top of the Gorongosa mountain (120 miles northwest of Beira). It soon became clear that the base would fall, and on 18 October Rhodesian helicopters lifted the non-Mozambicans off the mountain. On the same day, André led a diversionary raid on Gorongosa town, at the foot of the mountain. He was mortally wounded, and died while being taken back to Zimbabwe in one of the helicopters. The base fell on 22 October.

Agreement was reached at Lancaster House on 17 December, calling for a cease-fire in Zimbabwe and elections there in late February 1980. But the Rhodesians continued to support the MNR, and the delay in the withdrawal of Mozambican troops from Zimbabwe was linked to this issue. Finally, on 18 February, just days before the election, George Mitchell, then head of Rhodesian intelligence for Mozambique, called a meeting with Cristina and others to say it was over. The MNR radio stopped broadcasting two days later, and Cristina and most of the remaining MNR men went to South Africa along with Bishop Muzorewa's 'auxiliaries'. Remaining MNR fighters in northern Manica and Sofala Provinces were told to make their way to the Sitatonga mountain in southern Manica, near the Chimanimani mountains in Zimbabwe.

But on 30 June 1980, the Mozambican army captured the Sitatonga base, killing 272 men and capturing 300 more. At that point, the MNR was virtually shattered. It was leaderless and had only a few hundred men left inside Mozambique. With no base and no supplies, the remaining groups dispersed and turned to banditry. They began to attack the main north-south road, and killed several people working on the census in rural areas in August 1980. Even Alfonso Dhlakama, André's eventual successor, admitted later that 'when André died, the MNR was on the road to total destruction'. Sitatonga had been 'a shameful defeat'.

South Africa Takes Over the Reins

The remains of the MNR split into warring factions. One was headed by Dhlakama, who, like André, had been thrown out of the Frelimo army in the 1974 corruption purges. He became leader when he won a shoot-out between two groups at the Chisumbanje base in June or July 1980. As he later admitted, 'Many fighters died, including commanders and other heads. Others were maimed and crippled. All because of a power struggle.'

Cristina had backed Dhlakama, and then sold him to the South Africans. As early as 1979 South Africa had been providing some support, flying arms to Chisumbanje and then into Mozambique. A large quantity of South African arms were captured at Sitatonga.

The South African 'Special Forces' took over control of the group in 1980 and stepped up support. The MNR radio began to broadcast from the Transvaal, and by October the MNR was ensconced in a base called Zoabostad in the Transvaal. Cristina served as linkman between the MNR and the South Africans, and ran the radio, until he was assassinated at an MNR training camp near Pretoria in 1983 (much to the embarrassment of the South Africans).

Frelimo has a disconcerting habit of assuming it must be obvious that South Africa runs the MNR and that no proof is necessary. So Mozambique has produced very little direct evidence of the South African connection. It has, however, released a set of MNR documents found stuffed down a latrine when the Mozambican army captured an MNR base at Garagua in southern Manica on 7 December 1981. These typewritten documents appear genuine, and include reports and minutes of meetings between Dhlakama and the South Africans at Zoabostad in October and November 1980. (The earlier quotes from Dhlakama come from these documents.)

They draw quite a clear line. One report quotes Dhlakama as saying, 'you South Africans are like my parents' and that 'everything depends on you'. He also thanks them 'for evacuating my wife from Zimbabwe to South Africa'. In one meeting, an unidentified 'Colonel Charlie' says he will send specialists and instructors to teach the MNR how to use heavy weapons and do sabotage operations. And Charlie adds: 'The instructors who go to Mozambique will not only teach, but also participate in attacks.'

One of these 'instructors' was Alan Gingles, killed trying to mine the Beira-Zimbabwe railway in October 1981. Mozambican soldiers came across him and shot the mine; he was blown up and only his ear was found, which at least proved he was White. But in his pack was a partly finished novel about Northern Ireland, written in a school notebook. It contains, ironically, his own obituary: 'Death, as he now knew, was anything but pleasant or glorious.' The London *Observer* eventually showed the handwriting was that of Gingles. Born in Larne in Northern Ireland, he joined the Ulster Defence Regiment and went on to Sandhurst and the Royal Irish Rangers. Transferred to Germany, he became bored and resigned his British commission, moving to Rhodesia to join the Selous Scouts. With independence there, he joined the South African

Defence Force. An SADF statement in 1981 said Gingles was killed 'in action against terrorists' in the 'operational area'.

(Gingles had a similar history to Robert Hutchinson who moved from the British Army to the Rhodesian SAS to the SADF before being killed by the ANC in the raid on Matola in January 1981. About 300 former British servicemen are in the SADF, effectively with British government permission, according to the *Observer*.)

At first, the MNR tried to cover South African involvement. The minutes of the 9 November 1980 meeting quote Cristina suggesting that the MNR 'destroy the power line transporting energy from Cabora Bassa to South Africa to mask the existence of South African support'. The line was cut for the first time on 27 November 1980. Cristina told Dhlakama that as South Africa gained only a little power from Cabora Bassa, it would do no harm. This proved wrong during the unusually cold winter of 1981, when the lack of Cabora Bassa power meant electricity cuts in the Transvaal. The same mistake was not made during the 1983 winter, when the drought caused water shortages to power stations, restricting South Africa's electricity generating; this time, the Cabora Bassa line was not cut.

In the October 1980 meetings South Africa promised to step up supplies, although it said air drops were too expensive and that supplies would have to go by sea. Supplies are frequently left along the coast, apparently by the private South African boats that often fish illegally off the Mozambican coast. One Durban-registered boat was caught in 1982 returning from Inhambane with no fishing tackle and its refrigerator disconnected; this suggests it had not been there for the fishing.

But there were also many reports that air drops of food, arms and even uniforms continued. One of the most graphic was from a 17-year-old boy, Alexandre Zaqueu. In 1983 he was kidnapped and taken to Tome, the main MNR base in Inhambane. He later escaped and told the daily *Noticias*: 'Sometimes airplanes came at night. They didn't land. But they turned on lights so strong that in the camp it seemed like day. Then they began to drop crates tied to a kind of giant umbrella – obviously a parachute which he had never seen before. When the Tome base was finally taken by the Mozambican army on 23 August 1983, they found nine tons of equipment left behind by fleeing rebels. Navendra Bhay, a Portuguese national who was being held prisoner at the base when it came under attack, told me later that the material had only been air-dropped ten days before the Tome base fell.

Zaqueu also reported that while he was in the Tome camp there were six white men who spoke English and were teaching people to use radio equipment. South Africa is supplying sophisticated communications equipment; British-made Racal radios have been captured from the MNR. A British wildlife expert, John Burlison, who was kidnapped by the MNR in 1982, reported that his captors were in radio contact with a central base three times a day. Mozambican authorities claim that South African spotter planes keep track of troop movements and radio that information to the MNR.

It became increasingly hard for South Africa to deny its involvement, even without information from the Mozambican Government. In early 1983 the US State Department issued a public statement accepting that the MNR 'receives the bulk of its support from South Africa'.

The handover of the MNR to South Africa should not obscure the continuing links between South African and Rhodesian intelligence, nor the willingness of both to use the MNR for other purposes. This is most clearly shown by the case of Amaro Silva, who was executed in June 1982. A well-paid Maputo secondary school teacher, he crossed the border to South Africa in 1978 and turned himself in to the police there. He was sent to police headquarters in Pretoria, and passed on to the MNR training camp in Bindura, Rhodesia. Eventually he became an officer there, and under Special Branch instructions in 1978 assigned other Mozambicans to attempt (unsuccessfully) to bomb the Maputo house of Zanu leader Robert Mugabe. Silva returned to Mozambique and was arrested. In 1981 he escaped and went again to South Africa. This time the South Africans used him for the kidnapping of ANC member Joe Pillay from Swaziland. Next he was sent on an anti-Swapo mission to Namibia. Finally he returned to Mozambique with the MNR, and was caught again.

'Rhodesian'-South African links continued through the MNR well after Zimbabwe's independence. This is shown best by the sabotage on 29 October 1981 of the rail and road bridges linking Beira to Umtali (now Mutare). That attack was timed to coincide with the movement of four trainloads of arms for the Fifth Brigade then being trained by the North Koreans in Umtali. Thus the raid had the double purpose of cutting an SADCC link and blocking a vital weapons shipment. Only the Umtali Special Branch knew of the shipment. The Special Branch head had not changed since the late 1970s, and thus he was the same one who had been directing MNR activities; he left Zimbabwe shortly after the bridge raid.

Once the South Africans took over, the MNR became dramatically successful. In 1981 it was active in southern Manica and Sofala Provinces, forcing traffic on the main north-south road to travel in military convoy and eventually closing the road altogether. By the end of the year, it was moving freely through much of northern Manica and Sofala as well, and had moved south of the River Save. In February 1982 President Samora Machel toured Inhambane and Gaza Provinces to try to rally local people to oppose the MNR. But within weeks some of the areas he had visited were inaccessible.

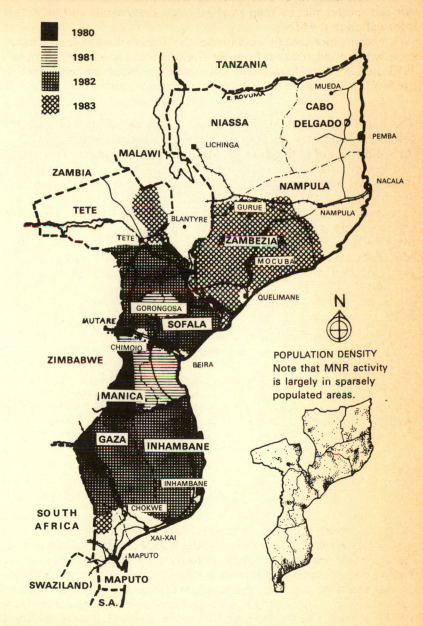

AREAS WHERE TRAVEL WAS DIFFICULT DUE TO MNR ACTIVITY

1980
1981
1982
1983

TANZANIA

R. ROVUMA

NIASSA

MUEDA

CABO DELGADO

PEMBA

LICHINGA

MALAWI

ZAMBIA

NAMPULA

NACALA

TETE

GURUE

NAMPULA

BLANTYRE

TETE

ZAMBEZIA

MOCUBA

QUELIMANE

GORONGOSA

N

SOFALA

MUTARE

CHIMOIO

ZIMBABWE

BEIRA

MANICA

POPULATION DENSITY
Note that MNR activity
is largely in sparsely
populated areas.

GAZA

INHAMBANE

INHAMBANE

SOUTH
AFRICA

CHOKWE

XAI-XAI

MAPUTO

SWAZILAND

MAPUTO

S.A.

Most of the areas affected by the MNR are sparsely populated. Part of southern Manica and Sofala was a huge Portuguese hunting reserve. The paved road had only been built by the Portuguese shortly before the end of the liberation war; I can remember driving along it in 1980 and not seeing anyone for more than an hour, in stark contrast to zones further south where the roads are always crowded by pedestrians. Northern Sofala contains the Gorongosa game park and mountain, and some of Mozambique's dense forest. Except for the coastal strip, Inhambane is dry and thinly populated; northern Gaza is semi-desert.

Thus until early 1982 the MNR was operating in largely uninhabited areas which were so vast that it was extremely difficult for Frelimo to pursue its forces. With South African supplies, they needed no contact with local people and could easily ambush traffic on remote roads and railway lines.

Bases were established in remote parts of Inhambane (like Tome) and Gaza, generally less than 200 miles from South Africa and thus within easy air-drop range. From there it was not hard to push out to the populated Inhambane coast and simply cut off the main road to Maputo.

But the push south failed to penetrate the populous Limpopo valley and came to a halt in mid-1982. Late that year in a much more open show of support, South Africa sent hundreds of MNR men across the border from the Kruger wildlife park. They tried to move to the sea south of the Limpopo valley and cut off the capital from the rest of the country. There was heavy fighting only 60 miles from Maputo. But this push also failed, leaving only border areas under MNR influence.

Thus in the south, the military situation changed little from mid-1982 until mid-1983. But in August 1982 South Africa made its most dramatic move. It set up bases inside Malawi, and pushed hundreds of well-armed and well-trained men into the border areas of Tete and Zambézia Provinces. During September and October they swept east through Zambézia virtually unopposed, burning tea factories and cotton gins, as well as mining roads and destroying dozens of vehicles. A number of foreigners were captured, including a six-person Bulgarian road survey team. In Gúruè, the town at the centre of the tea industry, an MNR band captured the army barracks and looted weapons and uniforms before marching down the high street singing and then disappearing into the surrounding tea estates. Attacks occurred only 25 miles from the coast and a similar distance from the provincial capital, Quelimane.

Then the offensive collapsed as quickly as it had started. After mid-November there were only sporadic incidents, except in the mountainous districts directly bordering Malawi. Two events precipitated the collapse. Mozambique said that South Africa had established bases in south Malawi for the MNR and on 27 October Foreign Minister Joaquim Chissano went to Malawi. He reminded President H. Kamuzu Banda that the MNR was also harming Malawi by cutting the railway to Beira and the road to Zimbabwe, thus cutting Malawi's fuel supply. Soon after the Banda-

Chissano meeting, the bases were apparently closed and emergency oil supplies for Malawi began to flow through the northern Mozambican port of Nacala.

It was never clear if Banda himself approved the South African bases. The *Economist* magazine *Foreign Report* (30 September 1982) argued that he did not, and that South Africa had specifically directed the MNR to cut off Malawi from Mozambique because of Malawi's increasing involvement in SADCC.

The second event was on 2 November, less than a week after the Banda-Chissano meeting. The Mozambican army captured the main MNR base in Zambézia, about 30 miles from the Malawi border, and freed the six Bulgarians.

Without bases in either Malawi or Zambézia, the MNR offensive collapsed. But that collapse was shortlived. In early 1983 bases in Malawi were reactivated, and the MNR again pushed across Zambézia. Mozambique had improved its defences, and the MNR could no longer attack towns like Gúruè. But it still spread across the province, and this time it reached the sea and easier access to supplies, although there were also reports of light planes flying from Malawi to bases in Gúruè district. By mid-year, the MNR had pushed into neighbouring Nampula Province, meaning it was active in nine of Mozambique's 11 provinces.

South Africa's much greater success with the MNR also reflects a change in tactics. Rhodesia wanted the MNR primarily for intelligence, particularly as to the location of Zanu bases. Only a secondary purpose was to attack economic targets. Thus the MNR under the Rhodesians made some effort to win over the population. It often distributed food and clothes brought from Rhodesia, which made it quite popular in northern Sofala during the 1979 drought there. Indeed, the MNR may have been moving to the creation of semi-liberated zones.

For its part, South Africa is not looking for intelligence and thus does not need the support of local people. Also it seems uninterested in supplying and supporting 'liberated zones'. Its main aims seem to be disruption and economic damage: a much more traditional policy of 'destabilization'. Indeed, reports from Gorongosa, an area that gave the MNR some support in 1979, suggest that the MNR in 1982 simply harassed people out of their homes and villages without ever trying to gain converts.

Thus the MNR concentrates on destroying economic targets and disrupting transport. It has destroyed 1,000 shops, hundreds of villages and vehicles, 40 locomotives, 20 sawmills, cotton gins and tea factories. New communal villages and their facilities such as health posts are a regular target. Crops are burned in the field and in peasant grain stores. In dry areas of Inhambane the MNR killed people and stuffed the bodies down wells to poison what little water there was. Party officials and militiamen are usually killed, and anyone linked to Frelimo, like the schoolteacher, may have ears and perhaps lips and breasts cut off.

Special attention is paid to attacking traffic, both by mining roads and by particularly nasty ambushes. Trains and buses have been machine-gunned. People driving along the roads in cars and lorries are forced to stop and stay in their vehicles while the rebels build a fire underneath, so the victims are roasted alive.

It is like Europe in the days of the highwaymen, and, not surprisingly, people are afraid to travel. There are parts of Manica and Sofala where no one goes and where there has not been a government presence for some time. In other areas, government officials still travel, but health, state farm, and agricultural marketing workers have been killed.

The aim seems to be simply to remove areas from Frelimo's control; there seem to be few areas under effective MNR control. The captors of wildlife expert John Burlison walked him for hundreds of miles but he never once visited an MNR-controlled village. Eduardo Ribeiro, a Portuguese trader, walked for more than 600 miles with the MNR after he was captured in December 1982. He told me: 'Whenever we passed a settlement, it was empty, because the people had fled.'

After one of my BBC reports on the MNR in 1982, MNR spokesman Evo Fernandes wrote to the BBC inviting me 'to visit the areas under the control of the MNR'. To his surprise, I accepted, but he was never able to arrange the trip.

Support?

Frelimo dismisses the MNR as 'armed bandits' who cannot be treated as a legitimate opposition; and they have not created liberated zones in the way Frelimo did during the liberation war. Yet all the fighters are Mozambicans, and it is clear from their rapid spread that some peasants feed and at least tacitly support them. How great is that support, and where does it come from?

There has been a steady stream of disaffected people switching to the MNR. The first group was obvious: Pides, flechas, commandos, and so on who had opposed Frelimo all along.

The second set, like commanders André and Dhlakama, were guer-rillas, soldiers, policemen and others who could not accept the rigid Frelimo morality and the lack of reward after the war. Attacks on re-education camps were a favourite way to recruit this sort of person. And there are still regular defections of disgruntled Mozambican soldiers unhappy with the discipline and poor conditions.

A third set of people are those who tried unsuccessfully to rise in Frelimo; it was noted especially in Inhambane that a number of candidates defeated in local elections in 1978 have since gone over to the MNR.

A fourth group are the witch doctors and Portuguese-appointed *régulos* deposed by Frelimo at independence. They still have some following, which they can sometimes take with them to the MNR. In turn, when the MNR moves into an area it often returns to power the old régulo and local witch doctor.

Mysticism and witch doctors are particularly important. Dhlakama tells his soldiers that the 'spirits' of the MNR will kill anyone who defects. In October 1979, the witch doctors told commander André that it was safe to attack Gorongosa town because all the Mozambican soldiers were on the mountain. In fact, the population and the witch doctors had turned against the MNR (reportedly because of abuse of local women) and the army was waiting. This was the attack where André was fatally wounded.

Tribalism is also important. The MNR recruited in Shona-speaking areas of Manica and Sofala by arguing that Frelimo is dominated by southerners. Southern Manica is fertile ground for this sort of recruitment because people there know little about Frelimo; Frelimo never fought there during the liberation war, and before it could do much post-independence organizing, the area fell under Rhodesian attack. In parts of Manica this has been sufficient to build a real local following. Several people were jailed by a military tribunal in 1983 for organizing local people into groups of 12 families to feed the MNR.

The limitations of this base are shown most clearly by the move south in 1982 into Inhambane and Gaza. Both are Shangana speaking and it is pointless to object to 'southern dominance' in the south. Furthermore, Frelimo was better known and had much stronger support, particularly because a drought relief programme in 1980 saved many lives. Thus the MNR was forced to switch to terrorizing the people there.

Recruiting tactics for ordinary soldiers are simple enough. Young men (and sometimes women) are kidnapped from buses or villages. In the army newspaper *Combat*, one young man told how during a 150-mile recruiting trip 500 people were collected in this way. As John Burlison reported, those caught escaping were shot. After some basic training, each new 'recruit' is sent out with more experienced fighters on raids. Then he is told that because of his killing, he will be executed by Frelimo if he is caught. So he becomes part of the group. But it is also clear that the excitement and promises of money, compared to the dull, poor life in the countryside, are enough to make many men quite happy to stay with the MNR.

Also, Frelimo tactics of press-ganging young men into the army send some over to the MNR instead. Often they just flee into the bush where they are picked up by the MNR, and then see little difference which side they are forced to fight for.

In a meeting in Vilanculos, Inhambane Province, in February 1982, the crowd complained to President Samora Machel about the brutality of the MNR and demanded arms and protection. Then Machel asked if the fighters were South Africans or Mozambicans. The crowd replied: 'Mozambicans'. 'Therefore, they are your children and your brothers', who you feed and support, said Machel. He went on to argue that they are like domesticated animals gone wild, or like the 'tsotsis' (thugs) of Johannesburg. And once a young man is in the MNR, his family does feel pressure to support it with food and intelligence.

Equally important, however, is peasant tolerance of the MNR. Peasants must actively support Frelimo before they will risk their necks to report the presence of anti-government guerrillas and join militias to fight them. The MNR's ability to move through densely populated areas of Zambézia (very different from the bush further south) means local people are not reporting them.

In part this comes from Frelimo's failure to carry out dynamic political mobilization after independence, so that some people know little about Frelimo. For its part, the MNR never puts forward an ideology and limits itself to vague anti-communism. But in its initial contacts with people, it does draw on local discontent, particularly about the lack of consumer goods. In some places the MNR gained local support by preferentially attacking traders who cheat the people and bosses who abuse workers. Forced villagization has also caused resentment, and some people must agree with the MNR when it says that destroying communal villages is 'liberating' the occupants. Some peasants forced off land to allow for state farm expansion also seem to have supported the MNR.

The Robin Hood aspect of the MNR also gains it support. When a shop is sacked, some of the goods are distributed to local people and the rest taken to feed the MNR. This point can be sharpened when the Mozambican army arrives and forces villagers to return goods given to them by the MNR. Sometimes, too, the MNR will introduce itself to local people with parties, usually cooking stolen food and cattle.

Thus the MNR ingratiates itself with the population while it gains control. Only later do people realize that the raided shop will not reopen and that they have even less to buy than before, and that they must feed the MNR guerrillas, too. By then, it is too late. In many areas there is considerable fear and bitterness about the MNR. Many people have had friends and relatives killed, kidnapped, raped and mutilated. In some areas captured MNR men are mutilated and left to die, or stoned to death. There was strong public support for the summary public executions of captured MNR guerrillas in early 1983.

The new harsher policy has not been totally popular, however. In February 1983 President Samora Machel announced flatly that, 'Those who give information to the bandits will die with the bandits, those who feed the bandits will die with the bandits, those who deal with the bandits will die with the bandits.' In Zambézia there were protests from doctors and priests that this was used as a licence to create 'free fire zones' and that innocent people were being killed near MNR bases and in villages occupied by the MNR. In combination with forced villagization, the policy seemed to be having some military success, but it was not bringing political converts to Frelimo.

In large measure peasants are trying to save their own skin and will support whichever side will protect them. They are not pleased when the Mozambican army passes through and beats them up for supporting the MNR and then the MNR comes through and beats them up for supporting Frelimo. Forced villagization causes even more resentment when the army cannot protect the villages after they are created.

The problem was illustrated when an MNR group moved across Sofala in 1982. In mid-July they hit the sawmill town of Savane, 35 miles north of Beira, and word spread (even to me in Maputo) that they were in the area. They stayed around Savane for a week and then moved 10 miles southwest towards Mafambisse, a large town on the main road with one of Mozambique's main sugar mills.

On Saturday, 31 July small groups moved into the outskirts of town. They interrogated and roughed up peasants in the fields and raided houses, taking food and clothing. They seemed anxious to make their presence known. Some played radios or drums, and danced and sang. As word spread, the most common response was for people to dig a pit and bury their recently harvested rice and any valuables. Many people moved nearer to the road or to town. The army barracks not far up the road was told, but did nothing.

That evening the MNR attacked a shop less than a mile off the main road and forced about 100 local men and women to carry the booty north into the bush to their camp. All were released and given salt to pay for the work.

On Sunday a group of local militiamen attacked, but had to withdraw when they ran out of ammunition. The Matzangaisas, as they are known locally after their first commander, stayed near town singing and dancing. Finally, on Sunday afternoon the army arrived and killed several MNR men. The rest escaped into the bush and regrouped at the nearby village of Mutua. There they asked who had been régulo. The villagers said he was no longer there, so the MNR named his brother as new headman, despite his reluctance. Two days later the army arrived and arrested the new 'régulo'. Then the MNR returned to ask about their new headman. Two women who did not give proper answers had their ears cut off.

Only then did the army move in reinforcements, but that just pushed the Matzangaisas further north. On the night of 9 August they were back in Savane where they raked a crammed passenger train with machine-gun fire, killing 14 and wounding nearly 100.

New Tactics

The rapid growth of the MNR, and of South African support for it, caught Frelimo by surprise, and led to a major change in tactics. After winning the guerrilla war against the Portuguese, the Mozambicans argued that the new threat was a conventional one like the 1975 South African invasion of Angola. This required a modern army, and Mozambique turned to the Soviet Union for heavy weapons, MIGs and training.

The merit of the choice was shown, first in April 1979 when a Mozambican artillery battalion helped the Tanzanians take Kampala from Libyan troops, and then in October 1979 when Mozambican artillery repulsed Rhodesia's largest attack of the war (providing an important boost to the Lancaster House talks then under way).

In mid-1980, the MNR really were 'armed bandits' as the Mozambicans claimed, and it seemed an easy job of mopping up. There was a peace euphoria in Maputo, and militias in the countryside were disarmed and disbanded.

Well into 1981, Frelimo officials still believed their own rhetoric about 'armed bandits' and refused to accept the extent of stepped-up South African support. Finally, Frelimo realized it had a different kind of war on its hands. Without dismantling the conventional forces, which were still necessary to face an Angola-style attack, Frelimo mounted an entirely new campaign based on its guerrilla traditions.

In March 1982, President Machel appointed military commanders for all the affected provinces. They are experienced guerrilla commanders, not Soviet-trained heavy weapons specialists. All come from the region where they are serving and speak the local language. Their main task is political mobilization, to ensure that people support Frelimo and will actively defend their villages against the MNR. Militias and provincially based army units were trained. Veterans of the liberation war were pulled out of other jobs and sent to help with training and organizing.

In a dramatic speech in June 1982, President Machel handed out weapons to the first of the new militias. By later in the year there were thousands of trained militiamen and women in the villages, factories, and state farms, and there were reports of them repelling MNR attacks and pursuing MNR bands into the bush.

The regular army, too, was better trained, fed and disciplined, and began to pursue the MNR. A doctor commented: 'The wounded soldiers I used to see were shot from behind. Now they are shot from the front.' After the second MNR offensive in Zambézia, the President visited there personally. He sacked the provincial military commander and demoted some local commanders who had failed to pursue the Matzangaisas.

Frelimo also realized that it could never have the helicopters and four-wheel drive vehicles to give it the kind of mobility required for modern anti-guerrilla tactics. So it began training commando-style units which actually follow MNR bands for days on foot, depending on local people for information.

The large expansion of the army put a heavy training burden on Frelimo, which called in several hundred Tanzanians for basic training and 500–1,000 trainers and advisers from the Eastern bloc (Cuba, Soviet Union, East Germany, Hungary, Czechoslovakia and North Korea).

Zimbabwe provided more than 1,000 combat troops to guard the pipeline, road, and railway from Beira to Zimbabwe, as well as to attack MNR concentrations near it. The combination of Mozambican and Zimbabwean troops kept the road, railway and pipeline open normally.

In the south, the combination of better tactics and training began to pay dividends, and the Mozambican army regained the upper hand. In late 1982 it repulsed the major MNR offensive from South Africa, and in early 1983 it reopened the railway from Maputo to Zimbabwe. Later in the year the army moved against bases in Inhambane, destroying the MNR provincial command at Tome.

If South Africa had not taken up the reins in 1980, the MNR would have disappeared. If South Africa withdrew support now, it would be much easier to suppress.

But whatever happens, Frelimo must make up for two years of inaction and disbelief. Half the country is disrupted. Economic damage is massive and many of the major development projects are affected; there is no point in talking about iron or gas if no one can safely get to the sites to do geological studies. Millions of people have been affected; many will be angry and embittered.

Regaining control from roaming bands of heavily armed men in a country as vast and sparsely populated as Mozambique will take years under the best of conditions. So long as South Africa steps up its support to match improvements in the Mozambican army, it will be extremely difficult for Frelimo to keep the initiative. And it will be all the harder for Mozambique to make the essential economic changes that will regain the support of the peasants.

It is depressingly clear just how well destabilization works.

22. Walking the East–West Tightrope

Frelimo has always tried to have a very open foreign policy while maintaining its own commitment to socialism. Thus it successfully retained support from both the Soviet Union and China during and after the liberation war, and has built links with the capitalist world. In general, though, it has tried to avoid the big powers and build closer ties with small ones, especially those who helped during the liberation war.

Its problem with the big powers is partly that Washington sees Southern Africa as an area of East-West confrontation (and thus Mozambique as an ally of the Soviet Union) while Moscow does not. So Mozambique gets a lot of stick from the West and insufficient help from the East.

Mozambique has been on and off the US aid blacklist, but during the later years of the Carter administration relations improved. In particular, Carter's human rights line and his pressure on South Africa did help keep Pretoria in check. With the election of Ronald Reagan, relations sank. The Reagan administration's policy of 'constructive engagement' with South Africa gave Pretoria a licence to attack its neighbours. And in the investigations following the first South African raid, in January 1981, Frelimo seems to have been genuinely shocked to find that the CIA had infiltrated even the Central Committee, and was apparently passing information on to South African security services.

The Soviet Union is Mozambique's main arms supplier. But its other help has been limited. It has provided a number of technicians such as doctors, teachers and geologists, although this has not been completely successful. Unlike other foreign teachers, many of the Soviets do not learn Portuguese and instead use interpreters. Soviet doctors are criticized for refusing to follow Mozambican prescribing rules and for not teaching Mozambicans. The Soviet Union has also built schools and has some Mozambican students in the USSR. But what Mozambique needs most is capital, and this has not been forthcoming. There is only a joint fishing company and a Soviet cotton project in Nampula Province, which is less than the involvement of several small countries.

The issue came to a head when Mozambique applied to join Comecon, the socialist economic community. The application was backed by East Germany and Bulgaria, which argued that the Soviet Union had a historic responsibility to support the new communist countries. But the USSR rejected the bid, on the grounds that it could not subsidize Mozambique to the extent it supports Comecon members Cuba and Vietnam. On his return from the unsuccessful bid, a frustrated Marcelino dos Santos noted that more developing countries were choosing socialism, and that 'Comecon must adjust to this new reality'.

The Soviet Union does not see any strategic interest in the region, especially as Mozambique refuses to give it a military base. One of Frelimo's most outspoken political stands, written into its constitution, is in support of 'the principle of turning the Indian Ocean into a non-nuclear zone of peace'. This means no US or Soviet bases in the coastal countries.

Finally the Soviet Union justifies its failure to support Frelimo on the grounds that it is not a full Marxist-Leninist party, but merely 'Marxist oriented'. Some Mozambicans comment that one thing the US and USSR have in common is that they do not believe Blacks can be Marxists.

Mozambique has much warmer relations with a number of European countries, particularly East Germany, Bulgaria, Sweden, Holland, France and Italy. There are three reasons for this.

First, with the exception of France, these are countries that helped during the liberation war, and Frelimo remembers and trusts its early friends. Marcelino dos Santos noted that the governments of Holland and Sweden (as well as other Scandinavian countries) 'recognized Frelimo during the armed struggle. None of us ever talked to members of the British, French, or West German governments then.'

Second, because Mozambique is a small country, it is easier to deal with other small countries. Mozambique's President can actually get to know the East German President, and ministers can meet their counterparts, which can never happen with the big powers.

Third, there is a sense of small countries clubbing together for mutual help in the face of exploitation by the big powers. Smaller countries like Italy or East Germany are at a disadvantage in their own economic groups, and can strengthen their positions through closer links with developing countries. This also provides opportunities to use the divisions between the big and small countries in the East and West blocs. This showed up in East German and Bulgarian backing for Mozambique's Comecon membership, and in Italian and Dutch support for EEC assistance to Mozambique in the face of West German and British objections.

All six of these smaller countries have provided significant aid and investment, as well as the more traditional technical assistance. East Germany provides the best credit terms of any of Mozambique's partners. And East Germany and Bulgaria take seriously their policy of joint long-term planning with Mozambique.

A seventh important partner is Cuba. Although it cannot provide capital, it has sent technicians and teachers to Mozambique, and is training 5,000 Mozambicans in Cuba. There are a similar number of Mozambicans being trained in East Germany, considerably more than in the USSR.

Mozambique's growing foreign exchange crisis led Frelimo to make several concessions. For example, Mozambique had refused to sign any agreement with the EEC or West Germany because of an almost theological argument over the 'Berlin clause'. All international treaties and agreements with West Germany include a clause which extends the agreement to West German-controlled parts of Berlin. In treaties with the East bloc, the clause refers simply to 'West Berlin' and Mozambique would have been happy to sign that. But in treaties with the rest of the world, West Germany uses a form of words which could mean that West Berlin is a state in the Federal Republic. East Germany objects, so Mozambique would never sign. (Tanzania and Zimbabwe, among others, dismissed this as a dispute of no worth to them and signed similar agreements.) Finally, however, in an attempt to unblock EEC development aid previously vetoed by West Germany and to try to gain some political support from Germany and Britain, Mozambique caved in and signed. It now seems likely to join the EEC's Lome Convention.

Having watched the International Monetary Fund (IMF) force both Tanzania and Zimbabwe to give up socialist goals, Frelimo remained implacably opposed to joining it and the World Bank. But as the balance of payments continues in the red and credit is increasingly hard to find, Mozambique opened talks with the IMF in late 1983, and may have to succumb to this as well.

Improved links with Western financial bodies are also seen in the light of growing South African aggression. Frelimo hopes that if it increases Western investment and involvement in Mozambique then these countries will stop South Africa from attacking their new property.

Relations with the United States have also improved significantly. Mozambique had joined the other Front-Line States in regular vitriolic denunciations of the US policy of support for South Africa. It threw out the CIA agents the same day as a USAID team arrived in Maputo, ensuring maximum impact. One of President Reagan's top advisers on Africa admitted to me afterwards that the pressure worked: 'Even our skins aren't that thick.' So the US eased off slightly.

Then Mozambique began courting the Americans. In less than a year five Mozambican ministers visited the US, all carrying the same message: Mozambique's main enemy is South Africa, not the US, and Mozambique does not have the same enemies as its friends in the East bloc. In response to US complaints, Frelimo toned down press criticism of the US inside Mozambique. (For all its trumpeting about its 'free press' at home, the US has an obsession with press criticism abroad which it believes is orchestrated by the government. So when US officials met Machel, at the top of their list was always the relatively mild press comment on the US.)

Foreign Minister Joaquim Chissano asked the US to take a public stand against destabilization, and it went part way with its statement that South Africa provides the 'bulk' of the support for the MNR. The US also named an ambassador to Maputo – filling a post left vacant for three years – and increased food aid. Mozambique named its first ambassador to Washington.

Foreign, and especially Cuban, troops are a key issue in US-Mozambique-South Africa relations. By late 1983, only Zimbabwe had provided combat troops, largely to protect its own access to the sea. Mozambican officials pointed out that when it had asked at the United Nations for international military help against the Rhodesians, only the East bloc had responded, and thus western countries should not complain now that all of Mozambique's military support came from the socialist bloc. Even so, they had never provided combat troops, and Mozambican officials make clear that they are most reluctant to bring in other foreign troops – but they will do so if there is no other choice. It was partly in order to reaffirm this right that Mozambique supported the presence of Libyan troops in Chad and Soviet troops in Afghanistan.

Chissano also warned that 'if international measures are not taken to stop South Africa from escalating its aggression, Mozambique in the long run will require more and more military assistance from the socialist countries.' The US responded by privately warning the South Africans that further escalation would bring in Cuban troops, which Washington did not want.

Not everyone in the South African leadership would be opposed; for some, it would be the excuse they want to invade Mozambique. In any case, private warnings are not enough.

South Africa does not want to overthrow the governments of Mozambique and the other Front-Line States. But it does want to bring them to their knees and keep them there, to ensure that they never present a viable alternative to apartheid.

Growing South African aggression preoccupied the eight of the nine SADCC heads of state who met in Maputo on 13 July 1983 (only Malawi's Banda was missing). Their final statement admitted that, 'South Africa can invade and occupy sovereign states, blow up vital installations, and massacre populations at no apparent cost to its relations with its main allies.' They pointed out that, 'Some of the friends of South Africa, who provide the racist regime with the capital, technology, management skills, and deadly weapons necessary to carry out such a policy also seek to improve their relations with SADCC.' The best way to improve these relations would be 'to use their influence to check the aggression being waged against SADCC member states'. They obviously felt that instead, South Africa's friends had given their imprimatur to destabilization by the approval earlier that year of a massive IMF loan to South Africa, as well as steady increases in sales of military equipment to South Africa.

For the first time as a group, SADCC actively backed disinvestment in South Africa. The heads of state called for 'a significant transfer of the resources which go to shoring up apartheid to the development of the independent countries of southern Africa. This would be an investment in peace and stability, and an investment in the future.'

Part VIII
The Future

23. Is Socialist Development Possible in Mozambique?

Riding on a bus in northern Ghana a few years ago I noticed several large yams under the driver's seat. But he was not taking food home for his family. At each police checkpoint along the road he had to hand over a yam as a bribe, or 'dash', in order to be allowed to pass. Yams are expensive, and I estimated that more than one-third of the passengers' fares had been paid out in that way. Mozambique, too, has many control points along the road. But the soldiers there apologetically ask for cigarettes only after they have said you can pass.

Public corruption is popularly treated as a condition of the Third World. And from a glance at the history of Britain and the United States, it is clear that corruption is often more common when countries are developing. But I lived for ten years in Boston where official corruption is so endemic and accepted that a member of the state assembly was re-elected while he was in jail for stealing state funds. Mozambique is vastly less corrupt than Boston.

In an important way, corruption and bribery reflect the citizen's attitude and relationship to the state. A doctor friend working in Mozambique, who has worked in several other developing countries, talks of hospitals in those countries where you have to bribe the orderly to get a bedpan and where you have to buy all your drugs at exorbitant prices. He says that, 'The importance of Mozambique is that it is one place where primary health care might work and might be shown to work. Whatever their shortcomings, the health posts are not corrupt.' After eight years, Frelimo has transformed the entire mentality of the population, so that most health workers and most of the general public do believe that the health posts and hospitals are there to serve people and not exploit them.

Mozambique *is* different from most other African and Third World countries. In general, neither the leaders nor civil servants are using their posts to enrich themselves. As I noted earlier, there are indications that at low levels this is weakening. And eight years of independence is still short, compared to more than 25 in Ghana. But it took much less time for a climate of self-enrichment to show in Zimbabwe. In part this is because Frelimo has made the choice to provide officials with houses, cars and so on so that they do not need to take bribes to live well. In part it is because of real social pressure; the wide publicity given to the suicide of Central Committee member Francisco Langa when he was caught with his hands in the till is constantly reinforced by press reports when corrupt officials are caught.

Most importantly, however, there is still a consensus that Frelimo and the Government are working for the common good. The initial enthusiasm for the revolution may have worn off, but there are now thousands of young Mozambicans with commitment, dedication, and growing experience and confidence. However many and repeated the mistakes made by Frelimo, and however frustrating the arrogance and incompetence that one sometimes faces, there is no sense that anyone else could do better.

This was shown most clearly by the popular response to the preparations for the Fourth Congress. People were angry, but they largely directed their anger *to* Frelimo, not *against* it. Again and again, right up to the Congress itself, there was a popular sense that if only the leaders knew what the problems were, they would be resolved.

I was riding on a train in neighbouring Malawi. Sitting opposite me in the packed carriage was a woman with several children and a crying baby. She opened a handkerchief containing all her money, and carefully counted the few coins; she thought for some time, and finally decided she could afford to buy one banana to keep the baby quiet. Sitting next to me was a young man who worked as a loom operator. His wage was low and half of it went on rent for a tiny one-room hut in a township outside Blantyre. He had no hope of sending his children to secondary school, he said, because the tuition for one child for one year was more than two months' salary for him.

The contradictory result of this is that markets in Malawi would make a Mozambican green with envy: stalls with bread and eggs, and no queues. And the reason is that most Malawians cannot afford bread or eggs. In Maputo, we get a few eggs each month and a loaf of bread a day from the consumer co-op, at a nominal price. Schools and hospitals may be crowded, but they are free and open to all. Life is hard for Mozambique, but for the poor it is a lot harder in neighbouring countries.

Shops in Maputo are empty *both* because of shortages of goods and because goods that are available are quickly and fairly distributed. No one is pressing their nose against the glass to look at goods which they cannot afford.

And that is a basic issue which has concerned me in writing this book, and which I hope has become clear to the reader. Mozambique must always be looked at in two different frames of reference: in comparison to other developing countries, and in comparison to its own goals of becoming a modern, developed socialist country. Thus in comparison to other developing countries, Mozambique has made spectacular progress in health, but in comparison to its own goals there is an intense and interesting struggle still under way.

Similarly, friends who come to Mozambique with experience elsewhere in the Third World often see Mozambique as a beacon of hope in a very bleak sea – one of the few Third World countries where a broadly based development is possible, one which benefits everyone and not just a tiny minority. But friends who visit from Europe without Third World experience see only the very real hardship. I have tried to show both, and to analyse the problems of socialist transition in both frameworks.

Differences and Similarities

Mozambique is different, but it is not unique. There are other revolutionary socialist developing countries, and Mozambique shares many of their experiences. In an introduction to the excellent book *Revolutionary Socialist Development in the Third World*, Gordon White points to the 'strikingly common elements' in the dynamics of socialist transition. He sets out three phases, detailed in Appendix 2, and summarized here:

*Revolutionary voluntarism. Initial post-revolutionary period with social structure in turmoil. Radical elements are dominant and the stress is on mass mobilization.

*Bureaucratic voluntarism. 'The revolution is being institutionalized.' State power is consolidated and 'the strategic task becomes rapid economic development'. A burgeoning state apparatus dominated by an urban elite undermines mass mobilization.

*Reformism and market socialism. 'The population wearies of postponed consumption', there is increased social differentiation, and a new group without experience of the revolution becomes more powerful. 'The traditional methods of directive planning become more and more ineffective as the economic structure becomes more complex.' There are moves for more cultural and economic diversity. The stress is 'on economic efficiency and productivity, intensive rather than extensive development'.

White wonders whether the newer socialist countries like Mozambique will follow this path. Mozambique has, and very quickly. The first phase was the period of the GDs (Dynamizing Groups). The second was one of 'acclerated development' and big projects, culminating in the ten-year plan. The third was ushered in by the Fourth Congress.

Indeed, many of Frelimo's mistakes have been made by assuming that Mozambique is unique; that it cannot make the mistakes of other developing countries and thus has nothing to learn from them. So Mozambique has swiftly moved through the disasters of state farms, big projects, squeezing the peasants to accumulate capital, urban bias and forced villagization – repeating similar mistakes made elsewhere.

Sjamboks and Passes

In 1983, Frelimo responded to the sharpening crisis in two ways: with the unexpectedly open Fourth Congress, and with draconian new laws. The death penalty was introduced for economic crimes, executions were held in public, and captured MNR men were summarily executed. In a rerun of *Antigone*, six 'collaborators' in Gúruè were executed without trial and their relatives refused permission to bury the bodies. Public flogging was introduced for a wide range of crimes. Only people with jobs were allowed to live in the cities.

Frelimo put on a brave face, but it was a climb-down from some of its most cherished principles. Frelimo had put great weight on clemency and re-education. There had been no death penalty at all until 1979, and until 1983 only for treason. Flogging had been one of the most hated (and propagandized against) of colonial punishments.

Comparison with South Africa was inevitable. Frelimo has always claimed, with justification, that it was building a fundamentally different society. And then it introduced what the Mozambicans themselves called passes and the sjambok (the name for the whip used in South Africa). Those without the right documents were being removed from Mozambican cities at the same time as South Africa was removing people from so-called 'black spots'.

There were good reasons. People were increasingly doing over captured criminals before turning them in to the police, to ensure they were punished, so exemplary and perhaps corporal punishment was needed. More important, in justifying the new laws, Politburo member Armando Guebuza said simply: 'We cannot allow the authority of the Government to be put in question.' In some areas, Frelimo was losing its authority. Perhaps the only way to reassert it was to return to the violent traditions of the régulos and Gungunhana.

In any case, underdevelopment means that Mozambique does not have the trained police, lawyers and judges to run a modern or sophisticated legal system; justice is necessarily rough and ready. The then Justice Minister, Teodato Hunguana, made clear that he knew there would be international protests about human rights when the new death penalties were introduced, but he argued: 'Before speaking of human dignity and human rights, it is necessary to first take account of the dignity and rights of the people. It is unacceptable to invoke human rights in defence of precisely those who violate those rights through the most odious crimes.'

The new measures met general approval. The extended death penalty is popular, just as the reintroduction of hanging in Britain would be. The specific penalty of flogging proved less popular than Frelimo may have expected, probably because of painful colonial memories; high officials were forced repeatedly to assert that Frelimo flogging is different from colonial flogging.

Anders Nilsson/AIM

At FRELIMO's 4th Party Congress. Marcelino dos Santos, Samora Machel, Joaquim Chissano (from left to right)

Anders Nilsson/AIM

Zimbabwe Prime Minister Robert Mugabe, Mozambique President Samora Machel (4th Party Congress)

And expelling the unemployed from the cities was popular. When Samora Machel announced the new policy at a rally in Maputo, the Mozambicans around me cheered spontaneously and loudly. City people could no longer support country cousins who had come to Maputo but were unable to find work. The queues were swelled by the unemployed who became professional queuers. Those who had jobs had no time to queue, so had no choice but to buy from the queuers.

Yet, the way these measures were carried out proved very heavy handed and sometimes unpopular. For example, the introduction of flogging led to a sharp increase in authoritarianism, as the police and local administrators took it as a licence for corporal punishment for minor offences and disrespect. Hunguana said that the newer harsher laws were aimed at the 'sharks, not the chicken thieves'. But in practice it has been mostly the petty criminals and runners who have been punished, while the bigger, more sophisticated criminals and black marketeers remain free. One of the first to be flogged was Raul Cumbe who, according to *Noticias*, sold 15 small cakes for 75 MT instead of the official price of 60 MT.

The expulsion of the unemployed, named Operation Production, created chaos and antagonized many who had supported the idea. City dwellers must carry four documents: identity card, work card, resident's card, and, for younger people, a national service card. Many people spent days in queues trying to ensure that all four cards were in order (and many people would probably prefer a single South African-style passbook to this fistful of documents). Tens of thousands of people without their cards in order were sent to 'verification centres', where some spent several days. Those declared unemployed, marginals, prostitutes, etc. were sent to 'evacuation centres' and within a couple of days flown to Niassa or Cabo Delgado. They could take only a few belongings, and sometimes relatives were not told. As I noted in Chapter 15, there was considerable trouble with single women being labelled prostitutes. There were many other irregularities and cases of people shipped off unjustly; I know one man who tried to free his sister who had been unfairly detained, and who himself was shipped off to Niassa for contempt of court. In Cabo Delgado, the provincial government had to send back to Maputo old people, asthmatics, cripples and others who should never have been expelled from Maputo.

The most worrying aspect of the get-tough policy is that it was partly a response to Frelimo's own mistakes. When workers cannot get lunch, they will pay extra to the black marketeer selling cakes; flogging the cake seller simply means workers get no food at midday. Similarly, the flood into the city is swelled because of Frelimo's bias towards the cities and its policy of mechanization on state farms that did not create jobs at a time of desperate unemployment. Indeed, the ten-year plan recognized that not

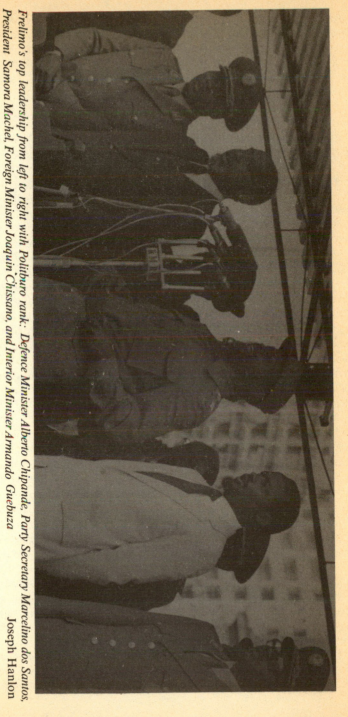

Frelimo's top leadership from left to right with Politburo rank: Defence Minister Alberto Chipande, Party Secretary Marcelino dos Santos, President Samora Machel, Foreign Minister Joaquim Chissano, and Interior Minister Armando Guebuza

Joseph Hanlon

enough was being spent to improve life in the countryside and that 'administrative measures' would be required to counter this urban migration. So it is a bit harsh to take the unemployed youth who desperately need jobs in order to start their families and for whom nothing has been done for eight years, suddenly dub them 'unproductive' and dispatch them to Niassa.

Indeed, the get-tough policy is a response to precisely those of Frelimo's mistakes which were pointed out frequently but never resolved. Consider:

*In 1981 the Party ideological work department admitted 'that the peasants for years have been complaining about a lack of hoes'. In 1983 they still were.

*In 1979 President Samora Machel talked about village shops with only tins of beans that no one wants because the village produces beans. In 1983 Marcelino dos Santos told the same story to the Fourth Congress.

Problems were recognized early and often, but the harsh measures were called for because the problems were never resolved.

The harsh measures arise from, and at the same time illustrate, one of Frelimo's biggest failings: its desire for quick results, whether it is victory over underdevelopment in a decade, or state farms as the 'quickest way' to produce food. Inevitably this leads to failure to consider the longer-term implications, for example for the unemployed. It also leads to the counterproductive habit of promoting people as soon as they have shown the slightest competence in a job; they are frequently not in posts long enough to understand the whole range of problems and establish good working systems, and when they are pulled out for something 'more important' the old job collapses. Coupled with this is the constant attempt to do too much. For example, the vaccination campaign falters because the Health Ministry is trying to give all possible vaccines, rather than concentrating on the one or two that are most vital. This, at least, seems to be improving a bit, with the Ministry of Agriculture, for one, concentrating only on selected districts.

Operation Production typified the worst of this. It was under the control of the Interior, Defence, and Security Ministries, which tried to ship tens of thousands of people out of the cities with no advance planning. In Maputo, people had only two weeks to update all four cards they had to carry (and no one asked, for example, if the ID card was really necessary since work and residents' cards could not have been obtained without it). Evacuation and verification centres were set up with no assessment of needs and the Maputo city council was called in to dig latrines only when the shit began to pile up. There was insufficient transport to evacuate the 'unproductive', so the national airline was simply closed down for a week and the planes commandeered, without notice, stranding people all over the country.

It was particularly sad because Mozambique had several very good experiences of organizing this sort of operation. The 1980 census, the 1980 currency change and the first distribution of petrol ration coupons were all done with spectacular success and minimal time wasting. They had been planned for months in advance so that everyone was organized and the bureaucracy and paperwork reduced to an essential minimum. Interestingly, the two Politburo members who are also provincial governors, Marcelino dos Santos and Mario Machungo, both delayed the start of Operation Production in their provinces for two months to allow better advance organization.

Building for Change

As Operation Production showed, there are divisions within the leadership. But they rarely surface, and Frelimo remains exceptionally unified. The leadership, still largely the victorious guerrillas, has remained unchanged since 1970. There have been a few additions, but no purges.

This unity arises from three elements: 1) strong commitment to consensus; 2) a tendency to institutionalize conflicts and keep them within the Party and within individual ministries; and 3) careful planning to ensure that trusted cadres are always used to their best advantage and not simply dismissed if they fail at a particular job.

Consensus has its problems in that where agreement is impossible, as on the Family Law, no action is taken. Important problems may remain unresolved for long periods. But Frelimo applies to its own top bodies two of its cardinal rules: democratic centralism and the belief that participation in making decisions guarantees that 'people are consciously committed to their implementation'. Thus once the Politburo or Central Committee has reached agreement, thre is a strong commitment to carry out that decision, and not to carp about it outside. (A problem for journalists, as it sharply cuts the number of leaks.)

This also means that Samora Machel, although the most important individual, is not all-powerful. In 1982, for example, the Politburo overruled his wish to visit Europe and said he should concentrate on the war instead. Thus, although his moral utterances are largely his own, his political statements are usually agreed and he often serves as spokesman for a Politburo view. Machel is an impressive and popular speaker. Not only does he sing, crack jokes and tell stories in his speeches, he can also deviate far from his prepared texts. Because of the nature of the Frelimo consensus, these improvizations usually reflect the general view. But not always. In a speech in 1982 he called for a curfew in Maputo; this had not been discussed and was clearly impractical, so it was deleted from the published text of the speech and quietly forgotten.

The second element, Frelimo's method of institutionalizing conflict, can be quite subtle. This is best shown in the Health Ministry. When Helder Martins was dismissed as Minister, he was replaced by two men. The new Minister, Pascoal Mocumbi, is a trusted Frelimo cadre who is also an advocate of primary health care. But a new post of Vice-Minister was created and filled by the former director of the Maputo Central Hospital, Fernando Vaz, who is spokesman for the curative hospital medicine clique. Both sides are represented within official structures. Frelimo hopes the tension will be creative rather than immobilizing. In any case, as both sides are inside, they are governed by the ethos of consensus and democratic centralism. They have to fight their battles inside and accept the outcome.

The third element is to ensure that trusted cadres, especially those who proved themselves in the liberation war, are never outside. They are given real and important tasks, usually with enough freedom of action to prove themselves anew (or rope to hang themselves again). Thus ministers never completely disappear, and it is hard to assess demotions and promotions. Frelimo often does two things at the same time. What did it mean in 1980 when Jorge Rebelo and Marcelino dos Santos were relieved of ministerships in order to concentrate full time on the Party? In practice, two different things were happening. Both were weak administrators and there was general relief when they were moved. Yet, at the same time, there was a desperate need to strengthen the Party. In the end, it was half and half. Rebelo became more powerful and did rebuild the Party. Dos Santos, on the other hand, clearly lost influence, in part because of his subsequent failure to negotiate Comecon membership for Mozambique, and he is steadily being eased into the role of Father of the Revolution.

All three of these elements, as well as an essential fourth one – going back to the people in time of crisis – can be seen in the way in which Frelimo in the Fourth Congress dealt with the intense struggles over economic and development policy.

The build-up to the Congress involved a mass mobilization and drew in many people not heavily involved before. They were often outspokenly critical. But these people were integrated into the process, rather than being left outside as a possible opposition. The critics became delegates to the Congress and some were elected to the new Central Committee. At the same time, Frelimo stuck to its tradition of not removing trusted militants. Thus, only nine of 54 members of the old Central Committee were not re-elected, and none of those nine were of note. Instead, it added 83 new people, largely from rural areas and including many critics, who will totally outweigh the old guard.

Similarly, no one lost his seat on the Politburo, not even Mario Machungo who had been publicly criticized by Machel for his running of the National Planning Commission. But the two Politburo members most associated with big projects, dos Santos and Machungo, have been given additional tasks as provincial governors. This will keep them out of Maputo, but it will also give them a chance to see how it really is out there.

The Politburo's small-project man, Jacinto Veloso, had created for him a new post of Minister in the President's Office for Economic Affairs. Another big-project opponent, José Forjaz, had created for him the new Secretariat of State for Physical Planning – inside the National Planning Commission, which is still headed by Machungo. In a classic Frelimo solution, Machungo, Forjaz and Veloso will have to work together to forge a new planning strategy from their very different approaches.

Similarly, the Congress maintained the tradition of consensus. There was agreement by the proponents of both the big-project line and the pro-peasant, small-project line that the state farms needed time to re-organize and consolidate, so the Congress approved what all could agree – a three-year economic plan. Both sides are convinced that afterwards the new enlarged Central Committee, and the general public, will see the merits of their lines: on the one side that the state farms have radically improved and become centres of efficiency, on the other that small projects will have sprung up throughout the country showing the merit of transferring resources away from the big projects. Thus both sides remain inside. The struggle will continue within the Ministries of Agriculture and Industry, and within the Central Committee. but as the three years pass, the choices and outcomes will become more clear, and people will be able to choose newer, more suitable positions without ever having been out-side the fold.

Thus the Fourth Congress did not so much make changes as set the stage for changes. It was still not clear how to organize agriculture, industry or planning; there were no simple or 'correct' solutions. The ministry reshuffles brought in the new people needed to try to find those solutions. And the new militant Central Committee is clearly separate from central Government and will demand answers from it, as well as demanding that the new guidelines are followed. More than anything else, this promises to stop Frelimo from talking, year after year, but not acting, about tinned beans in rural shops and the lack of peasant hoes. In effect, the Fourth Congress revitalized Frelimo and set the stage for changes in the same way that the Second Congress did in 1968. It would be foolish for me to try to forecast what will happen now; I only hope that this book provides suitable background and explanations for the changes that must occur.

Postscript

24. Destabilization Works

War and weather doomed any attempt to introduce the reforms agreed at the Fourth Congress, and precipitated the virtual collapse of the economy. When the previous chapters of this book were finished, in September 1983, the outlook was already gloomy. The reality was worse, and the next six months brought famine, flood, bankruptcy, and a non-aggression pact with South Africa.

Tens of thousands of people starved to death in Gaza and Inhambane provinces, in what was largely a man-made famine. The area had been hit by the worst drought in memory. But Frelimo had run a successful relief effort, which largely prevented starvation, in the same parts of Inhambane during a previous drought in 1979/80. This time, the deaths were caused by South African aggression, failure by donors to give food, and the collapse of communications channels within the Mozambican government.

Some of the areas worst hit by drought were badly affected by the Mozambique National Resistance (MNR). By August 1983, people had lost much of their remaining foodstocks and cattle to the MNR, and were running out of roots and berries in the bush. They began to risk their lives to flee to Frelimo-controlled towns and main roads, where camps were established. The major army offensive, which included the capture of the MNR's Inhambane provincial command headquarters at Tome, released a flood of refugees. Food relief efforts were begun, although the MNR attacked refugee camps and relief lorries. But there was a desperate shortage of food, lorries, and medical supplies, so that many of the victims died after they reached refugee camps.

Aid agencies often complain that countries are slow to warn of impending disaster, but in this case Mozambique gave six months advance notice. In January 1983, when it was clear the rains had failed completely, the government issued an aid appeal warning of the 'likely loss of the total 1982/83 crop in southern Mozambique'. Yet aid pledges actually *decreased*. In June, a worried Internal Trade Minister Aranda da Silva held a series of meetings with diplomats. He accused them of simply re-labelling normal food aid and calling it drought relief, and of being slow to deliver that. 'There is hunger now', he warned. 'If we do not receive more help, hundreds will die.' A week later, the International Red Cross circulated a report to diplomats calling the position 'alarming'. But no extra aid was forthcoming.

South Africa, however, was active in the area. The MNR's Tome base was in the heart of the worst affected zone. At the height of the drought, just two weeks before the base fell in August, the South Africans made an air drop to the base. It was not food for the starving, but nine tonnes of arms, ammunition, and mines for the MNR to use to disrupt relief efforts.

The war made the famine political. The United Nations World Food Programme (WFP) responded to the January 1983 appeal by helping in Maputo province, which was safe, but refused to work in worse affected Gaza and Inhambane. The WFP obstructed the June 1983 appeal on bureaucratic grounds, saying the request had not been properly formulated by the Mozambicans. Western diplomats reported to their home countries that because of security problems, they could not assess the severity. So donations fell.

For those accustomed to only emotional aid appeals and pictures of starving children, it is hard to appreciate how ponderous and petty the aid bureaucracies can be. It is sometimes a year between the promise of food and its delivery. But in this case, bureaucracy was used as a cloak. The Reagan administration policy of 'constructive engagement' with South Africa was widely seen as tacit US approval for South African destabilization of Mozambique. Since the famine was one result, Western countries, and supposedly neutral donor agencies, were reluctant to intervene, as it could be seen as taking sides. And they refused Mozambique's repeated requests to press South Africa to ease off its attacks.

Mozambique's courting of the West (see Chapter 22) was partly in recognition of this, and food aid increased only when the Western powers were convinced that Mozambique was really turning toward them. A key factor was a trip in October 1983 by President Samora Machel to Europe – Portugal, France, Britain, Belgium, Holland, the EEC, and Yugoslavia. Two states on the tour gave big grain donations – 30,000 tons from tiny Holland and 15,000 tons from Britain – and the US doubled its food aid to 43,000 tons. But the most important factor in Inhambane was the visit there in early October of Jeff Millington, the First Secretary of the US embassy in Maputo. His grim report was widely circulated by the US government. WFP in Rome learned officially of the gravity of the famine from that report, not from its Maputo office. The distribution of the Millington report was treated as a signal from the US that it was all right to support Mozambique, and it galvanised the United Nations system and other donors into action. Diplomats and aid officials flocked to Inhambane and Gaza to gawk at starving babies, and send shocked telegrams home. Bureaucratic obstacles melted away. Planes were chartered to fly in aid requested months before. Of course it helped, but by then the worst was over.

The Mozambique government was not entirely blameless in this man-made famine. Initially it was not candid about the impact of the MNR on the problem; at the last minute officials deleted all references to the MNR from the January 1983 appeal to diplomats, making the problem seem less serious. Another difficulty was Frelimo's curious faith in the international community. I was asked not to report Aranda da Silva's criticisms (in June 1983) of donors for cutting aid, because it was felt that Mozambique would do better going through 'proper channels' and that publicity would only offend the diplomats. I am ashamed to say I agreed to the request. In reality, publicity, and especially a TV film in Britain in late November, spurred aid donors into action.

Finally, Mozambique's own channels of communication proved ineffective; it took two months for Maputo to appreciate the magnitude of what had been happening in Inhambane. There was a similar communications breakdown in Tete province, where there was also a drought and thousands died. There peasants began eating baobab fruit in September 1983, a sure sign they had run out of food. Then the rains failed again, and starving peasants began dying on the streets of Tete city in December. *Noticias* commented later that 'nearly everybody in Tete city talks with horror of seeing bodies on the streets of the city.' Yet only when tens of thousands of Mozambican refugees began to flood into neighbouring Zimbabwe in February did Maputo take notice.

No one will know how many died, because so many starved uncounted in MNR-controlled areas. Estimates range from 30,000 to over 100,000. President Samora Machel talked of 'tens of thousands of deaths'.

And in the worst hit areas, especially Gaza, Inhambane, and Tete, the drought continued into a third year and the 1983/84 crops failed as well. But in Maputo province the worst drought in memory ended in the worst floods in 30 years. After heavy rains in Swaziland and South Africa during cyclone Domoina, water surged down three rivers killing more than 175 people and doing £70 million in damage. The surge was so sudden and so strong that near the Umbeluzi agricultural station a loaded railway wagon was washed off the tracks and across a road. People were rescued by boat and helicopter; a woman gave birth in a tree. At least 350,000 people lost their crops, and 51 small irrigation dams were destroyed. Some of those dams had been built as part of the Fourth Congress push for small projects, and were yet to be used.

Declaring bankruptcy

Reeling under the continued blows of war and weather, the government effectively declared bankruptcy. On 30 January 1984, it asked its creditors to reschedule its debts. Its total debts to banks, governments, and international organizations were more than £1,000 million ($1.4 billion). It admitted that it had already defaulted on over £145 million in debts. It asked that this, plus principal and interest of over £510 million due in 1984, 1985, and 1986 be rescheduled for repayment after 1990. Repayments of principal and interest are roughly equal to the normal balance of payments deficit; by deferring these payments for three years, the government hoped at least to be able to pay cash for normal imports. It also hopes that by 1987, it will have overcome the effects of war and drought, and that some of the big development projects will be earning foreign currency, so that it can begin to pay its debts again.

In asking for debt rescheduling, the government published economic figures for the first time in several years (see Economic Tables 13–15), and also gave details of the cost of war and weather. In 1982 and 1983, the MNR destroyed 840 schools, 212 health posts and centres, at least 200 villages, and 900 shops. Total losses due to the MNR in 1982 alone were £140 million, and it looked as if losses in 1983 were much higher. At the same time, South Africa had dramatically reduced traffic through Maputo port, from four million tons in 1979 to one million in 1983. The costs of South African destabilization, combined with losses due to drought, were double the £655 million in debts Mozambique was asking to reschedule.

Treating for peace

It had been clear for some time that Mozambique could not continue to sustain South African pummelling at this level. Since mid-1982 Frelimo had been trying to convince the West, and particularly the US, to put pressure on South Africa. Meetings in Komatipoort between Mozambican and South African Ministers in December 1982 and May 1983 were abortive. Then on 20 December 1983 Ministers met in Mbabane, Swaziland, and there was a totally new mood. After two more meetings, a non-aggression pact was signed on 16 March 1984. Both sides gained what they had wanted from the first: Mozambique wanted an end to South Africa's support and operation of the MNR; South Africa wanted major economic involvement in Mozambique, neutralization of the African National Congress (ANC), and a formal non-aggression pact (until then signed publicly only with the bantustans and, secretly in February 1982, with Swaziland). There was a strong feeling that South Africa had not been negotiating seriously at the two Komatipoort meetings, because it had demanded the complete expulsion of the ANC from Mozambique, which clearly would have involved an unacceptable loss of face for Frelimo.

The turning point was Samora Machel's trip to Europe in October 1983, which proved a diplomatic success and a financial failure. European governments made clear that no money was forthcoming, directly precipitating the declaration of bankruptcy. But Machel did convince his hosts that South Africa was not negotiating seriously and should be pressed to do so, which was exactly what happened when South African Foreign Minister Pik Botha followed Machel to Europe in November.

So Mozambique went to Mbabane knowing it was about to declare bankruptcy, and that a settlement with South Africa was a precondition for renegotiating its debts. On the other hand, a deal with South Africa and suspension of repayments together would give Frelimo an essential opening to concentrate on development. Finally, the Mozambique army's new tactics seemed to be working, and it was gaining ground on the MNR; without an agreement, South Africa would need to escalate the war, while with a deal, it was possible to beat the 'bandits'.

On the South African side, there was a significant change in tactics. Back in 1979, Prime Minister P. W. Botha had put forward his 'total strategy'. It envisioned a mix of military and economic pressure, combined with aid and investment, to push the majority ruled states of the region to join the bantustans in a South African dominated 'constellation of states'. This seemed blocked by the Mugabe victory in Zimbabwe and the subsequent formation of SADCC. Destabilization had always been part of the total strategy, but, shocked by Mugabe's victory and believing itself licensed by the newly elected President Reagan's policy of 'constructive engagement', South Africa shifted to a line of largely military pressure and economic blockade, ignoring the economic benefits side of the package. This imbalance was called into question, first with Zimbabwe, and later with Mozambique and Angola. The military budget was growing, and the May raid on Maputo, which hit a jam factory instead of non-existent ANC bases, raised questions about the validity of military tactics. At the same time, there were arguments that South Africa had been too rigid in its approach. In November 1983, for example, the Institute of Strategic Studies of Pretoria University, which has close links with the government, suggested that a non-aggression pact need only prevent the ANC from using neighbouring states 'as a springboard for acts of terror', and that it did not require the ANC's complete expulsion. In particular, the ANC could be allowed continued political representation in those countries.

It was in this already changing mood inside South Africa that Mozambique's diplomatic initiatives paid off. Western diplomats, particularly from the US, met repeatedly with the South Africans to say that the present level of destabilization was no longer internationally acceptable. But they went on to argue that, in any case, it was not in South Africa's interests. There was more profit to be made from economic dominance of Mozambique than simply destabilizing it, and they suggested that South Africa trade in the obvious military leverage it had gained from destabilization for a more useful economic leverage. This was accepted, and South Africa returned to the balance of the total strategy. This point was made particularly clear at the final signing of the Accord, when P. W. Botha talked of the Accord as a basis for 'an economic alliance', mentioning by name his proposed 'constellation of states'.

At the Mbabane talks, both sides accepted the other's preconditions: Mozambique said it would not do anything that might imply recognition of the bantustans, that it needed to maintain diplomatic and political support for the ANC and must still have an ANC office, and that South Africa must stop backing the MNR; South Africa said Mozambique must curb ANC military activities, and demanded parallel economic talks and an opening for South African tourists, goods, and capital. The rest followed quickly. On 16 January there were meetings of four working groups in Pretoria and Maputo: security, tourism, Cahora Bassa, and economic links. Further meetings followed on 20 February in Maputo and 2 March in Cape Town.

Machel and Botha met on the border, on the banks of the Incomati River on 16 March to sign The Accord of Nkomati, an 'agreement on non-aggression and good neighbourliness'. The two met for over an hour in a white railway coach, then signed the Accord in a circus atmosphere. More than 1,500 guests, including businessmen, journalists, and most of the ambassadors in the two capitals, drank wine and beer and ate prawns under huge tents pitched in the bush on the river bank.

Under the Accord, detailed in Appendix 6, Mozambique and South Africa agree to 'refrain from interfering in the internal affairs of the other'. Both agree to prevent the use of their territories for bases, transit, or accommodation of guerrillas – which applies to both ANC and MNR. But several sections apply only to South Africa, including an undertaking not to make land, sea, and air attacks or sabotage operations (which only South Africa has done) and to end 'radio broadcasting stations' and 'telecommunications facilities' between the command and guerrillas – both facilities provided only by South Africa for the MNR. A joint security commission was set up to monitor the agreement.

South Africa quickly shut down the MNR radio station. Two weeks after the signing, heavily armed Mozambican soldiers raided ANC houses to search for weapons, and the ANC was told it could maintain only a small diplomatic mission in Maputo. All ANC guerrillas and most ancillary staff had to leave Mozambique, although Mozambique did pledge its continued 'political, diplomatic, and humanitarian support for the ANC'. And there was a string of visits by South African and European businessmen promising new investments, particularly in tourist facilities. The head of the South African freight forwarding agency, Rennies, visited Maputo less than two weeks after the signing of the Nkomato Accord and promised within nine months to increase traffic through Maputo port by one million tons per year, a clear sign that the economic boycott was over.

Victory?

Both sides billed the Accord as a victory. South Africa saw the success of its tactics, and for the first time there was open recognition that it had been destabilizing Mozambique. The Durban *Sunday Tribune* (11 March) commented that 'Mozambique had been forced to the negotiating table by economic necessity and destabilization launched from South Africa'. The West, too, saw it as a victory – for the US policy of 'constructive engagement'.

Frelimo also talked of victory. The Nkomati Accord was to stand beside the Lusaka and Lancaster House accords, each of which ended a war. Frelimo stressed that every war ends in talks; since its founding 20 years before it had always tried to talk rather than fight, pressing repeatedly for talks with Portugal and pushing Robert Mugabe and Zanu to the Lancaster House conference table. Furthermore, the real battle had always been against imperialism, Frelimo argued. Portugal was the first line, and it was beaten. The second line was Rhodesia, and it too was beaten. South Africa was imperialism's last line – its final agent in the region as part of a world-wide campaign to destroy progressive and socialist governments. This campaign succeeded with Chile and Granada and failed with Cuba and Vietnam, Machel said. The objective of both Rhodesia and South Africa was 'to destroy our popular and revolutionary state'. The Nkomati Accord ended that attempt, and the continued survival of the first Marxist state in the zone is obviously a victory. Nkomati was also a victory in the sense that it came about only because of Mozambique's long diplomatic campaign with the West.

But the accords of Lusaka and Lancaster House did not only end the fighting, they also brought the independence of Mozambique and Zimbabwe. Nkomati may reduce the destabilization, but it does not end apartheid. Mozambique has been forced to accept South Africa's long-standing demand that it sign a non-aggression pact, and has agreed to push out the ANC and open the doors to South African capital in ways that would have been totally unacceptable in 1980. It is the victory of the seven-stone weakling being beaten by a bully, and who yells loudly enough to attract a crowd which stops the assault – the victory is in avoiding being beaten to death.

Mozambique's neighbours and the non-aligned movement were sympathetic but unhappy. Botswana's Foreign Minister Archie Mogwe, for example, recognized that Mozambique had been forced to sign, but said the pact would be 'futile and shortlived' because it did not deal with the fundamental problem of apartheid. They resented the circus atmosphere and claims of victory, and clearly agreed with the ANC Executive Committee that the Accord 'cannot but help to perpetuate the illegitimate rule of the South African white settler minority'.

At the non-aligned summit in New Delhi in March 1983, Machel had given a stirring speech declaring apartheid 'the Nazism of our time', and declaring that 'racial discrimination in South Africa is just cause for all humanity to wage total war against it'. Apartheid was one of the few issues which united the non-aligned movement, and now Mozambique, which pushed it so hard, was the first to break ranks.

Indeed, in statements at the time of the signing, Frelimo leaders stressed the new view that apartheid, although still objectionable, is an 'internal' problem for South Africa – a direct reference to the Accord's prohibition against interfering in 'internal' affairs. The style of the signing effectively broke South Africa's international isolation. If Machel could have friendly chats with the 'Nazis', and if Frelimo could lunch with the pariah, why not play rugby with it?

South Africa agreed. There was euphoric talk of other possible non-aggression pacts with Zimbabwe, Lesotho, and Botswana (and fear in those countries that, as in Mozambique, South Africa would step up destabilization to gain an accord). Some South African politicans even suggested that South Africa might be so acceptable as to join the Organization of African Unity.

In part, Frelimo was putting on a show. It was effectively screaming: 'Of course I love you, just don't hit me again'. But it did feel that South Africa needed to be convinced Frelimo was serious, and protestations that it only signed under duress would not be helpful.

Equally important, however, were growing doubts about the whole tactic of isolating South Africa, as well as disillusionment about the ANC. A few in Frelimo were even saying that the oil boycott was an obvious failure, the arms embargo had only encouraged South Africa to develop its own arms industry, and the cultural boycott seemed to hurt liberals inside South Africa more than the government.

Disagreements with the ANC

The Nkomati Accord was a blow to the ANC, both politically and militarily, even though Frelimo had never given the ANC the full backing it gave Zanu. From independence in 1975, Frelimo took very different lines on Rhodesia and South Africa. Rhodesia was seen as an issue of decolonization; Zanu, like Frelimo, was fighting for independence. South Africa, however, was accepted as a sovereign state with whom Mozambique was forced to be neighbours. Frelimo repeatedly stressed that one chooses friends, not neighbours. However abhorrent its internal political system, Mozambique would press for peaceful coexistence and good neighbourly relations. The ANC was the sole legitimate representative of the South African people, but it was fighting an internal, revolutionary struggle.

Zanu was given the same total support that Tanzania gave Frelimo during its liberation war. It was allowed to establish camps and to use Mozambique as the rear base for its operations; eventually Mozambican troops went into Rhodesia. By contrast, the ANC was never allowed bases in Mozambique, and was expected, at first, to keep a very low profile.

This distinction was as much pragmatic as political. Ian Smith could be beaten, and had to be, because Marxist Mozambique could not survive nearly surrounded by hostile neighbours. By contrast, Frelimo and the ANC were no match for the military might of South Africa, and in 1975 the ANC was moribund. With an independent and sympathetic Zimbabwe, Mozambique assumed it could survive with the apartheid state as its neighbour.

The January 1981 raid on ANC houses in the Maputo suburb of Matola shocked Frelimo. Despite Frelimo's oft-expressed desire to be a good neighbour, and its holding back of the ANC, South Africa still attacked. At a rally in Independence Square in Maputo on 14 February, two weeks after the raid, Machel stood side by side with ANC President Oliver Tambo, and publicly pledged full support to the ANC for the first time: 'We and the South Africans will fight side by side, shoulder to shoulder, until the final victory – until apartheid falls'. The ANC was allowed to open an office; Frelimo turned a blind eye to guerrillas and political cadres going across the border. The only restrictions – always observed – were that the ANC should not have bases in Mozambique and that it enter South Africa via Swaziland and not directly.

The struggle inside South Africa had grown since Mozambican independence and the ANC had come to life again. Even before 14 February 1981 it had been using Mozambique, but the new freedom made Mozambique the ANC's most important entry route into South Africa. The struggle intensified, with the ANC playing an important role. The armed wing, Umkhonto we Sizwe, carried out spectacular bombings. More important, however, was the ANC's involvement in both legal and illegal political activity. Its colours, slogans, and jailed leaders became the symbols of the struggle; it pushed the Freedom Charter back into the forefront.

Support for the ANC was genuine and wholehearted. Mozambique's leaders seem to have been convinced that they could not live with a hostile South Africa, as they had hoped, and that Frelimo's own survival depended on defeating apartheid, just as it had on defeating Ian Smith. Backing the ANC seemed the obvious way to do this. The rhetoric changed. From an internal revolutionary struggle, the ANC's fight became that of a liberation movement for independence from internal colonialism, thus elevating it to the same plane as Frelimo's and Zanu's. Support reached a high point in March 1982 in Maputo when Front Line heads of state promised to increase support for the ANC so that it 'can intensify the armed struggle for the attainment of national independence'. But by late 1982, it was clear that South Africa was just too strong, and the ANC was warned that Mozambique would negotiate peace and be forced to restrict the ANC.

The settlement was delayed, but when it occurred both Frelimo and the ANC acted badly, as the Nkomati Accord brought to the surface long simmering disagreements. From the warm friendship of 1981, Frelimo turned cold. There were, for example, no comradely discussions between

Frelimo and the ANC as to how to face up to South African demands (as the ANC had with the Lesotho government when it faced a similar problem a year earlier). ANC President Oliver Tambo was kept waiting in Maputo for a month before simply being told by Machel the rough outlines of what was to happen. The weapons search by Mozambican soldiers a week after the Accord was done without warning, and confiscated guns given to ANC officials for personal protection by the Mozambican government. And it was only after the Accord's signing that the ANC was told that it meant the total expulsion of all but a diplomatic mission.

Furthermore, Frelimo changed its line without explanation or comment – to the ANC or to the general public. In February 1981 President Machel said 'we are 35 million' – 12 million Mozambicans and 23 million South Africans – fighting to end apartheid. In March 1984, a Mozambican Minister was obviously referring to that pledge when he said: 'Our international policy is linked to our national policy – we must think of our 12 million people'. And they returned to the pre-1981 line that apartheid is an internal problem and that the ANC is fighting an internal revolution.

For its part, the ANC responded to the Accord like a petulant, jilted lover. The ANC Executive Committee issued a statement that suggested that by signing the Accord, Mozambique had been reduced to the level of a bantustan. The ANC had failed to read the writing on the wall. After the 1982 warning that an agreement would be signed, ANC members began to complain of being cold-shouldered by Frelimo. Yet the leadership was caught off guard both by the Accord and by its severity as applied to them.

This stems from one of the ANC's main mistakes in Mozambique – that most of its members had little interest in the Mozambican revolution. They failed to learn Portuguese, which often isolated them from both the press and their neighbours, so they did not see the depth of the crisis that was to force Frelimo's hand. At one extreme, some ANC members arrogantly argued that Mozambique could never be truly free until South Africa was free, so that Frelimo must subordinate its revolution to the South African one. This had two results. First, it made it easy for the ANC to be lulled by Frelimo's continuing public statements of support. And second, it offended some in Frelimo, and this annoyance may have been at the root of Frelimo's cavalier treatment of the ANC when the Accord was signed.

Such attitudes were not universal. For example, Ruth First, as research director of the Centre for African Studies, committed herself to Mozambique and argued both that the ANC should contribute to Mozambique's revolution, and that it could learn from Frelimo's experiences. But not enough of her compatriots listened. Since many felt they had little to learn from Frelimo, they failed to pay attention to what was going on around them. Some in the South African Communist Party even laughed derisively at Frelimo's attempts to build a Marxist-Leninist party from illiterate peasants. On its side, some in Frelimo accused the ANC of only playing at armed struggle, and said it was wasting its limited time of free access from Mozambique. In part, this must reflect the ANC's failure to explain its struggle to Frelimo and to the Mozambican people. Nevertheless, South Africa's insistent demands for the expulsion of the ANC show both that Mozambique was backing the ANC, and that the ANC was using that support to build its struggle inside South Africa.

Socialism Under Siege

In reality, the Fourth Congress came too late. However wise its assessment of the problems and proposals for change, the collapse had become too rapid to halt. Bankruptcy and an agreement with South Africa were inevitable. Nine years of war had stretched Frelimo's management capacity beyond the breaking point; by 1983 it was simply overwhelmed by problems. One result was a further shift away from people's power and toward authoritarianism. There was, for example, no attempt to prepare the people for the Nkomati Accord and little effort to explain it; there was no discussion, and the Party study guide for the Accord said flatly: 'Only those who are against the Mozambican revolution are against this Accord.'

Pass-like controls of the people were increased. In January 1984 Interior Minister Armando Guebuza announced that no one could travel from one district to another without a *guia de marcha* (travel permission), a document issued by a ministry or local authority authorizing the travel and giving the reason for it. Shortly afterwards, Manica Governor Manuel António in a speech in Chimoio said that people absent from their neighbourhoods without the knowledge of the officials should be turned over to the police for investigation when they returned.

In parallel, there was a sharp increase in arbitrary orders and punishments. This reached such a stage that Governor António was forced to publicly order a halt, at least, to 'the practice of flogging people who criticise incorrect actions of officials'.

Indeed, Frelimo's own high-handedness seemed to be creating an opposition where none existed before. In December 1983 I talked with captured MNR men in Sofala province. It was apparent that many people there were bitter and angry about the MNR, and brutally beat them when given the chance. But also clear was the growing phenomenon of *madjubas*, or collaborators, who regularly and voluntarily bring food to MNR bases and warn the MNR of the approach of Frelimo soldiers. In Gorongosa, I talked with Elishu Shabant, who had been captured by the army while on a reconnaissance mission. He said some people in his base were there only because they had been kidnapped and were afraid to run away. But others were there because they opposed Frelimo. 'They are against communal villages and cooperatives. They say Frelimo does not represent the people, and they are still fighting to free their country,' Shabant said. Gorongosa was an area of forced villagization in 1980, when the army created its own opposition.

Perhaps most depressing is that Frelimo failed to learn this lesson. In late 1983 the MNR swept across Nampula province, virtually unopposed, as had been the case in Zambezia before. In Erati district the army responded by forcing people into villages, and burning the homes of those who resisted.

In a speech on 5 April 1984, Samora Machel argued that imperialism, acting through Rhodesia and South Africa, had a 'plan to destory our state'. Thus Nkomati is a victory becuse it is 'the defence of our sovereignty', Machel explained. 'With the signing of the Accord of Nkomati, the main project, the destruction of our state, failed.'

But the President also noted that 'the objective was to destroy the alternative civilization which Mozambique represents'. What the President did not point out is that it is possible to destroy 'the alternative civilization' without destroying the state or overthrowing the government. Nine years of war and hardship have smashed not only the economy, but also the early enthusiasm, ideals, and good political intentions. Destabilization has remoulded Frelimo in the South African image of sjamboks and passes – in the Portuguese colonial image of 'protected villages'. South African troops and saboteurs may have been expelled, protecting Mozambique's sovereignty; but that will be a hollow victory and South Africa can happily withdraw if people's power and those things that make Mozambique progressive and socialist – Machel's 'alternative civilization' – have been destroyed.

Nor has Nkomati brought peace. In January and February 1984, the South Africans pushed hundreds of heavily armed men across the border, and set up supply caches for them in Mozambique. The level of attacks actually increased. After the signing of the Accord, the war moved closer to Maputo than ever before; the typing of this final chapter was disrupted by the MNR's first cuts of Maputo's electricity. The MNR has the means and the will to continue fighting well into 1985. Destabilization is cheap and effective; South Africa can always pick up the reins of the MNR again, and can use the threat to do so in order to extract further concessions from Frelimo.

Nor does Nkomati mean immediate prosperity. Except perhaps for isolated islands of tourism, it will be years before any significant amount of South African capital moves in. Rescheduling of debts will also require time, and is likely to be conditional on a promise from Mozambique to join the International Monetary Fund (IMF). That, in turn, will require further concessions by Frelimo to increase the role of the private sector and cut back on the health and education programmes that are the base of its popularity.

But South Africa and the IMF may not have to apply too much

pressure, because the whole process is in the interests of some of the aspirants to the bourgeoisie (see chapter 18). They have been putting their own interests first as the crisis worsened. For example, the Beira newspaper, *Diário de Moçambique*, reported from Chókwè that there were complaints that officials were only redistributing land to friends or those who offered bribes, and that in the consumer co-operative there, goods were going only to officials and their friends. Similarly, as food became short, there were reports from Niassa that in prisons, re-education centres, and camps for the 'unproductive' expelled from Maputo, the police and others who ran the facilities were concentrating on feeding themselves first, allowing those in their care to become malnourished. With the Accord, the aspirants will again put their interests first; they will be at the front of the queue for the consumer goods South Africa is anxious to sell to Mozambique.

Similarly, the whole stress on Western and South African capital investments is in the interests of the technocrats and big project advocates. Foreign investors will not be interested in small projects and co-operatives. And joint ventures with the capitalists will be even more beneficial to the elite than projects with the socialist bloc.

This has not passed unnoticed within Mozambique. In April the Mozambique news agency AIM published a special commentary noting that the Nkomati Accord 'unleashes a new area of struggle – foreign investment'. It argued that 'imperialism, having failed to destroy socialism in Mozambique by military means, will try to do so by economic means'. It will try to create a local petty bourgeoisie and corrupt the government. 'Defending socialism in Mozambique in the face of this onslaught of capital will not be easy.'

In practice, the Fourth Congress did not resolve the class struggle. The new radical Central Committee did not meet for a year after the Congress. Thus it had no say in the Nkomati talks or in economic changes, and it could do nothing to force the implementation of Fourth Congress decisions. Within weeks of his appointment as Vice Minister of Agriculture with special responsibility for family and co-operative farming – *the* Fourth Congress priority – Francisco Pateguana was given a 'temporary' transfer out of Maputo to be acting governor of Tete; he largely stayed there, but no one in the Ministry of Agriculture took over his brief. And in his year end message, Politburo member Marcelino dos Santos said that although small projects were necessary, it was important not to forget 'the grand projects that are the props of the development of the country'. The backsliding was obvious.

The Nkomati Accord and the rescheduling of debts could give Frelimo a vital breathing space and unleash its creativity to resolve both the internal disputes and the related problem of how to rebuild the economy, just as peace in 1980 released a burst of energy.

It is essential to remember that Frelimo did not inherit a going concern, as did many new governments at independence. Instead it took over an economy with a massive and permanent balance of payments deficit, and then faced the withdrawal of a major subsidy (by South Africa) and the dramatic fall in the prices of key exports that in colonial times could be produced profitably only through super-exploitation. Even a financial wizard could not have made that work, and radical restructuring was required. However many mistakes Frelimo may have made, it is hard to blame it for trying one great leap out of the economic pit. But destabilization ensured that it was never given a chance. Now the problem remains: the economy must be restructured, whether by capitalists or socialists, big projects or small. The real test of whether destabilization has succeeded or failed will be how Frelimo now chooses to rebuild the economy. Has 'the alternative civilization' been destroyed? Will South Africa, the West, and Frelimo's aspirants to the bourgeoisie allow it to re-establish socialism and people's power as its goals?

Even if the shooting stops, the revolution will still be under fire.

Appendix 1: Producing Food at a Loss

Mozambique actually loses money by increasing food production. This nonsensical result comes from low world commodity prices and high costs of imported machinery, fuel, fertilizers, and so on. To demonstrate this I will compare the foreign exchange (US dollar) cost of producing maize with the average cost over the past few years of importing it from the United States, which has been about $160 to $180 per tonne.

There are no official figures for the cost of producing maize in Mozambique, but it is possible to do some very rough sums. The cost of buying tractors, harvesters, and other machinery for a typical state farm in Mozambique is $2,500 per hectare (ha = 2.5 acres), and in present Mozambican conditions such machinery will last about five years. So the machinery cost is $500/ha/yr, all in dollars. Similarly, fuel, chemical and other consumable imports cost $500/ha/yr. So the foreign exchange cost of state farm is about $1,000/ha/yr. Thus, at the Fourth Congress target for state farms of 2.5 tonnes of maize per hectare in 1985, it will cost $400/tonne to produce maize, which is two-and-a-half times the import price.

With better maintenance and more skilled operators, machinery could last seven or eight years, bringing the capital cost down to $350/ha/yr and thus the total foreign exchange cost to $850/ha/yr. Because of the normal vagaries of weather, the best average production that could be expected in Mozambique is 4.5 t/ha. So the cheapest Mozambique can expect to produce maize is $190/t. (This is not out of line internationally. When I visited Zimbabwe in 1982 there were still hidden subsidies to commercial farmers and they were still paying their black workers literally starvation wages, yet they complained they could not make a profit on the government purchase price for maize of US$ 160/t.)

There is even a high foreign exchange cost for maize produced for sale by peasant farmers. The producer price for maize is 6 MT/kg, and it costs between 5 and 10 MT/kg for the state to actually buy and store it. Although these are officially in local currency, there is a sizeable foreign exchange component. Thus when consumer goods are imported to stimulate production they are normally sold at not much above the official rate of exchange, and it is virtually like paying the peasants in dollars. Also, about half the marketing costs are in foreign exchange, for fuel, lorries, chemicals, etc. Thus the real cost of a tonne of peasant màize is 2,500 to 5,000 MT in local currency *plus* $225 to $290. This is still more expensive in foreign exchange than US maize, but cheaper than the Fourth Congress $400/t for state farm maize. If only half the producer price of 6 MT/kg was paid in foreign exchange (say, because Mozambique devalued, imposed a high import duty, or produced more consumer goods locally), then the foreign exchange cost of peasant maize would come down to a more reasonable $145–210/t.

These calculations are very approximate, but they make two things clear: Mozambique does *not* save foreign exchange by producing food for the cities rather than importing it, and it costs less foreign exchange to stimulate peasant production than to support state farms.

This comparison ignores an essential point, in that it applies only to marketed food; in other words, to food for the cities. To spend foreign exchange to import food or to support state farms is to spend that money directly on the urban population. To spend that money to import capulanas and other goods for the peasants is to accomplish two things at once: provide the peasants with essential goods they now lack, and provide food for the cities, and industrial raw materials. It is necessary to assume (as I have done here) that all the extra consumer goods must be imported precisely because of the economic crisis and the collapse of the trading circuits: peasants don't produce cotton because there is no cloth to exchange for it because the peasants did not produce the cotton to make the cloth. Dollars are needed to break that cycle, by initially importing essential consumer goods for peasant farmers. Development should mean more local production and eventually fewer imports.

Nevertheless, the nonsense remains that even efficient large farms in Mozambique cannot compete with food imported from similar farms in Europe and America. This is because European and American governments subsidize their farmers, either directly or through cheap transport, credit, etc. In addition to the political need to subsidize their own farmers, the developed countries have a vested interest in keeping food prices low. It allows them to encourage developing countries to produce export crops and import food, thus keeping them tied to the industrialized countries. This dependence can create serious problems, especially because of the wide fluctuation in commodity prices. According to the UN Food and Agriculture Organization (FAO) the world recession caused the average price of developing country agricultural exports to fall by 30% between 1980 and 1982. By mid-1982, world sugar prices were only one-fifth what they had been at the beginning of 1981.

The industrialized countries compensate through food aid. But this is largely a way of getting rid of their own surpluses. Would any country be prepared to give tractors and fertilizer or capulanas and other consumer goods to allow Mozambique to produce its own food instead of giving the food itself? This encourages dependence. Mozambique, like so many developing countries, diverts resources to produce export crops because it counts on a certain amount of food aid.

Yet Mozambique does not profit from many of these export crops. Cotton requires repeated applications of imported pesticides. In 1980, $19 million in pesticides were imported for cotton, more than two-thirds of all of Mozambique's pesticide imports for that year. It cost another $4 million in foreign exchange for fuel, aircraft, tractors, and so on to apply the pesticides – $23 million in all. Yet cotton exports in that year earned only $22.5 million. Taking into account all the other imported inputs, Mozambique will lose money on cotton even if it increases productivity.

Similarly, millions of dollars are being invested in the sugar industry, yet the precipitous drop in world sugar prices means that it costs Mozambique three times as much in foreign exchange to grow the sugar as it earns from the sale. Tea, too, is unprofitable.

Appendix 2: Phases of Revolutionary Socialist Development

(This appendix is quoted from Gordon White's introduction to *Revolutionary Socialist Development in the Third World*, edited by Gordon White, Robin Murray, and Christine White, and published by Wheatsheaf Books, Brighton, England.)

. . . The basis thesis is that state socialist countries undergo certain characteristic transitions and stages of development which reflect the influence of structural changes in society and state, historical conditions, and ecological constraints (both internal and external) and certain basic problematic features of 'planned' economies and 'Partycratic' polities.

Each major transition manifests itself in specific policy changes but these are the tip of the iceberg. The key determining factors in each phase are first, the strategic context – domestic and international, economic and political, technical and social; second, the evolving nature of the social structure, notably the emergence and consolidation of new class forces; third, the nature of the state both as an agent of class formation and a matrix of political relations. At each stage, these conditions and pressures shape, and are shaped by the specific mix of institutional alternatives characteristic of socialism – state intervention, markets, and mass participation – and the specific policy agenda of the period.

Using this broad analytical framework, one can distinguish three key phases and transitions in revolutionary socialist development:

(i) *Revolutionary voluntarism and its limits*: this involves the classic problem of transition from a revolutionary era of fierce politico-military struggle to the post-revolutionary stage of socialist construction. In the initial post-revolutionary period, the nascent state is dominated by radical elements representing the political aspirations of the revolutionary mass coalition; the social structure is in turmoil and transformation; and internal and external politico-economic conditions are threatening. Institutionally, state-building combines with mass mobilization; markets are seen as matrices of antagonistic class power and subjected to increasing controls. The policy agenda calls for rapid social and institutional transformation. In this context, the methodological heritage of the revolutionary period is appropriate; as conditions change, however, its applicability is brought into question.

(ii) *Bureaucratic voluntarism and its limits*: to the extent that the strategic tasks of the immediate post-revolutionary period are achieved, the revolutionary model of social mobilization is undermined. The burgeoning state apparatus is increasingly manned by people without

270

revolutionary experience, a reorganized social structure is taking shape with institutionalized patterns of social mobility and a strategic role for educated, primarily urban, strata; as the state is consolidated, it manages to marginalize domestic counter-revolutionary opposition and establish a *modus vivendi* with the external world. The strategic task of the era becomes rapid economic development and the state takes on the key role in steering the social economy in the prescribed direction through a network of increasingly complex bureaucratic organizations. This is the era of bureaucratic voluntarism. In Weberian terminology, the revolution is being institutionalized; from the perspective of many former revolutionaries, 'revisionism' and 'degeneration' are setting in. Thus the transition between stages is usually marked by political conflict and ideological disagreement among the Party leadership. . . . However, the new phase of bureaucratic voluntarism also digs its own historical grave (but is remarkably resistant to being lowered into it).

(iii) *Reformism and market socialism*: in a transitional process much analysed in socialist countries and abroad, bureaucratic voluntarism becomes increasingly irrational economically and increasingly unacceptable politically. The new state apparatus has bred 'new men', reared in a post-revolutionary environment, who develop interests which are increasingly incompatible with those of the politico-administrative elite and press them by technocratic means. The population wearies of postponed consumption, and increased social differentiation leads to proliferating sectional interests and demands which beat on the doors of Party hegemony. The traditional methods of directive planning become more and more ineffective as the economic structure becomes more complex and social demands diversify. There are thus moves to change the institutional mix, with more scope for markets, greater political pluralism, and cultural diversity. The policy agenda focuses on economic efficiency and productivity, intensive rather than extensive development.

Appendix 3: Top Government and Party Officials (1983)

Key to abbreviations:

Party posts:

> *PB* = Politburo
> *PS* = Party secretary
> *CC* = Central Committee
> and all positions in italics

Notes: 1) all *PB* and *PS* are also *CC*, and 2) all party posts held continuously since the Third Congress in 1977 unless indicated otherwise.

Government posts:

> M = minister   A = ambassador
> G = governor   PMC = provincial military commander
> PG = *PB* member serving as governor
> TGF = Frelimo member of Transitional Government
> TGP = Portuguese member of Transitional Government
> TGM = Frelimo representative on Transitional Military
>   Commission
> + = held two government posts for part of period

(Vice ministers and secretaries of state not listed)

The Top Thirteen

Samora Moisés Machel: *President*; President
Marcelino dos Santos: *PB, PS*; Planning M (75–80), PG Sofala (83–)
Joaquim Chissano: *PB, PS*; Prime M (TGF), Foreign M (75–)
Alberto Chipande: *PB*; TGM, Defence M (75–), PG Cabo Delgado (+83–)
Armando Guebuza: *PB, chairman of control commission* (77–83), *political commissar of the army*; Interior M (TGF–77, 83–), Deputy Defence M (77–81), PG Sofala (81–83)
Jorge Rebelo: *PB, PS*; Information M (75–80)

Mariano Matsinhe: *PB, chairman of control commission* (83–   ); Labour M (TGF–78), Interior M (77–83), PG Sofala (+80–81), Security M (83–   )

Sebastião Mabote: *PB*; TGM, Deputy Defence M (75–   )

Jacinto Veloso: *PB*; TGM, Security M (80–83), M in President's Office for Economic Affairs (83–   )

Mário Machungo: *PB*; Economy M (TGF), Industry M (75–78), Agriculture M (78–81), Planning M (+80–   ), PG Zambézia (83–   )

José Oscar Monteiro: *PB* (83–   ), *PS* (77–83); Information M (TGF), M in President's Office (75–83), Justice M (83–   )

Armando Panguene: *PS* (83–   )

José Luis Cabaço: *PS* (83–   ); Transport M (75–80), Information M (80–   )

Other Ministers

Graça Machel: *CC*; Education and Culture M (75–   )

Julio Carrilho: *CC*; Public Works M (75–78, 80–   ), Industry M (78–80)

José Carlos Lobo: *CC* (83–   ); Minerals M (83–   )

Pascoal Mocumbi: *CC* (83–   ); Health M (80–   )

Rui Baltazar: Justice M (TGF–78), Finance M (78–   )

Joaquim Ribeiro de Carvalho: *CC* (77–78); Agriculture M (75–78), Foreign Trade M (83–   )

António Branco: Industry & Energy M (80–   )

Luis Alcantara Santos: Transport M (TGP), Ports & Railways M (80–   )

Rui Lousa: Post & Telecommunications M (80–   )

Aranda da Silva: Internal Trade M (80–   )

João Ferreira: Agriculture M (83–   )

Other Central Committee Members in High Government Posts

Raimundo Pachinuapa: state inspector

Tomé Eduardo: vice-chief of general staff

Joaquim Munhepe: Sofala PMC

Manuel dos Santos: A United Nations (Internal Trade M 78–80)

Eduardo Nihia: Nampula PMC

José Moiane: Maputo Province G

Fernando Matavel: Gaza PMC

João Mpfumo: air force commander

Aurelio Manave: Gaza G

Domingos Fondo: Inhambane PMC

Manuel António: Manica G

Sergio Vieira: Niassa G (M-Governor of Bank of Mozambique 78–81, Agriculture M 81–83)

Tobias Dai: Manica PMC
Matias Juma: Tete PMC
Pascoal Zandamela: Inhambane G
Felíciano Gundana: Nampula G
João Baptista Cosme: A Portugal (Public Works M 78–80)
José Ajape Ussene: Zambézia PMC

Appendix 4: Social and Political Statistics

Area and Population (1980 Census)

Province	Area (1,000 square miles)	Population (1,000s)	Density (people (per square mile)
Niassa	50	514	11
Cabo Delgado	32	940	31
Nampula	31	2,402	79
Zambézia	40	2,500	64
Tete	39	831	22
Manica	24	641	28
Sofala	26	1,065	42
Inhambane	26	997	39
Gaza	29	990	35
Maputo Province	10	491	51
Maputo city	0.2	755	3,380
Total	*309*	*12,130*	*41*

Note: Maputo city is considered the country's eleventh province

Communal Villages (1981)

Province	Number of Villages	Population (1,000s)	% of Population of Province
Niassa	52	53	10
Cabo Delgado	514	782	80
Nampula	234	151	6
Zambézia	50	53	2
Tete	23	33	4
Manica	133	196	29
Sofala	69	188	17
Inhambane	48	26	2
Gaza	118	270	26
Maputo Province	25	16	3
Total	*1,266*	*1,769*	*14*

Delegates to the Frelimo Fourth Party Congress

According to the Mandates Commission to the Congress, there were 677 delegates, categorized as follows:

OCCUPATION	*Number*	*%*	
Workers	173	26	
Peasants	195	29	67%
Soldiers	85	13	
Other defence and security	44	6	
Commerce and service workers	53	8	
First secretaries of districts or localities	35	5	
Officials of mass organizations	15	2	
Directors of state companies	11	2	

(Other delegates were, apparently, non-elected, for example members of the previous Central Committee)

SEX		
Men	572	85
Women	105	15

AGE		
Under 25	49	7
26–35	248	36
36–50	319	46
Over 50	67	10

EDUCATION		
Illiterate	54	8
Four to nine years' schooling		more than 60
Higher education	53	8

POLITICAL BACKGROUND		
Delegates to Third Congress	85	12
Frelimo militants before 1977	192	28

Party membership
The Central Committee told the Fourth Congress that Frelimo has 110,323 members organized into 4,244 cells. Of these, 54% are peasants and 19% are workers; 26% are women.

Health

Health Units and Beds (1980)

	Number of:	
	Units	*Beds*
Health posts	629	—
Health centres	285	5,710
Rural and general hospitals	26	2,308
Provincial hospitals	7	1,489
Central hospitals	3	2,564
Psychiatric hospitals	4	1,109
Total	*933*	*13,180*

Increases in Facilities

	1979	*1981*
Health posts	628	788
Health centres	265	281
Maternity beds	3,240	3,781
Pediatric beds	898	1,317

Health Staff

	1980	*1981*
Total	*12,261*	*12,830*
Doctors	323	365
Nurses	2,156	2,134
Midwives	457	490

Geographic Distribution of Resources (1979)

	Maputo City	*Ten Provincial Capitals**	*All Other Districts*
% of population	5.9	17.5	82.5
% of doctors	52.5	89.8	10.2
% of all health workers	32.1	66.1	33.9
Number of people:			
per doctor	4,450	7,750	257,500
per health worker	180	290	2,670
per bed	385	420	1,512
per primary care unit	12,416	13,095	13,600
Yearly expenditure for personnel, per head	$15	$9.30	$0.85
Out-patient consultations per head	1.4	1.1	0.4

(*including Maputo city)

Distribution of Doctors (1981)

Ministry of Health	23
Maputo Central Hospital	111
Other Maputo city	46
Other cities	128
Rural areas	56

Health Budget

	million £	£ per capita
1975	9	0.9
1976	14	1.3
1977	20	1.8
1978	23	2.0
1979	24	2.0
1980	29	2.4
1981	35	2.8
1982	38	2.9

Education

Enrolment has more than doubled since independence:

	1973	1977	1979	79/73
PRIMARY				
Total pupils	666,600	1,363,000	1,495,000	2.2
Teachers	11,000	16,000	17,000	1.5
Pupils per teacher	61	85	88	
Pupils completing primary education	13,560	—	74,000	5.5
SECONDARY				
Total pupils	33,000	48,000	93,000	2.8
Teachers	1,800	1,872	2,500	1.4
Pupils per teacher	18	26	37	

But the failure rate is very high:

	Pass rates (1982)			
	Starting year	Pupils Finishing year	Passing	Pass/Start
PRIMARY				
K	60,000	48,000		
1	373,000	272,000	176,000	.47
2	267,000	198,000	121,000	.45
3	156,000	112,000	66,000	.42
4	95,000	68,000	44,000	.46

SECONDARY

5	43,000	38,000	23,000	.53
6	28,000	23,700	12,000	.42
7	5,000	4,600	3,400	.69
8	3,300	2,900	2,100	.64
9	2,700	2,300	1,500	.57
10	700	700	540	.79
11	480	460	280	.57

Appendix 5: Economic Statistics

Mozambique publishes very few statistics. Those which are issued are sometimes confusing and conflicting. More statistics were published in colonial times, but they were often fraudulent. Thus, to compile a statistical picture of the Mozambican economy is extremely difficult.

Except where noted, the tables that follow are my own estimates compiled from a mix of official and unofficial sources, and must be treated with caution.

In general, 1973 was the year of highest pre-independence production so it is usually taken as the base.

Rates of Exchange

The Mozambican metical has been steadily devalued against the US dollar, and thus has varied against the UK pound according to the $/£ exchange rate. The official rate, at mid-year, has been:

	1969	1970	1971	1972	1973	1974	1975	1976	1977	1978
Meticais/$	29	29	28	27	25	25	27	31	33	33
Meticais/£	70	70	67	65	57	60	56	53	57	62

	1979	1980	1981	1982	1983
Meticais/$	32	32	37	38	40
Meticais/£	71	75	67	66	61

Throughout this book, I have used the following exchange rates:

At all times: To 1975: 27 MT = $1
63 MT = £1   1976–80: 32 MT = $1
                       1981–83: 38 MT = $1

Note that until 1980, the unit of currency was known as the escudo.

National Social Product (1,000 million meticais)

	1975	1977	1981	1982	1985 target *	†
Agriculture		30.6	33.3	32.5	43	
Industry		27.8	31.6	27.5	31	
Construction		3.6	4.5	4.7		
Transport & Communications		7.8	9.0	8.4		
Commerce & Other		5.2	5.3	5.1		
Total	71.1	75.0	83.7	77.9	87	175
Total in $1,000 million	2.2	2.3	2.6	2.4	2.7	5.5
Per capita, US$	210	210	210	191	197	400
Total in £1,000 million	1.1	1.2	1.3	1.2	1.4	2.8
Per capita, £	107	107	107	97	100	203

Official government figures at constant 1980 prices (and 1980 exchange rates)

*1985 target set by Fourth Congress in 1983
†1985 target set in 1981 in the ten year plan

These figures are for 'Global Social Product Produced' (*produto social global produzido*) which is analogous to Gross National Product (GNP), and within the limits of the available statistics can be taken as a measure of GNP. (Mozambique has another figure, not published, for Global Social Product Used, which is analogous to Gross Domestic Product.)

Balance of Payments (million £)

	1973	1974	1975	1976	1977	1978	1979	1980	1981
Merchandise:									
Imports	181	186	166	144	168	273	295	368	409
Exports	88	120	80	73	77	85	132	188	208
Balance	−93	−66	−86	−71	−91	−188	−163	−180	−201
Invisibles:									
Payments	37	42	48	50	47	40	38	49	50
Receipts	85	105	134	127	105	104	105	124	130
Balance	+48	+63	+86	+77	+58	+64	+67	+75	+80
Overall balance	−45	−3	0	+6	−33	−124	−96	−105	−121

Invisible receipts include remittances of miners' wages and some foreign assistance. Other foreign assistance, capital investment, and loans help to cover the deficit.

Not included is capital of over £100 million taken out by departing Portuguese during 1974–77, nor profits from gold sales resulting from the difference between the official and free market gold prices which were about £150 million during the same period.

Exports by Product

	Value (£ million)						
	1973	1976	1977	1978	1979	1980	1981
Oil products	4	3	5	11	17	31	*
Cashew nuts	16	17	23	23	23	34	33
Prawns	2	6	6	8	12	18	32
Sugar & molasses	9	10	5	4	18	26	25
Tea	4	3	6	6	11	18	19
Cotton	19	9	5	7	12	12	16
Copra	4	3	5	7	9	5	*
Timber	5	3	2	2	3	3	*
Sisal & sisal cord	3	2	2	2	4	2	*
Coal	—	2	2	1	3	2	*
Citrus	1	1	—	1	1	1	*
Total	*88*	*73*	*77*	*85*	*132*	*188*	*208*

	Volume (1,000 tons)					
	1973	1976	1977	1978	1979	1980
Oil products	403	90	133	257	271	314
Cashew nuts	30	21	17	18	17	16
Prawns	2	4	3	3	4	5
Sugar & molasses	281	148	78	77	184	106
Tea	18	13	12	13	23	23
Cotton	51	16	6	13	16	*
Copra	48	41	36	34	29	19
Timber	128	62	38	31	26	21
Sisal & sisal cord	27	13	14	12	19	7
Coal	50	205	173	39	152	98
Citrus	21	9	3	12	16	14

* = not available
— = less than £500,000

Main Imports

	Value (£ million)			% of total imports		
	1973	*1978*	*1980*	*1973*	*1978*	*1980*
Total Imports of which:	181	273	368			
Crude oil*	7	34	80	4	12	22
Machinery	49	34	50†	28	13	14
Vehicles	19	35	42	10	13	11
Grain	5	25	39	3	9	11
Textiles	14	27	33	8	10	9

*Note that one-third to one-half of oil is re-exported as refined products
† = 1979

Detailed import lists have not been published since 1980.

Trade Links

	Value (£ million)			% of total		
	1965	*1973*	*1979*	*1965*	*1973*	*1979*
Imports from:						
Iraq	4	7	52	5	4	18
South Africa	8	37	42	10	20	14
East Germany	—	—	28	—	—	10
Switzerland	—	—	20	—	—	7
UK	8	14	16	10	8	5
West Germany	6	24	14	8	13	5
Portugal	27	35	14	35	19	5
France	2	15	12	3	8	4
US	4	9	11	4	5	4
Romania	—	—	8	—	—	3
Exports to:						
US	2	12	31	5	14	24
Portugal	18	31	19	37	36	15
Netherlands	1	2	11	2	3	8
East Germany	—	—	11	—	—	8
UK	2	5	8	5	6	6
Japan	0	2	8	0	2	6
South Africa	6	8	6	11	10	5
France	1	2	4	1	2	3
West Germany	2	3	3	4	3	2
Madagascar	—	—	3	—	—	2

— = not available

Data on trade by country have not been published since 1979.

Marketed Crops (1,000 tonnes)

	1977	1979	1980	1981	1982	Target for 1981	Target for 1985
Rice	33	56	43	29	42	82	60–65
Maize	34	67	65	78	89	137	155–165
Sunflower	6	5	12	12	11	17	—
Raw cotton	53	30	64	74	60	105	75–80
Potato	25	20	9	14	9	53	—
Beans	5	13	10	14	8	13	20–25
Citrus	—	39	32	37	38	40	—
Copra	—	56	37	54	24	53	45–49
Tea (green leaves)	—	—	95	99	111	—	111

— = not available

1981 target set in state plan for that year
1985 target set by Fourth Congress

Industrial Production

	As percentage of 1973 1979	1980	1981	1982	Actual 1973 production
Coal	—	103	136	—	394,000 tons
Sugar	61	58	60	41	294,000 tons
Cashew nuts	43	59	56	44	30,000 tons
Textiles	84	95	97	60	23,000 square metres*
Edible oil	—	82	94	78	23,000 tons
Soap	72	86	125	112	20,000 tons
Beer	—	70	66	58	77 million litres
Bottles	—	56	51	46	43 million
Cement	45	39	43	44	611,000 tons
Hoes	—	24	55	90	895,000
Bicycles	94	15	33	38	33,000
Railway wagons	3	0	66	82	304

Notes: — = data not available   *1974 production

	Industries for which 1973 baseline data not available: As percentage of 1980: 1979	1981	1982	Actual 1980 production
Salt	72	108	110	80,000 tons
Tyres	59	139	110	120,000
Radios assembled	—	138	128	80,000
Dry cell batteries	82	65	79	17 million

Structure of Industry (1973)

% of Total Industrial Production				% of Raw Materials: Local	Imported	Category	Notes
33			**Exports**				
	30		Processed agriculture	100	0	I	
	3		Refined oil	0	100	—	a
67			**Domestic consumption**				
	43		Consumer Goods				
		15	Processed food	82	18		
		6	Textiles	69	31		
		3	Tobacco	100	0	II	—
		1	Shoes & leather	100	0		
		1	Soap	100	0		
		5	Beverages	5	95		
		4	Printing	0	100	III	—
		3	Clothing	0	100		
		5	Other	10	90		
	15		Intermediate Goods				
		3	Cement	100	0	—	c
		3	Refined oil	0	100		b
		9	All other	0	100	III	
	9		Other	45	55	II, III	—
100	100						

Overall, 60% of industry is based on local raw materials, but only 44% of products for local consumption used mainly local raw materials.

Categories:
   I: Processing local agricultural products for export (30%)
   II: Processing local agricultural products for local consumption (30%)
   III: Processing imported raw materials for local consumption (33%)

Notes:
   a. Half of refined oil is exported and does not fit into any of these categories.
   b. Half of refined oil is used domestically and is thus category III.
   c. Cement is the only intermediate good made from local raw materials and thus does not fit in to any of these three categories.

Port Traffic

	(million tonnes loaded and unloaded)							
	1968	*1971*	*1973*	*1975*	*1979*	*1981*	*1982*	*1990 SADCC projections*
Total	16.2	19.3	18.0	14.7	10.6	8.9	8.7	30
By port:								
Maputo*	12.1	14.9	14.2	10.9	8.1	6.4	6.3	22
Beira	3.4	3.4	3.0	3.0	1.7	1.7	1.6	6
Nacala	.4	.6	.7	.5	.8	.8	.8	1
Transit for:								
South Africa	—	—	6.2	4.4	3.2	3.0	—	5
Zimbabwe	—	—	3.3	2.2	0	.9	—	8
Swaziland	—	—	3.0	2.8	1.7	.7	—	4
Malawi	—	—	.7	.6	—	.8	—	1

*Maputo includes Matola   — = not available

Government Expenditure

Current Budget (calendar year, £ million)

	1979	*1980*	*1981*	*1982*
Total	245	270	296	339
of which:				
Health, Education	66	76	86	103
Defence	64	75	87	99
Economic sectors	48	28	22	37
Expected deficit	−38	−32	−42	−46

This does not include capital expenditures.
No current budget was published in 1983.

The government has never been able to spend its entire budget allocation:

	1979	*1980*	*1981*	
Actual expenditure	178	217	268	
Actual deficit	+3	+16	−14	(+ indicates surplus)
% of budget not spent	28	19	9	

Actual expenditures on health and education have been published for two years:

	1980	*1981*
Health	24	30
Education	37	43

Foodgrains

Marketed grain, 1982 (1,000 tons)

	Wheat	*Maize*	*Rice*	*Total*
Commercial imports	46	20	42	*108*
Donations arrived	82	71	45	*198*
Local marketed production*	1	89	42	*132*
Total	*129*	*180*	*129*	*438*

*Does not include black market sales or production for self-consumption.

Estimated grains imports (1,000 tons)

	1960	*65*	*70*	*75*	*76*	*77*	*78*	*79*	*80*	*81*	*82*
Total	40	90	110	180	200	200	300	300	300	300	300
of which:											
Commercial purchases		150	100	100	200	150	200	150	100		
Delivered food aid			30	100	100	100	150	100	150	200	

Table 13
Foreign Debts and Trade
(£ million, as of 15 April 1983)

Algeria	152	BADEA (Arab Bank for	
Brazil	130	Economic Development)	23
East Germany	128	Angola	18
France	77	USA	18
Italy	61	Japan	18
Britain	61	OPEC Fund	15
Portugal	55	Romania	12
Libya	49	Kuwait	11
African Development Fund	41	India	10
African Development Bank	36	Sweden	7
Iraq	34	West Germany	7
Holland	32	South Africa	6
USSR	26	Others	143

Total 1,061

Of the loans by countries, £407 million is from banks in those countries.

Expected repayment rate
(£ million, before debt rescheduling)

	To centrally planned economies		Others		
	Capital	Interest	Capital	Interest	Total
1984	28	7	119	34	189
1985	25	5	102	25	155
1986	27	4	119	21	170
1987–90	42	6	242	37	327
1991 onwards	na	na	192	30	222

na = not available.

Central planned economies = Angola, East Germany, Bulgaria, Czechoslovakia, China, North Korea, Cuba, Hungary, Yugoslavia, Poland, Romania, Vietnam, and USSR.

Others = other countries plus international financial institutions.

Data given by National Planning Commission with request to renegotiate debts, 30 January 1984.

Table 14
Trade Balance by Groups of Countries
(million pounds)

	1973	*1975*	*1977*	*1979*	*1981*	*1982*
OECD countries:						
Exports to	66	51	59	93	82	55
Imports from	125	104	102	121	197	196
Balance	—59	—53	—44	—28	—115	—141
Countries with centrally planned economies:						
Exports to	0	0	0	12	32	18
Imports from	0	1	2	53	63	114
Balance	0	—1	—2	—41	—31	—96
Other countries:						
Exports to	22	29	19	27	43	64
Imports from	56	65	68	120	190	191
Balance	—34	—36	—48	—94	—147	—126
Total:						
Exports to	88	80	78	132	158	136
Imports from	181	171	172	295	449	501
Balance	—93	—90	—93	—163	—292	—364

Data published by the National Planning Commission as part of request to reschedule debts. Does not correspond precisely to Table 3.

Table 15
Oil Imports
(million pounds)

	1980	*1981*	*1982*	*1983*
Total imports	80	94	128	na
of which the following were on special credits:				
from Iraq	31	0	0	0
from Algeria	0	67	72	0
from Libya	0	0	47	26
from Angola	0	0	17	18

na = not available.

Appendix 6: Excerpts from the Nkomati Accord

I. Mozambique and South Africa 'undertake to respect each other's sovereignty and independence and . . . to refrain from interfering in the internal affairs of the other.'

II. The parties agree to resolve disputes by peaceful means and not to resort to force or threat of force, including '(a) attacks by land, air or sea forces, (b) sabotage, (c) unwarranted concentration of such forces at or near the international boundaries, [and] (d) violation of the international land, air, or sea boundaries.'

III. (1) the parties 'shall not allow their respective territories, territorial waters, or air space to be used as a base, throughfare, or in any other way by another state, government, foreign military forces, organisations or individuals which plan or prepare to commit acts of violence, terrorism, or aggression against the territorial integrity or political independence of the other, or may threaten the security of its inhabitants.'

(2) With respect to the 'elements contemplated in paragraph (1)'

(a) The parties agree to: 'forbid and prevent in their respective territories the organisation of irregular forces or armed bands, including mercenaries.'

(b)–(e) They also agree to 'eliminate from the respective territories': 'bases, training centres, places of shelter, accommodation, and transit'; 'centres or depots containing armaments'; 'places for the command, direction, and coordination of the elements'; and 'telecommunication facilities between the command and the elements'.

(f)–(k) Further, they agree to: 'eliminate and prohibit the installation . . . of radio broadcasting stations . . . for the elements'; 'exercise strict control . . . over elements which intend to carry out or plan the acts contemplated in paragraph (1)'; 'prevent the transit of elements . . . from a place in the territory of either to a place in the territory of the other or to a place in the territory of any third state which has a common boundary' with Mozambique or South Africa; 'take appropriate steps to prevent the recruitment of elements'; and 'prohibit the provision . . . of any logistic facilities.'

IV. The parties 'shall take steps, individually and collectively, to ensure that the international boundary between [them] is effectively patrolled.'

V. The parties 'shall prohibit within their territory acts of propaganda that incite a war of aggression, . . . acts of terrorism, and civil war in the territory of the other.'

IV. The parties agree to establish 'a joint security commission with the aim of supervising and monitoring the application of this agreement.'

Signed 16 March 1984 by Pieter Willem Botha, Prime Minister of South Africa, and Samora Moises Machel, President of Mozambique.

Bibliography

General

Issacman, Allen and Issacman, Barbara. (1983) *Mozambique: From Colonialism to Revolution 1900–1982*.

Kaplan, Irving. (1977) *Area Handbook for Mozambique*. Washington, DC, US Government Printing Office.

Munslow, Barry. (1983) *Mozambique: the Revolution and its Origins*. London, Longman.

Vail, Leroy and White, Landeg. (1980) *Capitalism and Colonialism in Mozambique*. London, Heinemann.

Resisting Change

Coccia, Giancarlo. (1976) *The Scorpion Sting*. Johannesburg, Livraria Moderna.

Gibbs, Richard. (1972) *African Liberation Movements*. London, Oxford University Press.

Swift, Kerry. (1975) *Mozambique and the Future*. London, Robert Hale.

Winter, Gordon. (1981) *Inside Boss*. London, Penguin.

Post Independence Euphoria

Frelimo. (1977) *Central Committee Report to the Third Congress*. London: Mozambique, Angola, Guinea Information Centre.

Searle, Chris. (1981) *We're Building a New School*. London, Zed.

Sketchley, Peter and Lappé, Frances Moore. (1980) *Casting New Molds*. San Francisco (2588 Mission Street), Institute for Food and Development Policy.

Watt, G. and Melamed, A. (1983) *Changing Health Care in Mozambique*. London, Zed.

Harsher Realities

First, Ruth. (1983) *Black Gold*. Brighton, Harvester.
Frelimo. (1983) *Out of Underdevelopment to Socialism*. Maputo, INLD.
————— (1983) *Frelimo Party Programme and Statutes*. Maputo, INLD.
————— (1983) *Building Socialism: The People's Answer*. Maputo, INLD.
  (These three books contain the documents of the Frelimo Fourth Congress and are available for US$8.50 plus 85c postage for the set from INLD, CP 4030, Maputo, Mozambique.)
Isaacman, Barbara and Stephen. June (1980) *Mozambique: Women, the Law, and Agrarian Reform*. United Nations, Economic Commission for Africa.
Saul, John. (to be published) New York, Monthly Review.
White, Gordon *et al* eds. (1983) *Revolutionary Socialist Development in the Third World*. Brighton, Wheatsheaf. (Introduction by Gordon White and Mozambique article by David Wield.)

Periodicals

(1983 prices; inst = institutions)

AIM Bulletin (monthly news summary). Agencia de Informação de Moçambique, CP 896, Maputo (per year: US$15, inst $25).
Facts and Reports (fortnightly press cuttings on southern Africa). Holland Committee on Southern Africa, Oudezijds Achterburgwal 173, 1012 DJ, Amsterdam, The Netherlands (per year: Dfls 90, inst Dfls 125).
Mozambican Studies (annual; translation of *Estudos Moçambicanos*, the journal of the Centre of African Studies of Eduardo Mondlane University, Maputo). Eduardo Mondlane Stichting, Oudezijds Achterburgwal 173, 1012 DJ, Amsterdam, The Netherlands (4 issues: US$22, inst $30).
People's Power (quarterly journal on Angola and Mozambique). Mozambique Angola Committee, 98 Great Russell Street, London WC1B 3LA (per year: £4, outside UK £6).
News Review (fortnightly summary). Mozambique Information Office, 34 Percy Street, London WC1 9FG (per year: £6, outside UK £12).

9079 ==